ROYAL GREENWICH

THROUGH TIME

David Ramzan

AMBERLEY PUBLISHING

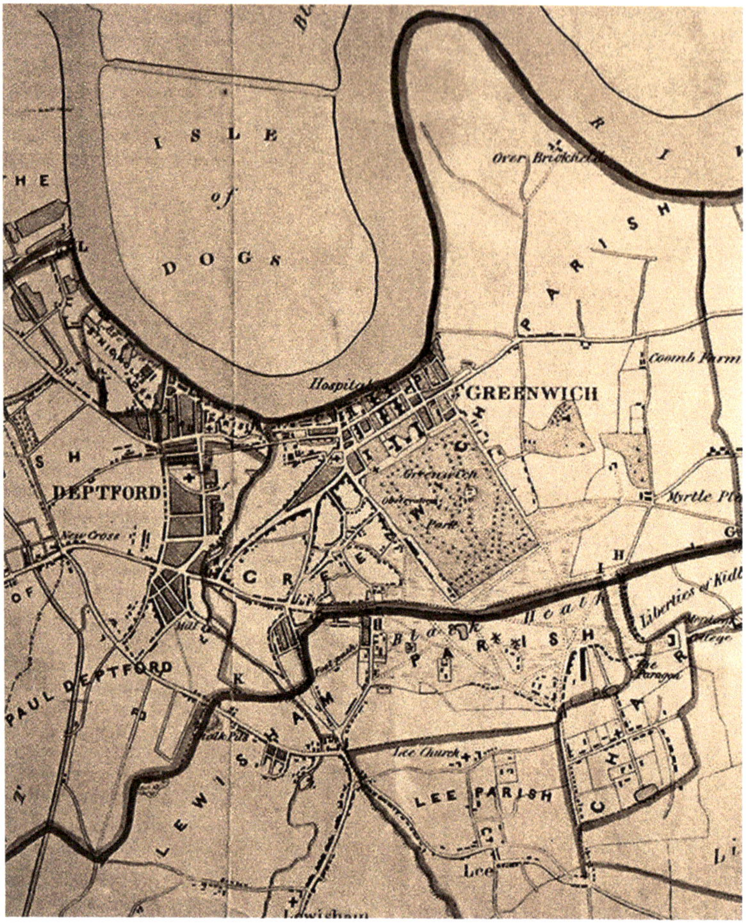

Greenwich Borough Boundaries
A map of Greenwich showing the boundaries of the parishes, townships and river in 1832.

First published 2010

Amberley Publishing Plc
Cirencester Road, Chalford,
Stroud, Gloucestershire, GL6 8PE

www.amberley-books.com

ISBN 978 1 84868 544 4

British Library Cataloguing in Publication Data.
A catalogue record for this book is available from the British Library.

Typeset in 9.5pt on 12pt Celeste.
Typesetting by Amberley Publishing.
Printed in the UK.

Introduction

Greenwich was a small village situated on the south bank of the River Thames when the first settlers, the Anglo-Saxon's, gave the settlement the name 'Grenewic' green village or village on the green. There is evidence of pre-Roman activity in the area and remains of a Roman temple have been found within Greenwich Park. To the west of the temple are a series of mounds, thought to be Bronze Age barrows, used as burial grounds by those first settlers who put Greenwich on the historical map.

The Danish invaders made Greenwich their base while carrying out attacks upon Kent and Canterbury. Alfege the Archbishop of Canterbury was taken hostage during one of these raids and after months in captivity was stoned to death by his captors. The Archbishop's martyrdom assured him saintly status and a church was built on the site where he died.

After the Norman invasion William the Conqueror's half brother Odo of Bayeux held lands at Greenwich. The manor was seized by the crown after Bishop Odo was found guilty of fraud. The manor gained royal patronage after Edward III had a chapel and hunting lodge built at Greenwich. Henry IV signed his will at the manor which was inherited by the king's half brother Thomas Beaufort Duke of Exeter who resided at a riverside property Bella Court. On his death the property passed to Humphrey Duke of Gloucester, the building was enlarged and given the title Bella Court Palace.

Henry VI inherited the palace and manor after the death of his uncle Humphrey and Bella Court Palace was renamed Placentia. Extensive rebuilding work took place during the Tudor period under the instructions of Henry VII, the medieval buildings were demolished and replaced by the magnificent Greenwich Palace.

Henry VIII was born at the palace as were his daughters, Mary and Elizabeth. The king spent many years of his reign at Greenwich overseeing the development of his naval dockyards at Woolwich and Deptford. After the turn of the sixteenth century the whole area would go through a dramatic transformation through the successful development of the ship building industries. As working opportunities grew so did the population which resulted in a change to the whole industrial and social development of Greenwich.

By the time of the English Civil War the monarchy had fallen out of favour with the people and the Tudor palace had fallen into disrepair. The palace remains were demolished when plans to build a new palace were commissioned by Charles II after the monarch's restoration to the throne. This new palace was never completed and when William and Mary succeeded the throne the Queen instructed Sir Christopher Wren to design and build a hospital for sailors upon the site of the old palace.

During the sixteenth and seventeenth centuries the dockyards at Woolwich and Deptford had grown and expanded. New industries were required to compliment the shipbuilding which included ironworking, milling, munitions manufacturing, barge and boat building.

By the end of the nineteenth century industry and housing had grown beyond compare, to the east of Greenwich row upon row of Victorian terraced houses had been built to accommodate the families and workers employed in the trades and industries on Greenwich Marsh and along the river from Woolwich to Deptford. The properties to the west of Greenwich consisted of elegant regency houses and shops with a prosperous market square at the centre. Dividing East and West Greenwich were the magnificent Royal Hospital and the Royal Hospital School buildings, with the wide green expanse of the Royal Park situated to the south.

Greenwich was not only divided by social and industrial necessity but also by the Meridian Line passing through the town's centre running north and south from the Royal Observatory in Greenwich Park. Positioned at zero degrees longitude the line divided the globes western and eastern hemispheres with Greenwich at the centre.

After almost two thousand years of living history Greenwich was awarded World Heritage status and made a Royal Borough, an honour granted by Queen Elizabeth II in recognition of the monarchy's long associations with Greenwich.

Being born in Greenwich I spent all of my childhood years playing with friends in the streets, the park and along the river front of a Greenwich which has seen continued change and re-development. I hope that within *Royal Greenwich Through Time* a have been able to reflect the ever changing image of Greenwich which I have no doubt will continue to change through the passage of time.

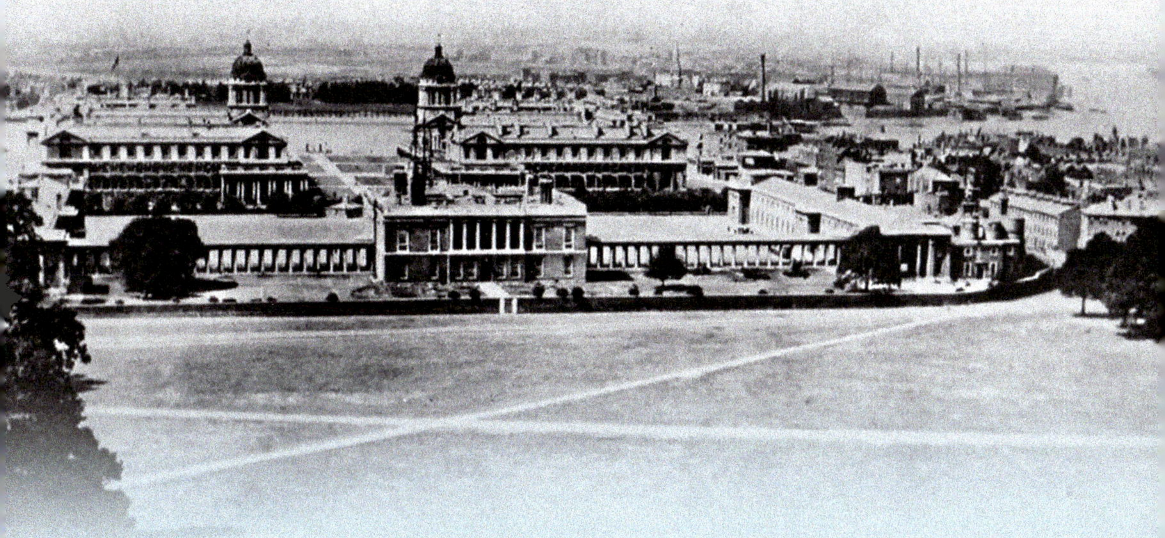

CHAPTER 1

Historic Views

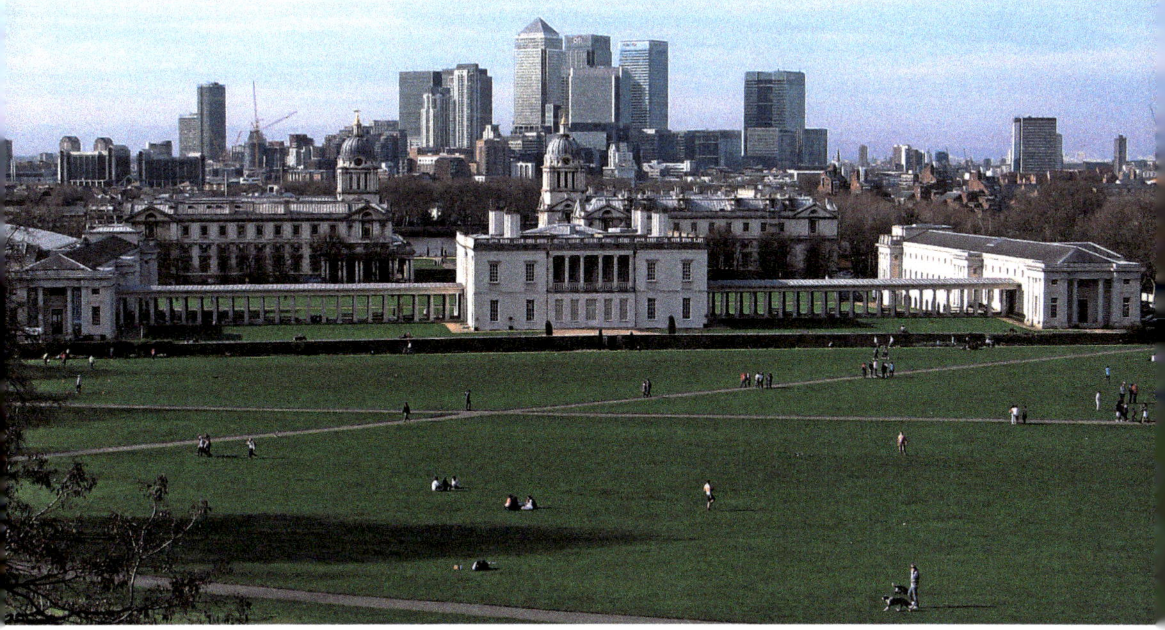

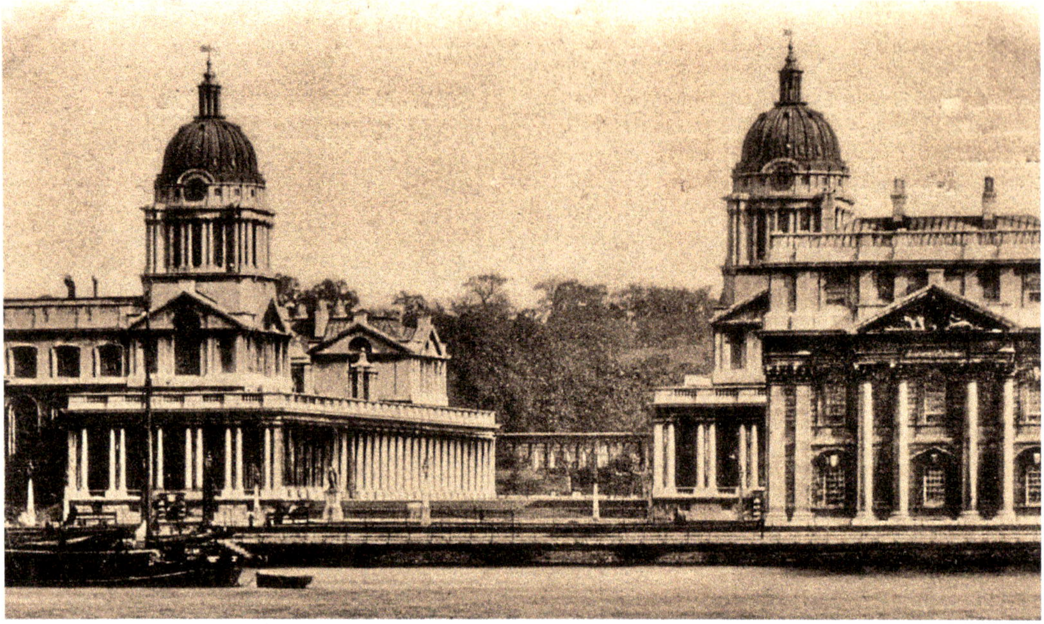

Greenwich Royal Naval College

In 1660 King Charles II commissioned architect John Webb to design a magnificent new building to replace the Tudor Palace at Greenwich which had fallen into disrepair. With only one wing built when William and Mary ascended the throne in 1689, the queen commissioned Sir Christopher Wren to complete the buildings as almshouses for injured and retired seamen. The buildings were acquired by the Royal Navy in 1873 and used as a college for training officers. Today these elegant buildings on the Thames are part of the University of Greenwich.

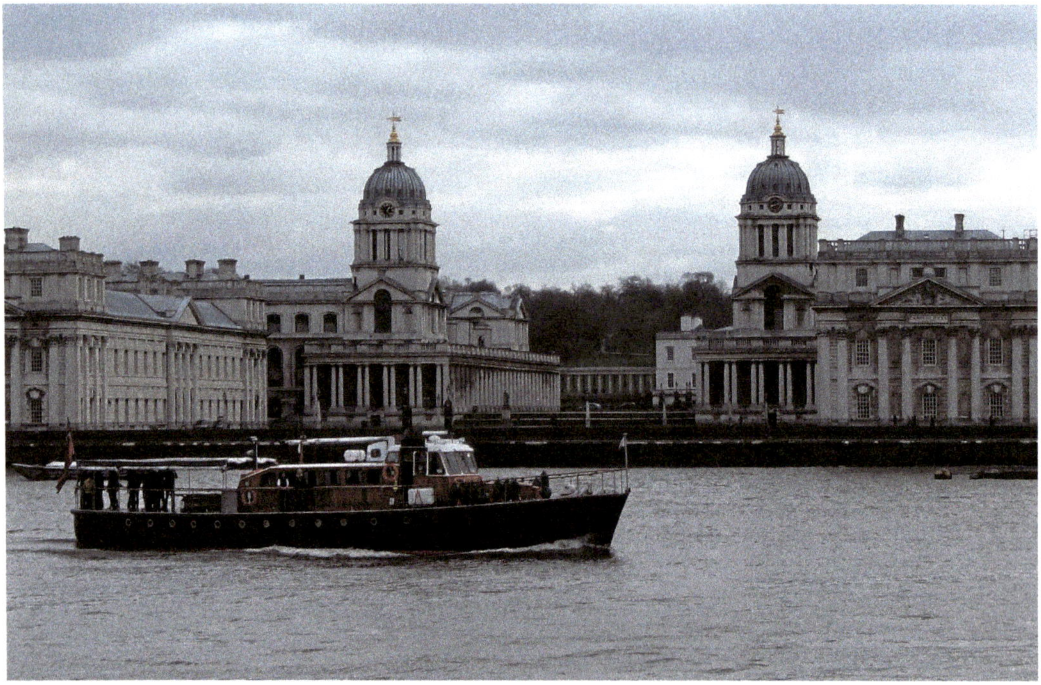

Cutty Sark – Greenwich Pier

Built and launched at Dumbarton in 1869 the *Cutty Sark* is the only existing clipper ship to have sailed the tea and wool trade routes of the world. Placed in dry dock during 1954, close to the entrance of the Greenwich foot tunnel, the clipper was open to the public for almost fifty years. While undergoing restoration in 2007 a fire on board almost destroyed this historic monument to seafaring. A majority of the ship's superstructure, masts and decking had been removed for storage and restoration and the raging fire did not cause as much damage as was first feared. On completion of the restoration the ship will be back in her dry dock sailing on a sea of glass, which is an architectural feature of the roof of a new tourist attraction centre positioned below the waterline of the clipper.

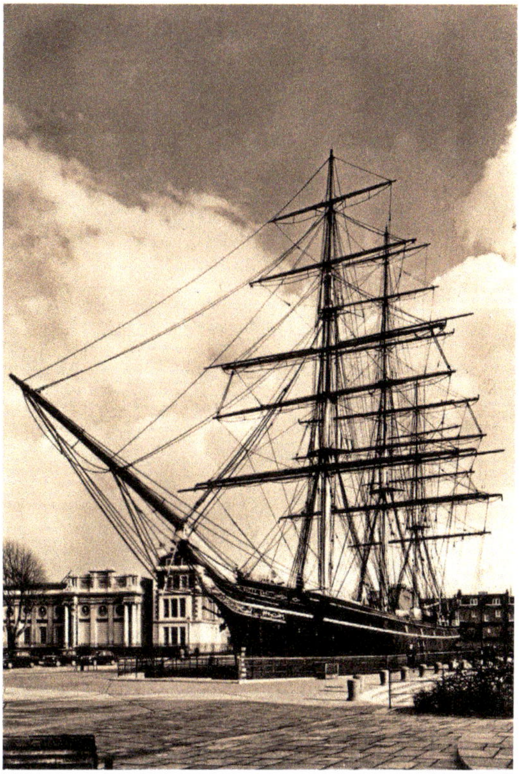

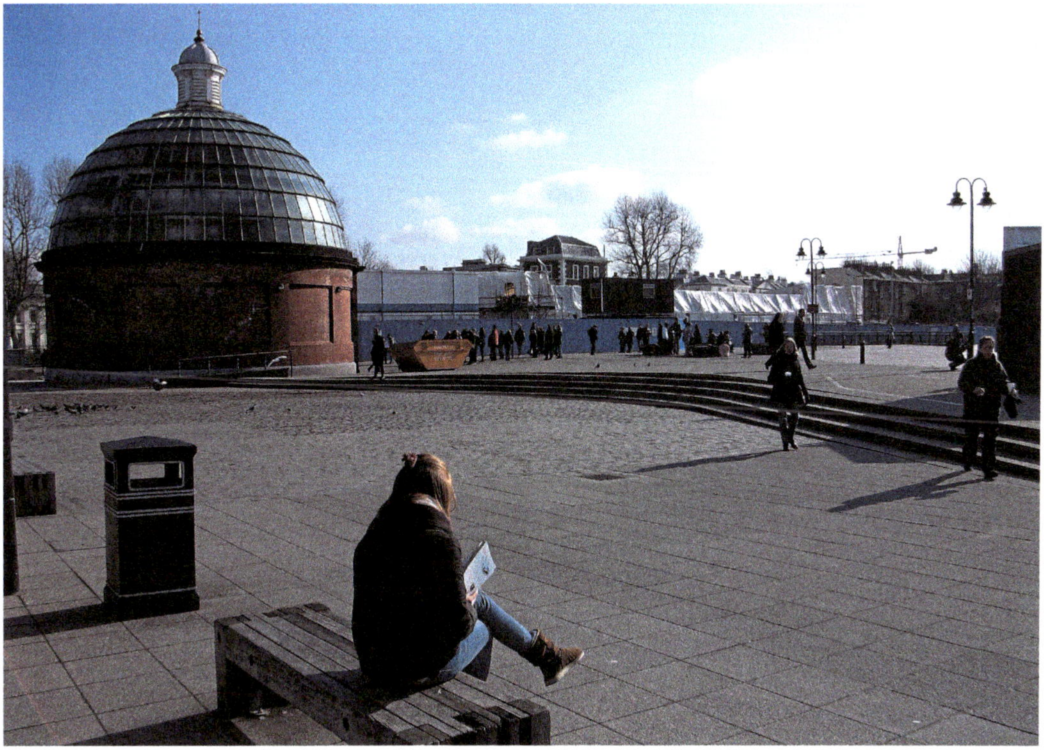

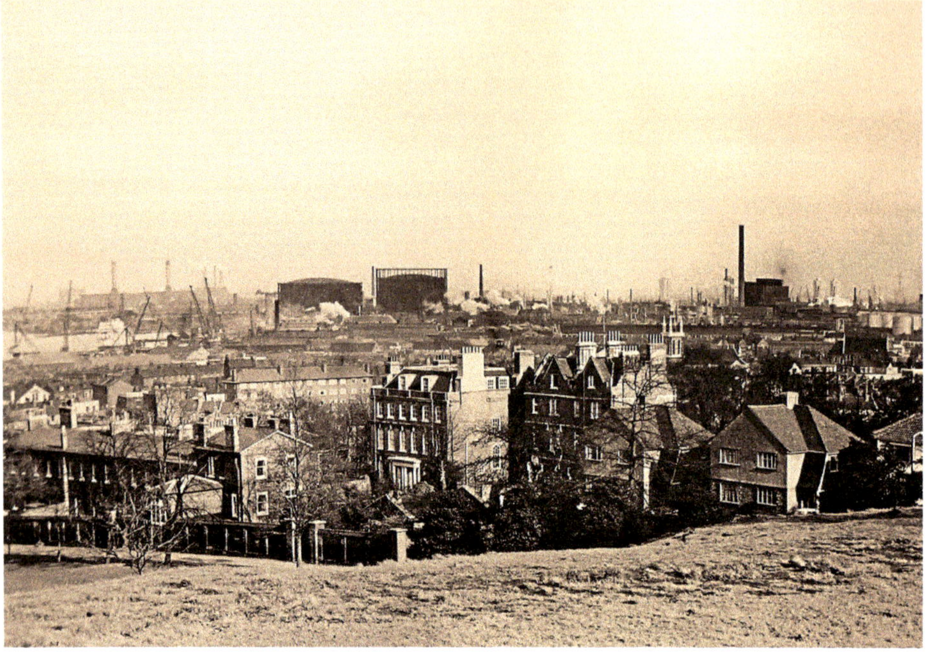

Greenwich Marsh from Greenwich Park

During the great shipbuilding era of the seventeenth and eighteenth centuries Greenwich Marsh had become a huge industrial site supplying commodities needed for shipbuilding and the production and refining of chemicals, gas, glucose, cements and building aggregates. Along the river's edge there were lighterage and boat building yards. Many of the industries had gone before the marsh was redeveloped for the 2000 millennium celebrations. The Dome was built as the central showpiece for the festivities and can be seen in the distance of the picture below with the high yellow support towers reaching up to the sky, replacing the tall chimneys that were once part of the industrial skyline.

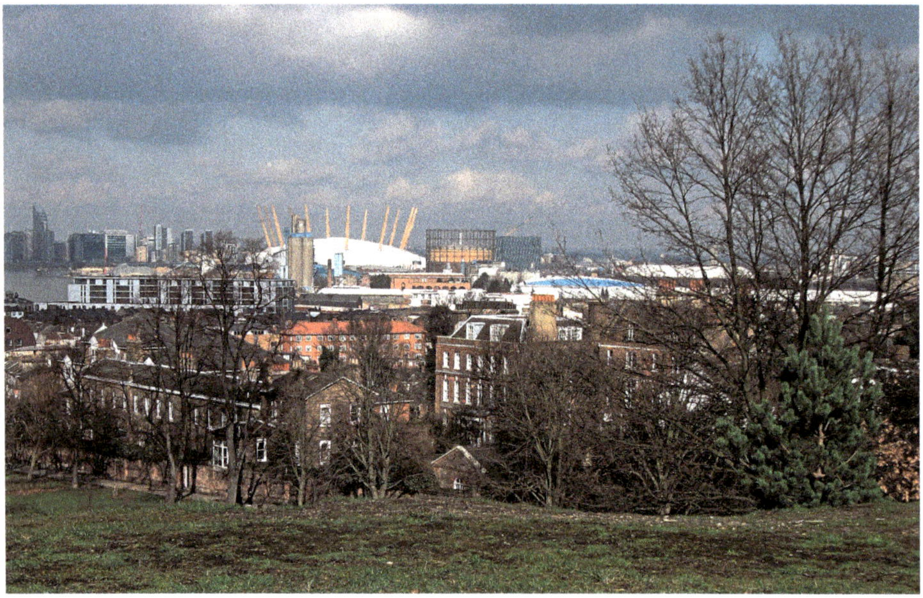

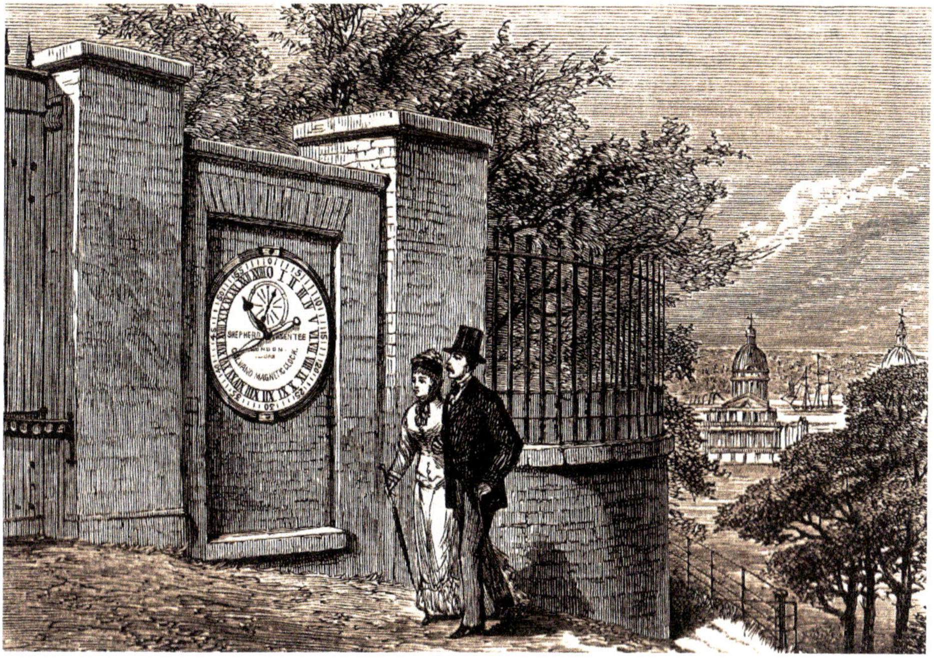

Greenwich Mean Time – Shepherd Gate Clock

The Royal Observatory in Geenwich Park was designed by Sir Christopher Wren in 1675. From here all time zones around the globe were set and measured after Astronomer Royal George Airy proposed that a standard time should be used throughout world provided by the Greenwich Royal Observatory. A twenty-four hour clock showing Greenwich Mean Time, built by Charles Shepherd, was installed in the outer gate wall of the Observatory in 1852. The clock is still in use today and tourists can set their own time pieces at the Shepherd Gate Clock.

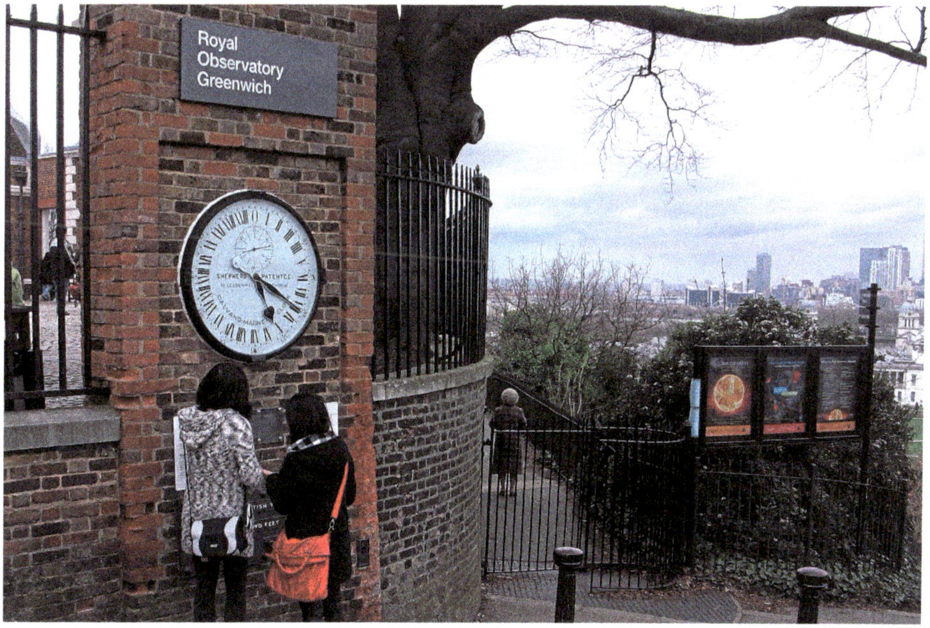

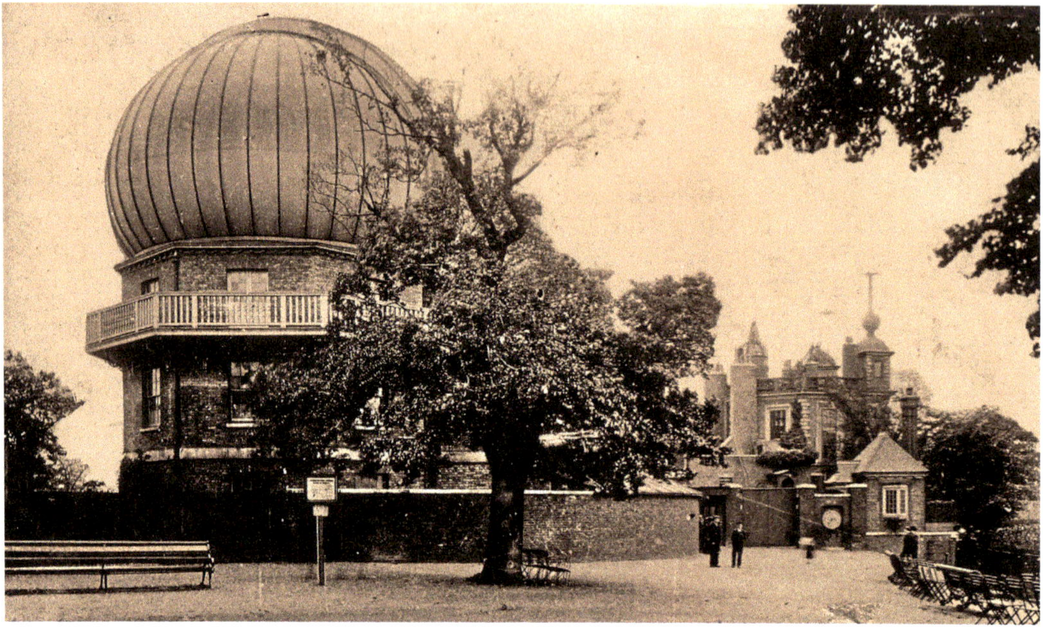

Greenwich Royal Observatory

King Charles II donated £500 and reclaimed material from a Tower of London gate house and unused bricks from Tilbury Fort for the building of the Royal Observatory. The observatory's function was to develop the use of astronomical navigation at sea. Now part of the National Maritime Museum the observatory houses collections of scientific and astronomical equipment including the navigational time pieces designed by John Harrison. To the right of the observatory stands the statue of General James Wolfe, resident of Greenwich, erected in 1930 as a monument to the fallen hero of Quebec who commanded British forces in a victory over the French in 1759.

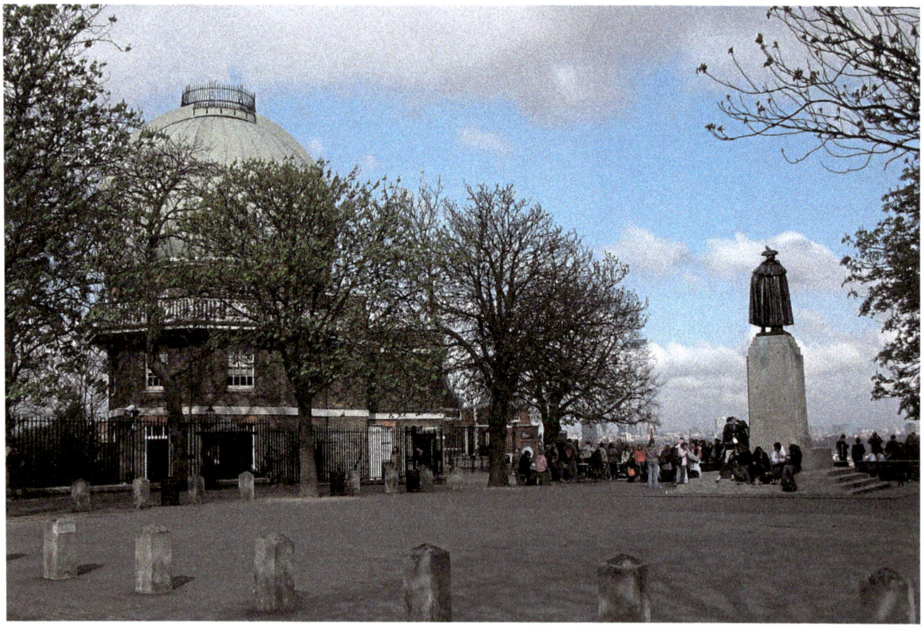

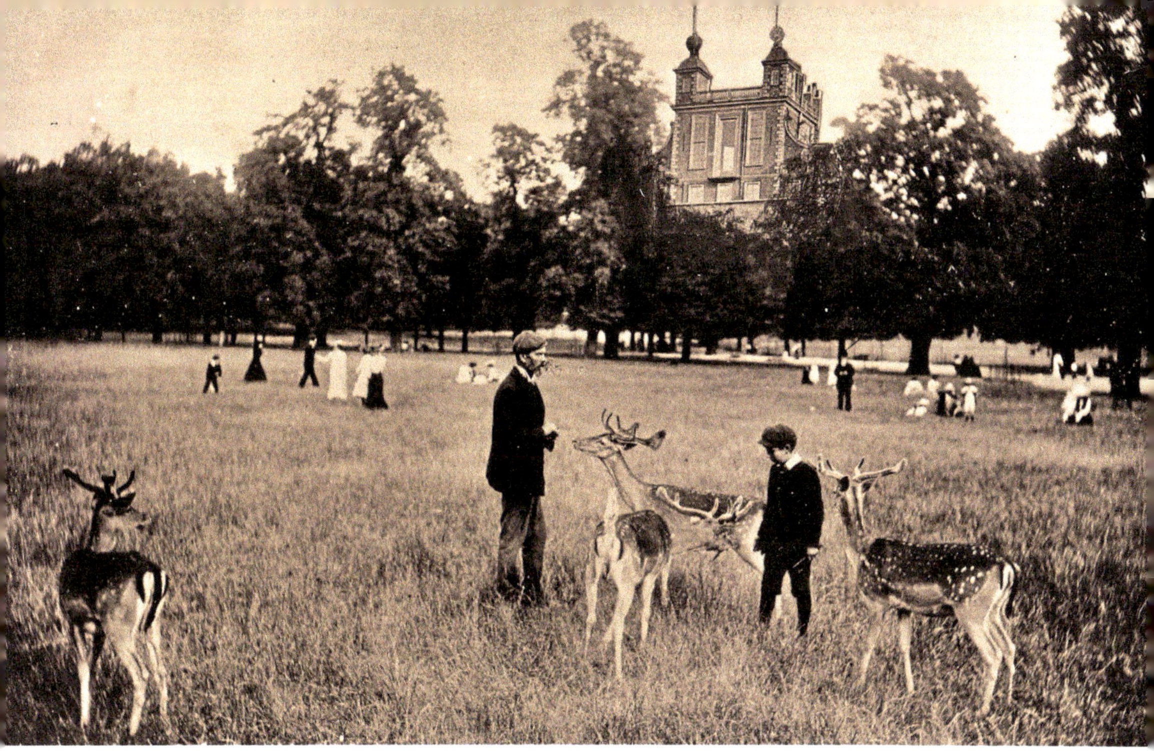

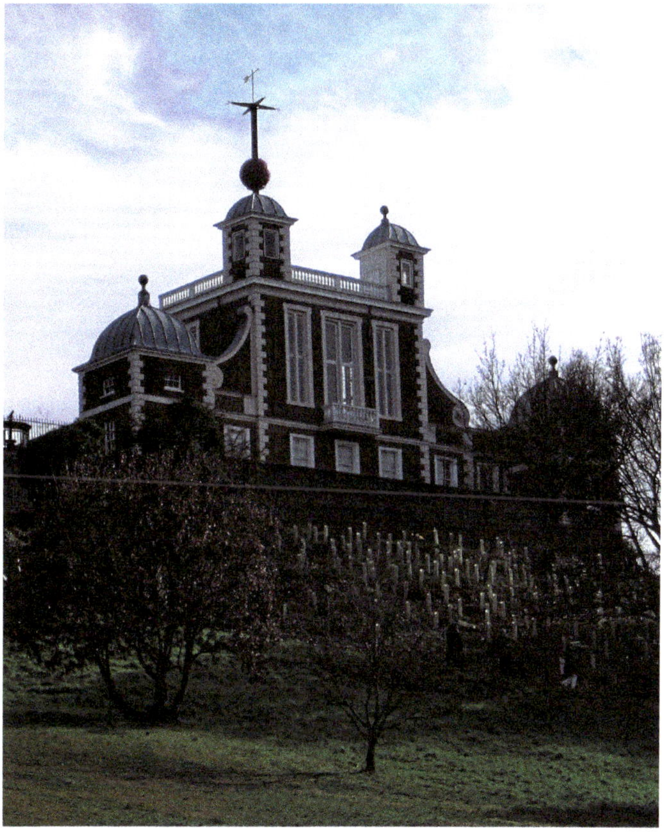

Flamsteed House – Greenwich Time Ball

A bright red ball on a tower of the Royal Observatory was first used as an aid to distributing time to ships on the Thames and the residents of Greenwich in 1833. Each and every day the ball rises to the top of the mast at 12.58pm and then drops down at exactly 13.00 hours. Shipping would set their time pieces at this signal and in 1884 a delegation made Greenwich the centre for world time. Greenwich had already been chosen as the Prime Meridian, Longitude 0º, and within the grounds of the Royal Observatory you can stand astride the Meridian Line with one foot in the east and one foot in the west of the globe's hemispheres.

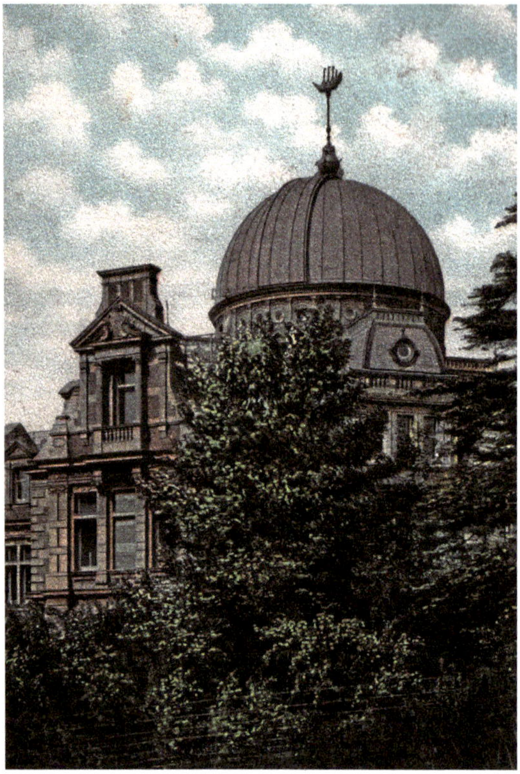

South Building – Greenwich Royal Observatory

Built between 1891 and 1899 the South Building at the Royal Observatory was used specifically for the study of astrophysics. The dome of the South Building housed the Thompson Equatorial telescope. When the observatory relocated to Herstmonceaux in 1957 the Royal Observatory turned towards tourism and the buildings were opened as a museum of astronomy, navigation and time keeping. The South Building was later refurbished to hold four galleries of modern astronomy, an education centre and a seminar room in the dome. Next to the South Building is the new ultra modern 120 seated Peter Harrison Planetarium which opened in 2007.

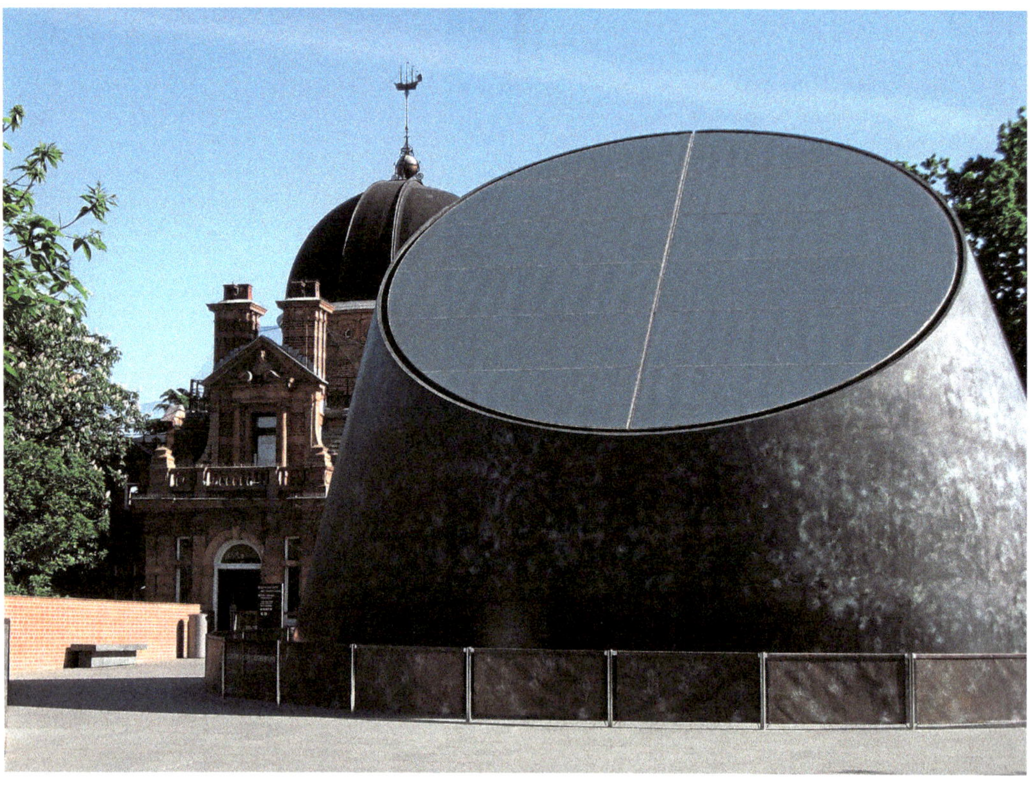

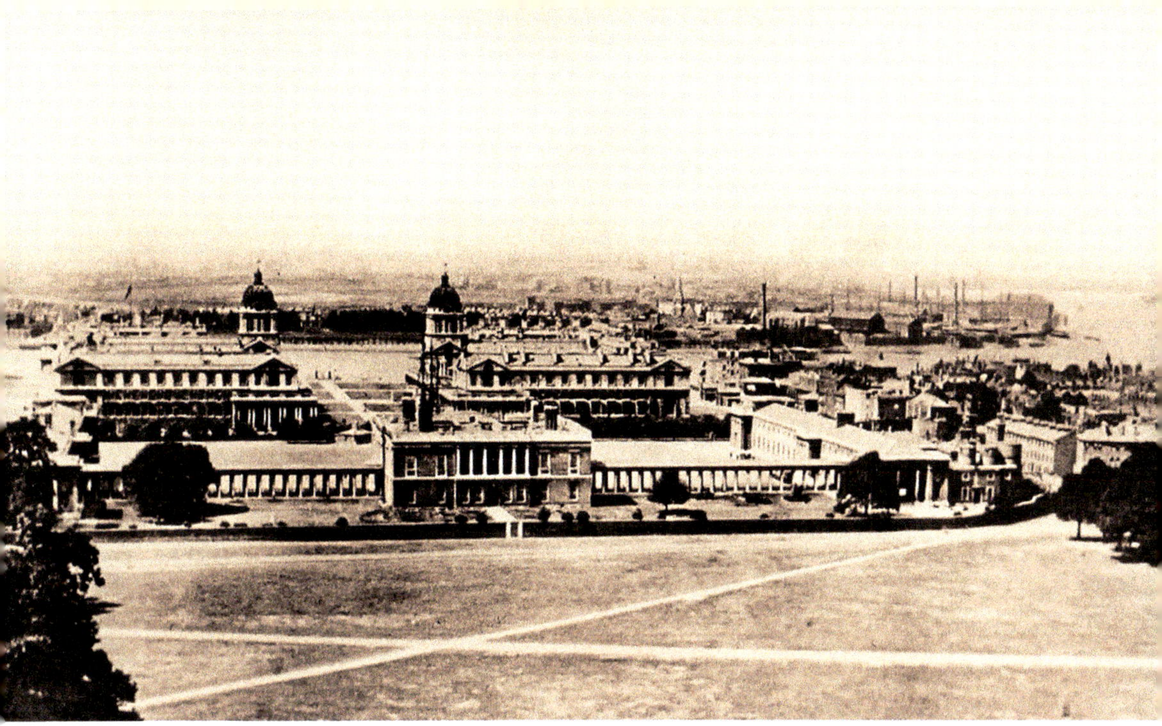

Greenwich Hospital School

A view of the Hospital School buildings from Greenwich Park. The central block was designed and built as the residence of Anne of Denmark, consort of King James I. In 1806 the building was given over to the schooling of boy sailors. Young boys, some orphans, were educated at the school in the ways of seamanship and many would be destined to serve in the navy. In 1933 the school moved to larger premises at Holbrook in Suffolk, since moving out the view across the Thames has changed considerably with high rise offices and apartments replacing the industrial buildings and wharfs which once covered the Isle of Dogs opposite.

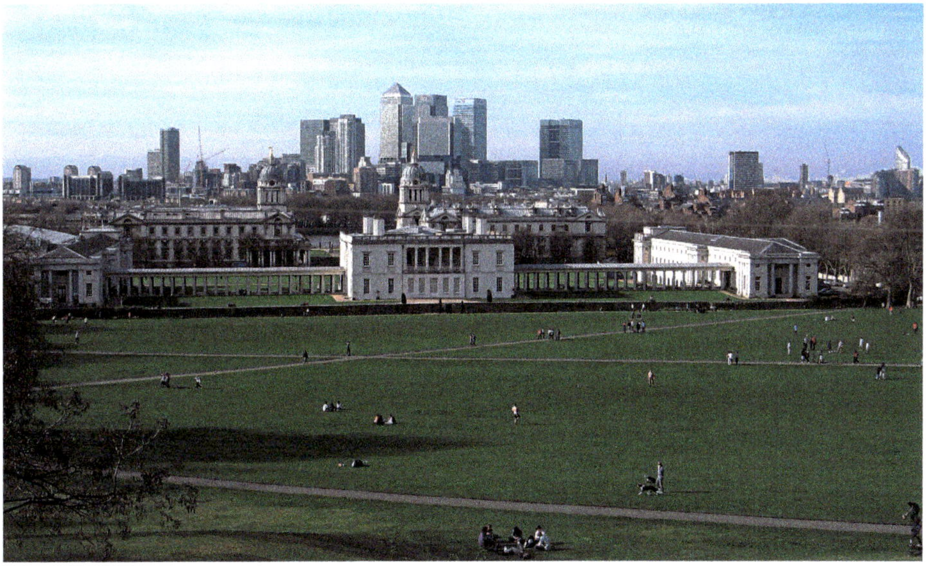

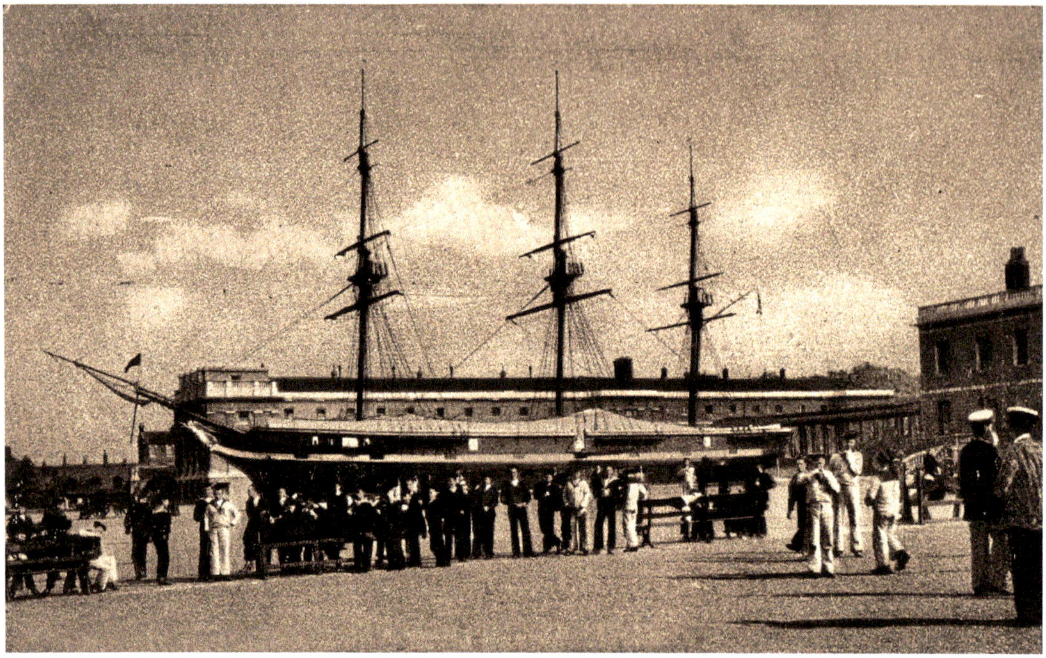

National Maritime Museum

Boy sailors of the Royal Hospital School line up during the 1920s by the training vessel *Fame*, built as a scale replica for teaching seamanship. After the school moved out the buildings were acquired by the National Maritime Museum to display naval artifacts stored at the Royal Naval College. The collections of naval and seafaring exhibits were put on display to the public when the museum doors opened in 1937. The museum now has the largest collection of maritime exhibits in the world.

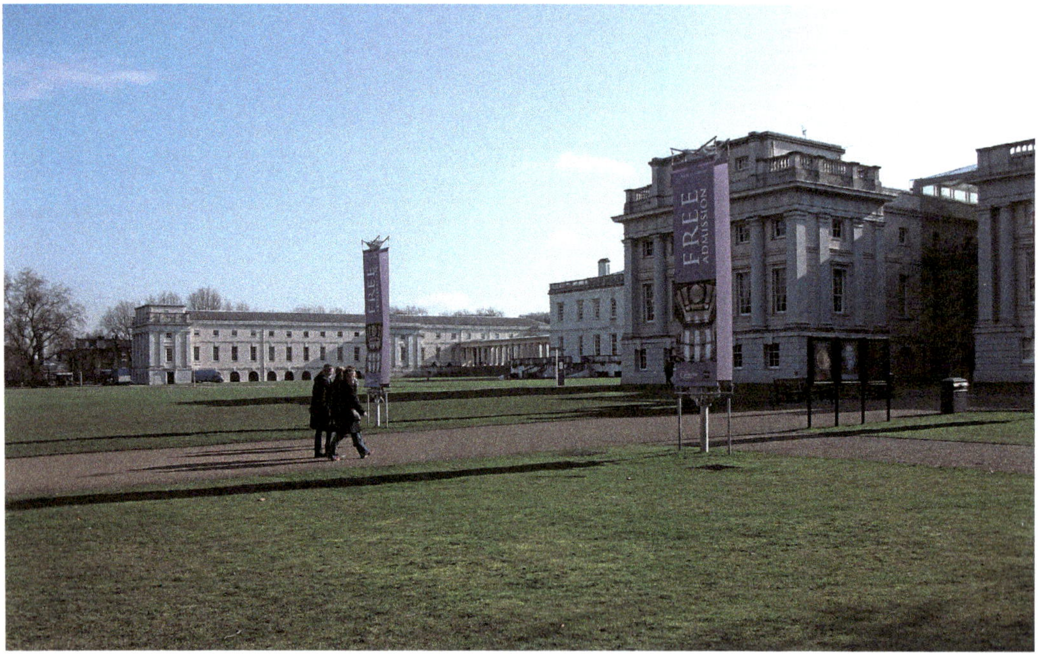

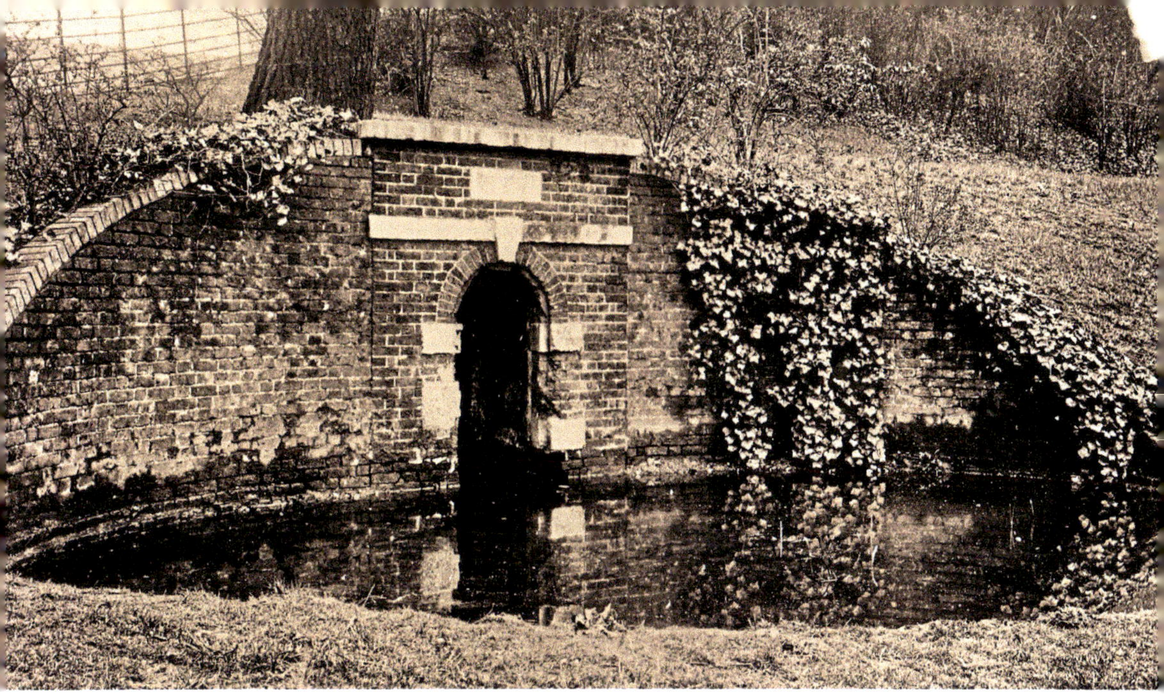

Greenwich Park Conduit – Greenwich Park

Below the surface of Greenwich Park are a series of brick tunnels believed to have been built in Tudor times running down to Greenwich Palace. At the foot of One Tree Hill is a large brick entrance to one of these mysterious tunnels where many local myths and legends surrounded these hidden passageways. This bricked up entrance was rumored to be a tunnel which ran all the way to the Neolithic caves at Chislehurst in Kent. The tunnels were conduits built during the 1600s taking water which drained through the upper surfaces of the park down to the old Greenwich Seamen's Hospital, although there is some evidence that a water drainage system did exist during the Tudor period.

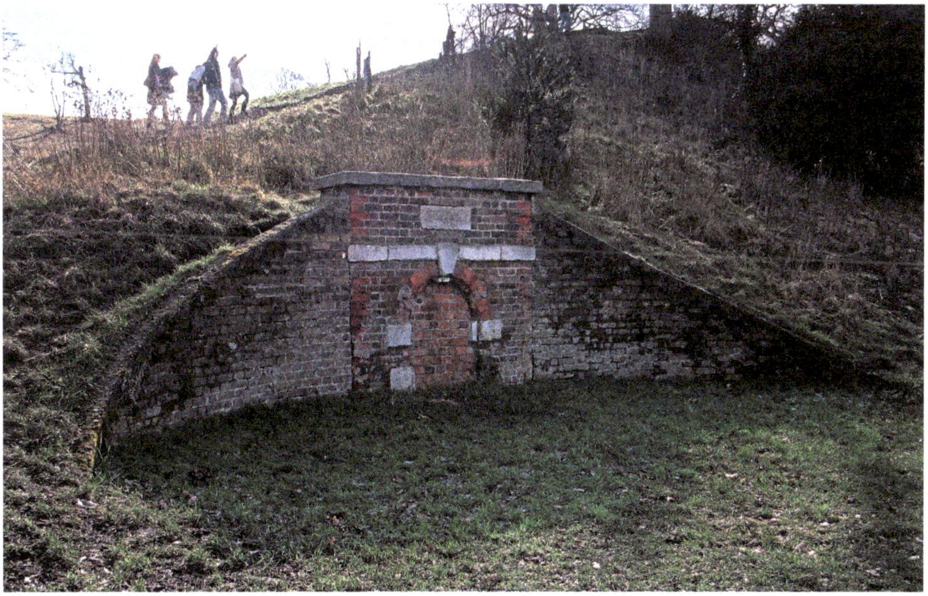

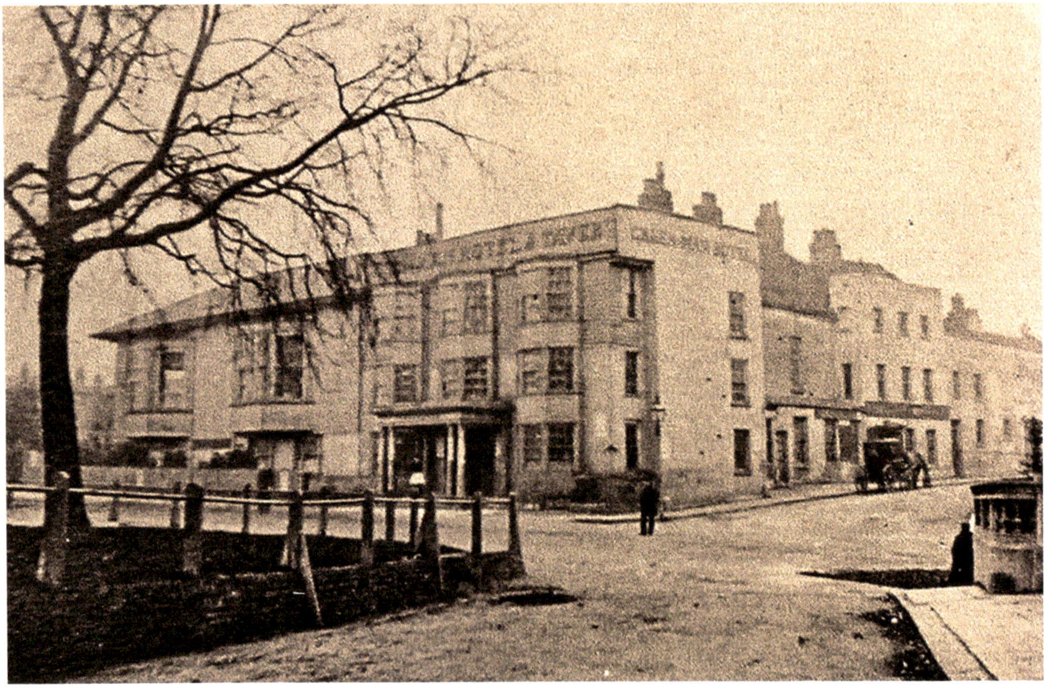

The Green Man – Blackheath Hill

This famous seventeenth-century coaching inn stood at the top of Blackheath Hill. The Green Man was rumored to have been named after Herne the Hunter, whose followers had supposedly worshipped in a cavern found below the inn. Used as the headquarters of the oldest golf club in the world, Royal Blackheath, the inn was demolished in 1868 and replaced by a grand Victorian building which stood at the same site for over a hundred years. The public house, hotel, rock and jazz venue was knocked down to accommodate a block of flats.

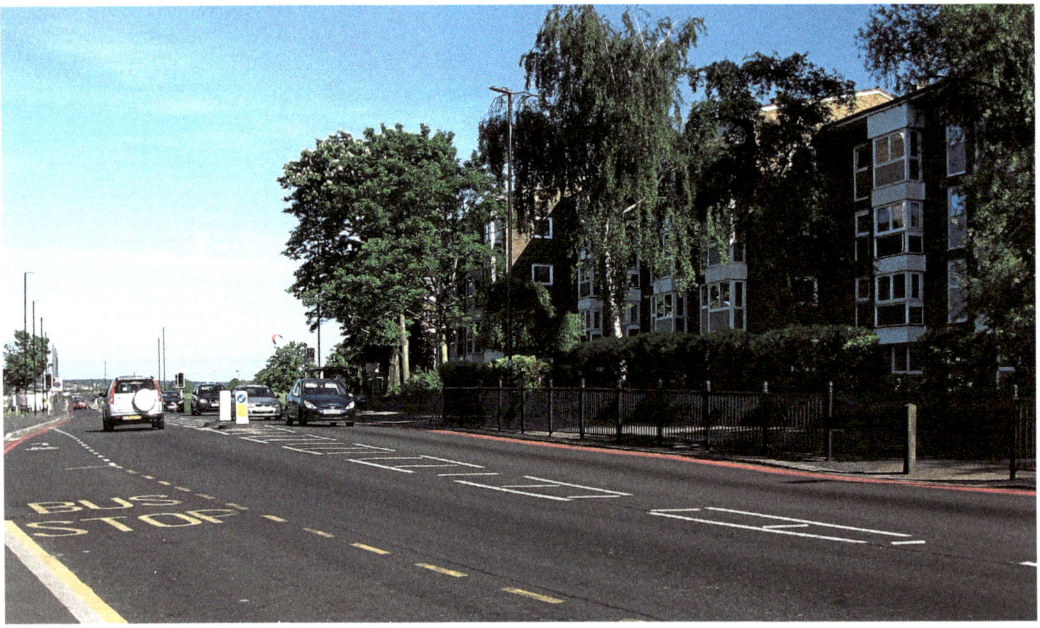

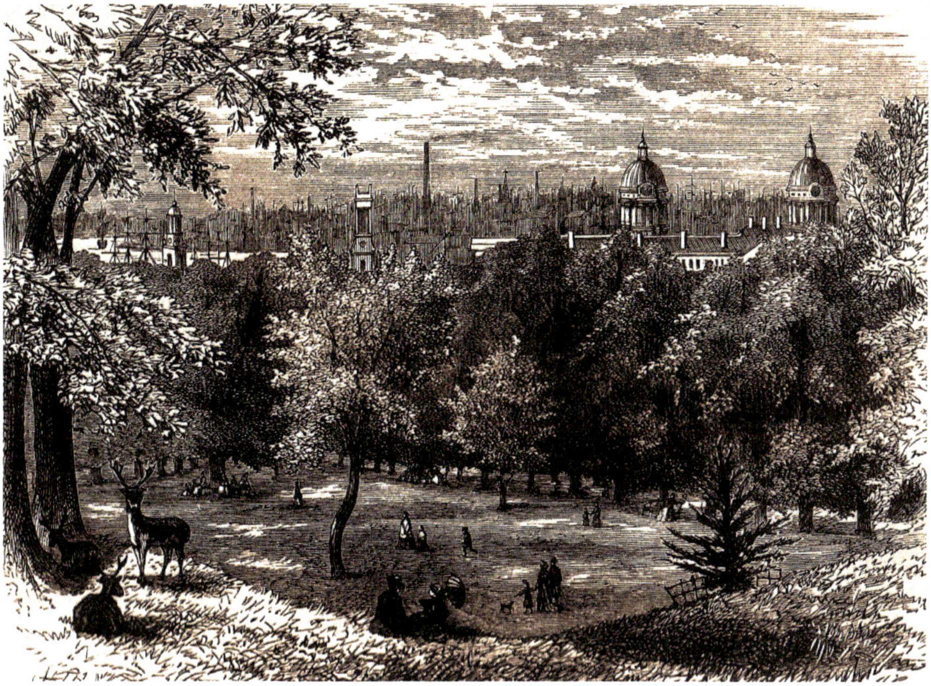

The City of London from Greenwich Park

Greenwich was a favourite destination for city dwellers who wanted to escape the smoke and smog of Victorian London. From the top of One Tree they would be able to look out across roofs of Greenwich and the Royal Naval College towards the city and beyond. The only change to the view is the distant skyline where office blocks have replaced the tall chimneys from the industrial revolution.

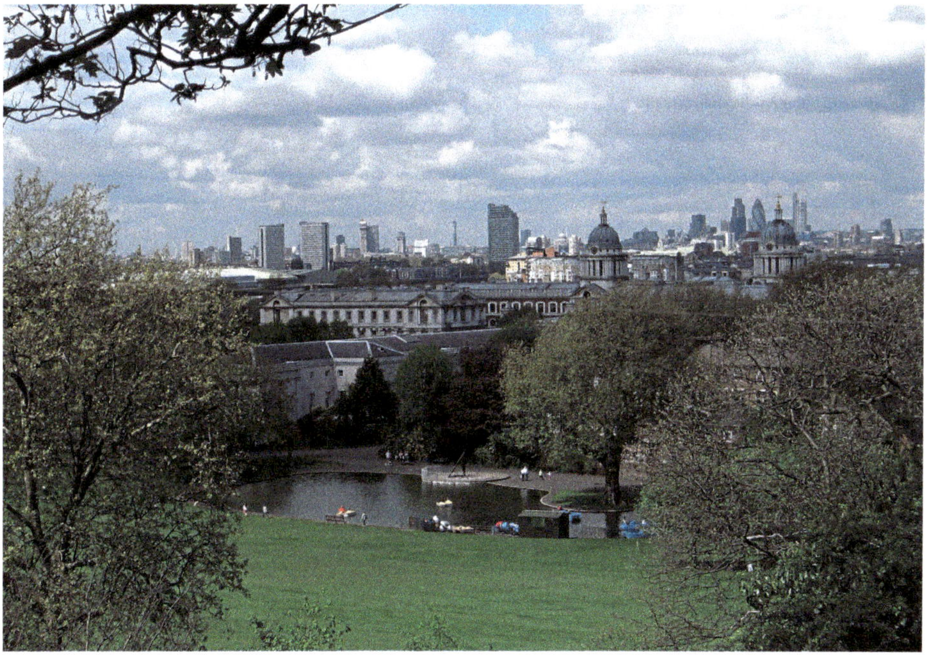

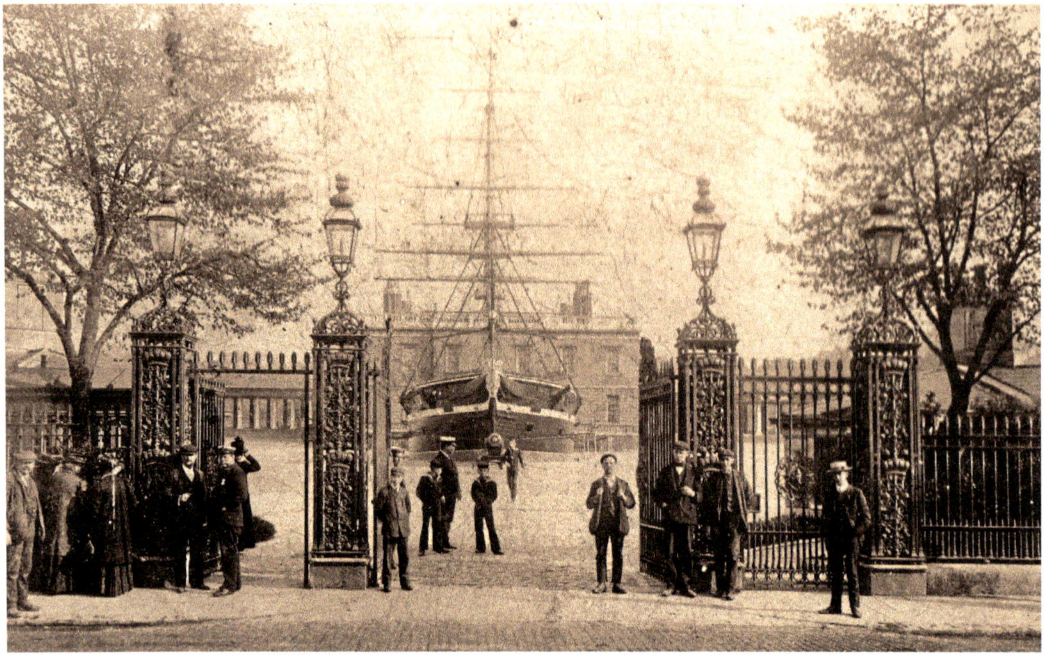

The Gates of the Royal Hospital School

The Royal Hospital School gates on Romney Road during the early 1900s, open for thousands of young boys to be schooled in the art of seamanship. Today tourists now pass through these gates *en route* to the National Maritime Museum where visitors experience a thousand years of maritime history when visiting the galleries, exhibitions, events and activities which take place throughout the year.

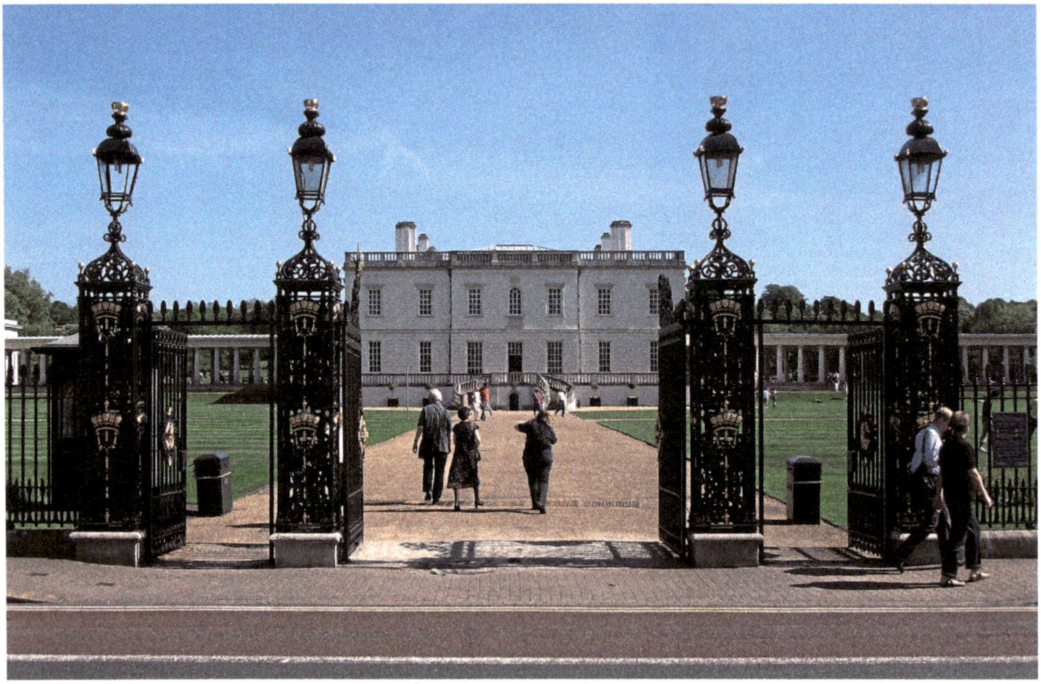

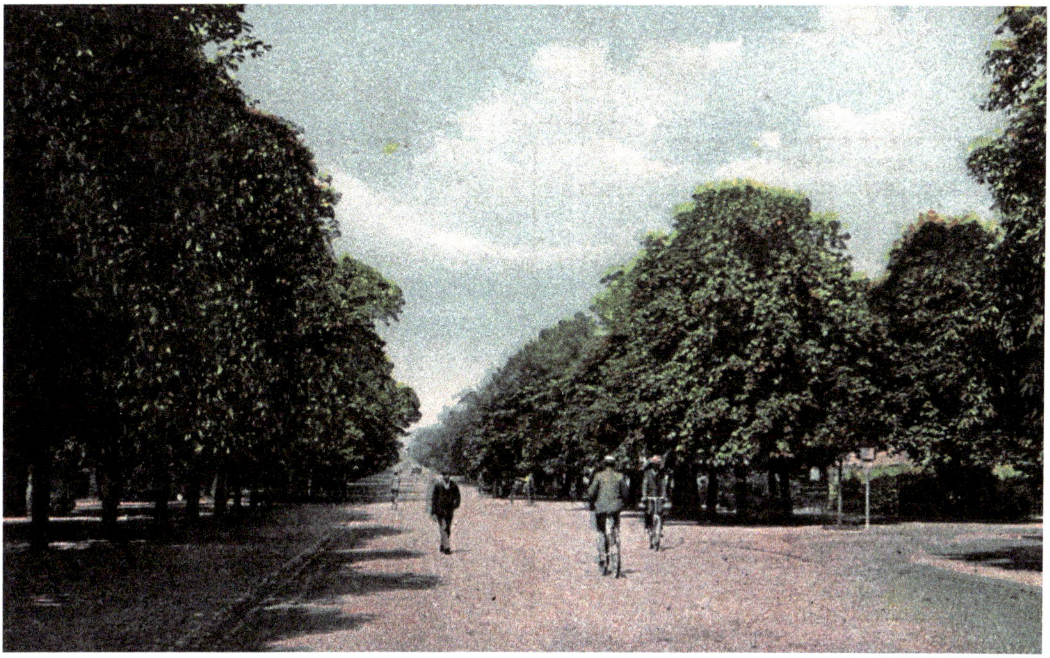

Blackheath Avenue – Greenwich Park

Visitors to the park during the early 1900s could take a walk down the tree-lined Blackheath Avenue during summer months and where children would try knocking chestnuts off the these trees during the autumn. At certain times during the day the avenue is now used as a thoroughfare for traffic running back and fourth from Blackheath to lower Greenwich and where visitors can park their cars below the same chestnut trees which still run the length of Blackheath Avenue.

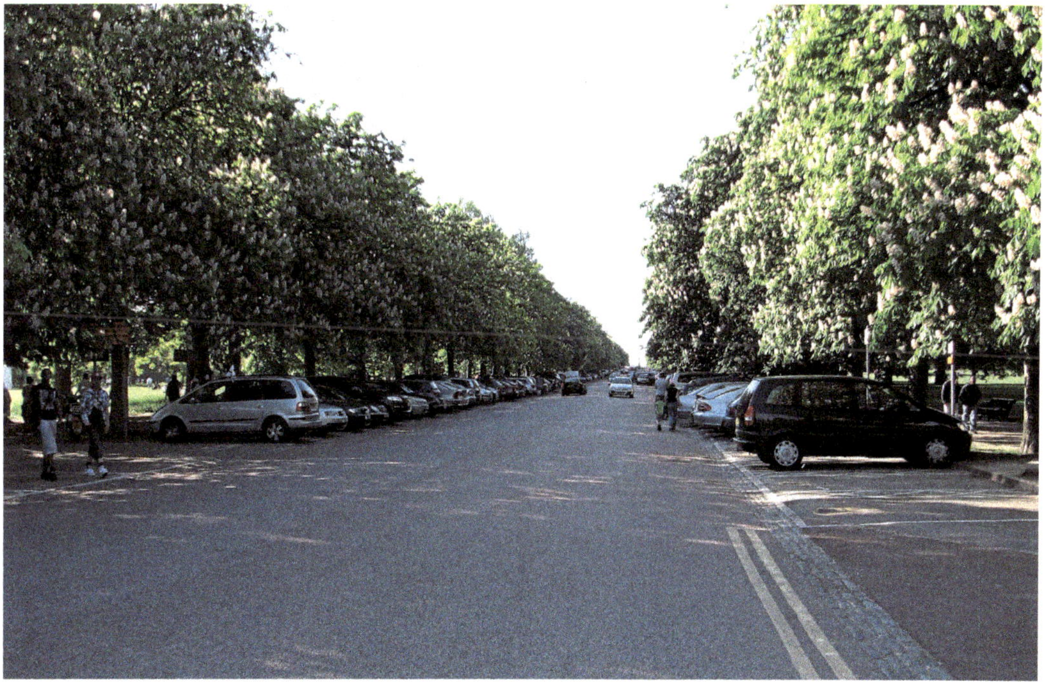

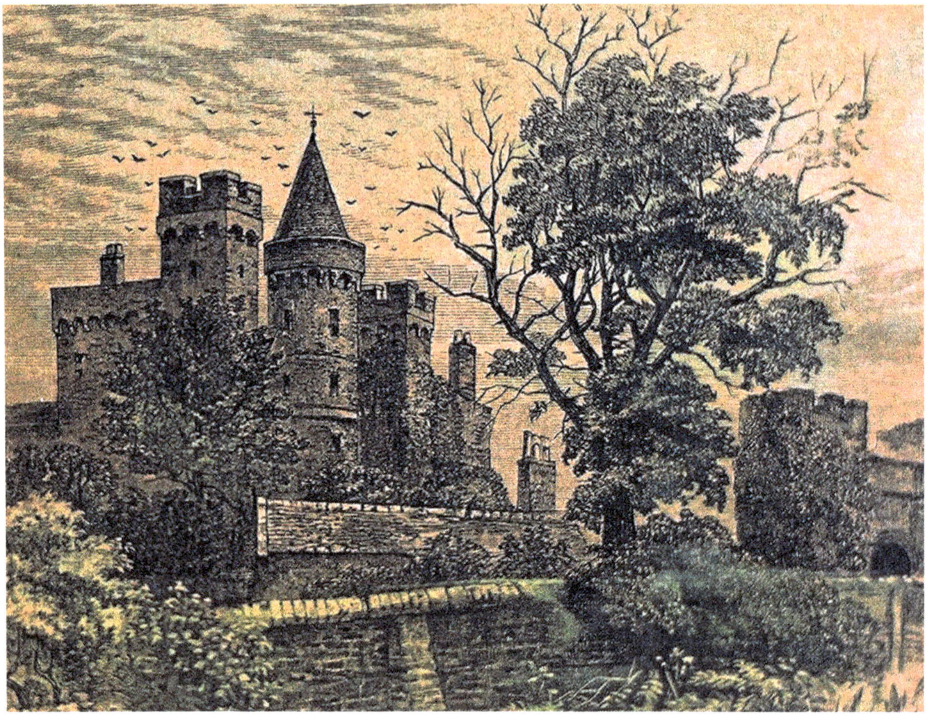

Vanbrugh Castle

Opposite Maze Hill Gate to the east of Greenwich Park is a private castle built in 1717 by architect and dramatist Sir John Vanbrugh. The castle was modelled on the French Bastille where Sir John Vanbrugh had been imprisoned in 1690 accused of being a British spy. The castle remained a private residence until it was used as a school for the children of RAF personnel during the mid 1900s. The castle was returned into private ownership and has now been converted into flats.

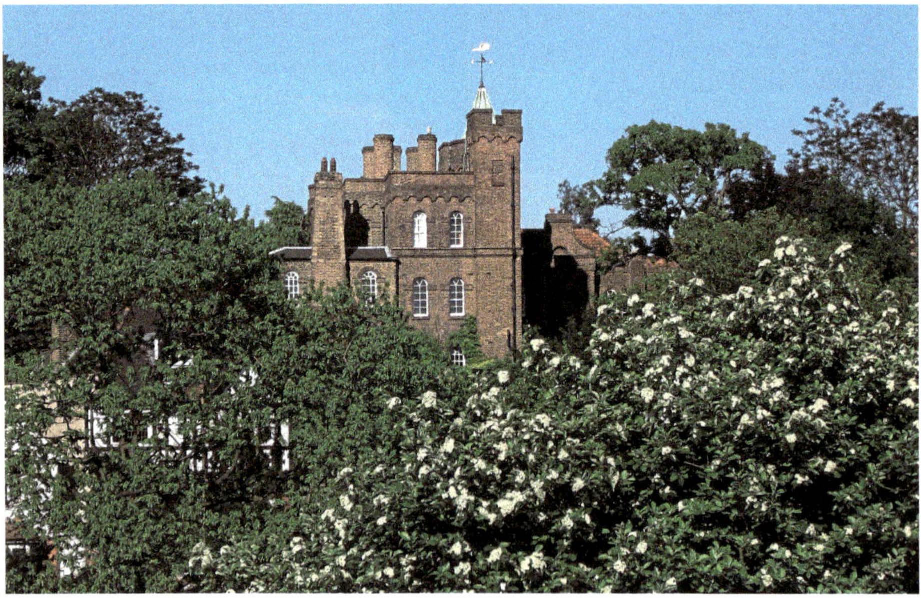

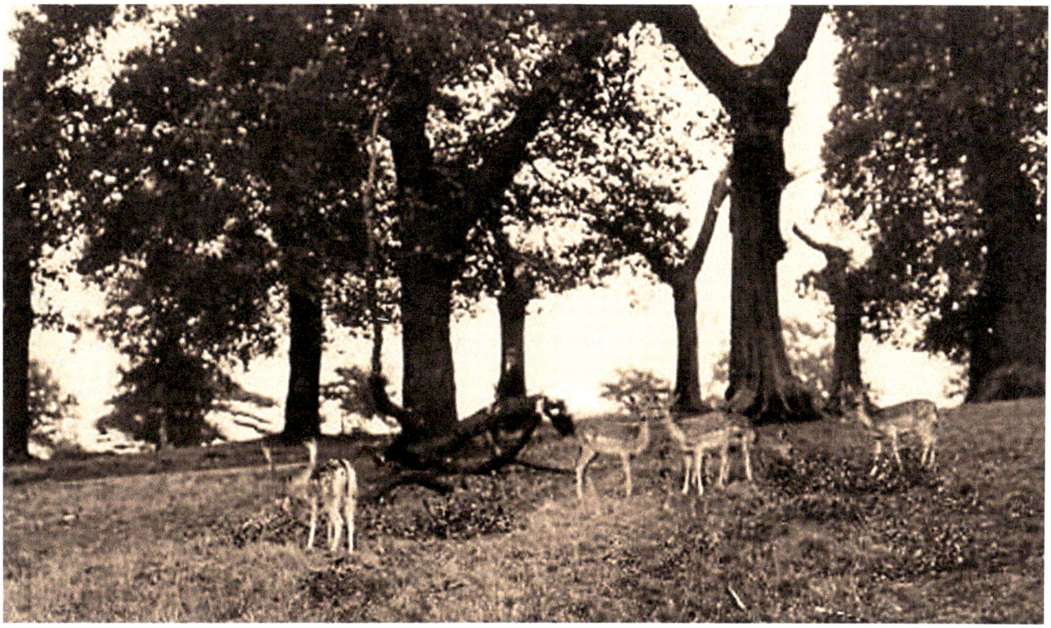

Greenwich Park Deer

Edward III hunted in Greenwich Park during the fourteenth century and Henry VIII introduced the first herds of deer into the park while holding his court at Greenwich during the early 1500s. The sport of hunting deer in the park carried on throughout the next few centuries. The herds of red deer and fallow deer are no longer roaming free in the park but can been found at their enclosure in an area known as the Wilderness.

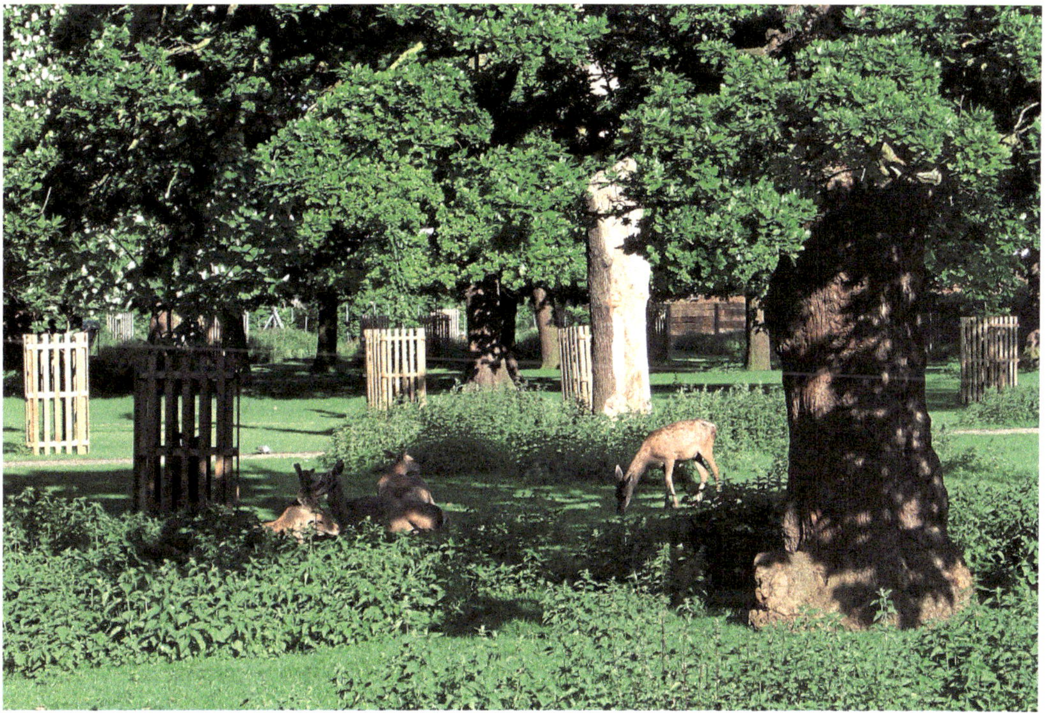

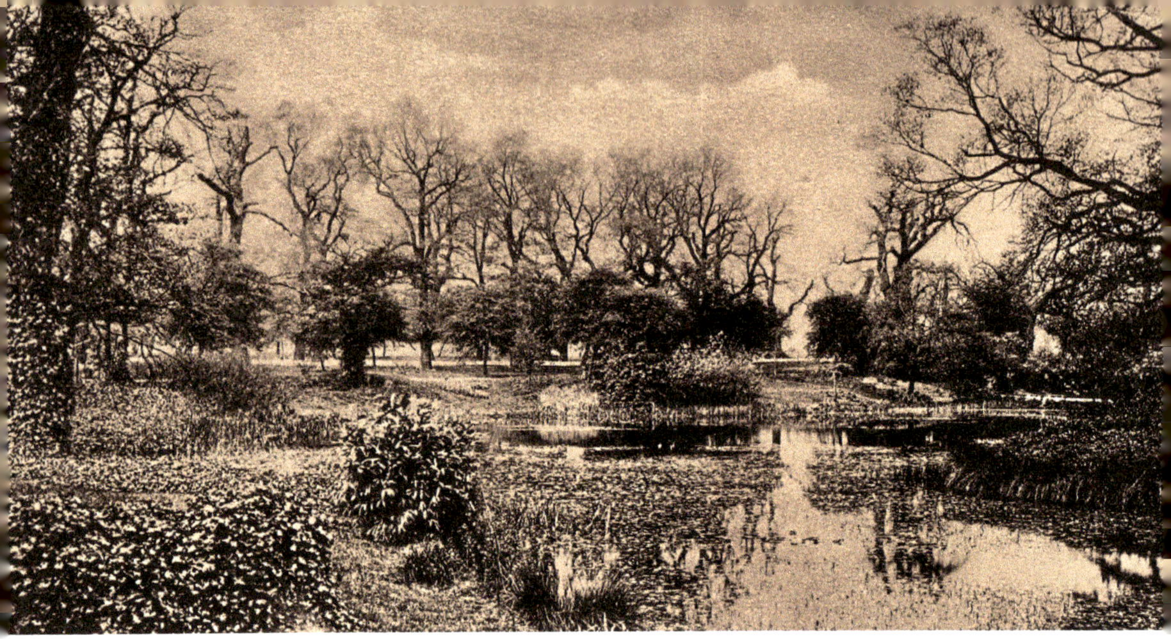

The Pond – Greenwich Park

In the seventeenth century Charles II commissioned the royal park to be formally landscaped, which included the planting of a flower garden and woodlands in an area known as the Wilderness. The flower gardens at the south east corner of the park later incorporated a large ornamental duck pond. The pond was surrounded by various trees and shrubs which became a haven for many species of wildfowl where children were taken with bags full of bread crusts to feed the ducks on the pond.

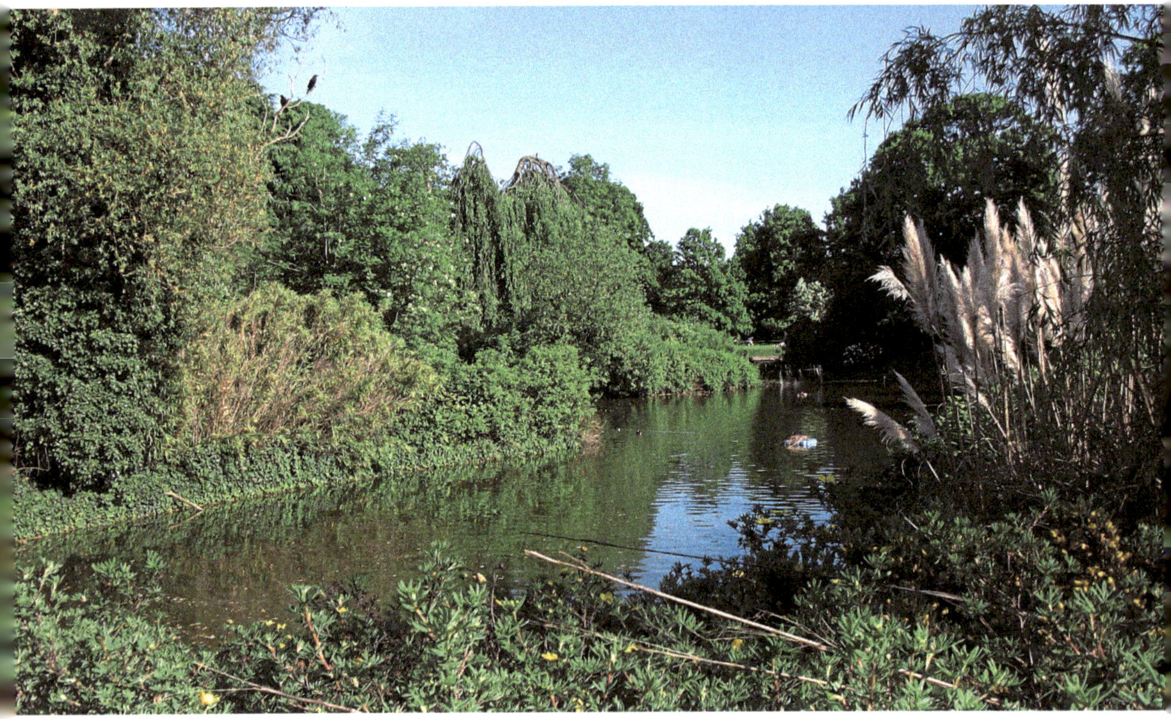

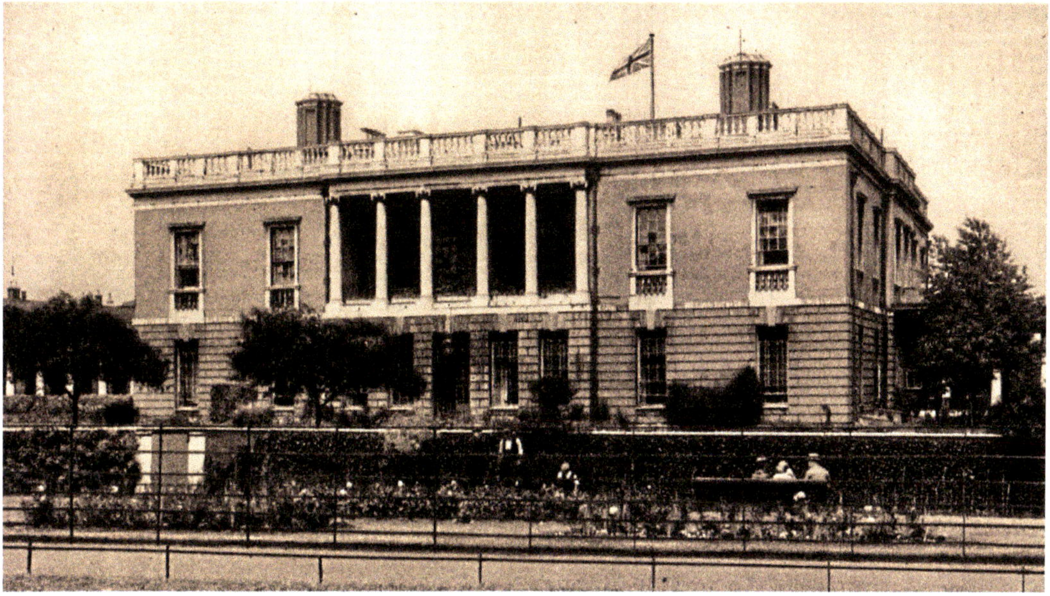

The Queen's House – Royal Hospital School

Commissioned by Anne of Denmark in 1616 the Queen's House was designed by the Surveyor of the King's Works Inigo Jones built to bridge the main Greenwich highroad. George III donated the Queen's House to the Royal Hospital School in 1806 which was later enlarged by adding colonnaded walks each side of the main house connecting to the east and west wings. Maintained by the National Maritime Museum and restored as a place of royal residence, the elegant house, which includes the Great Hall, Orangery and Undercroft, can be hired for corporate events and wedding receptions.

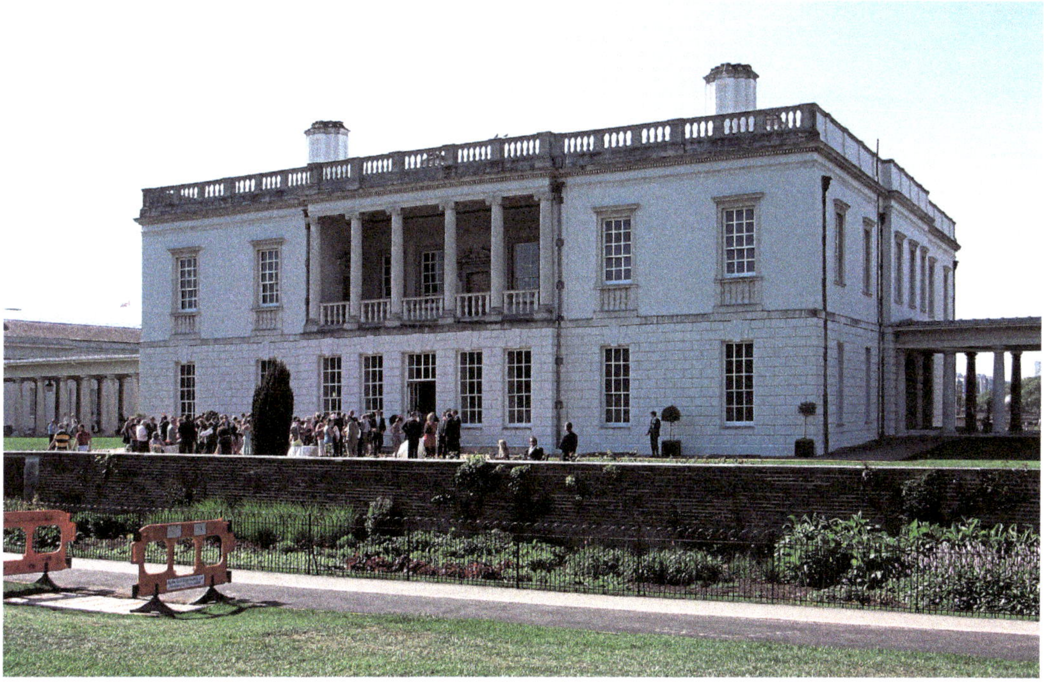

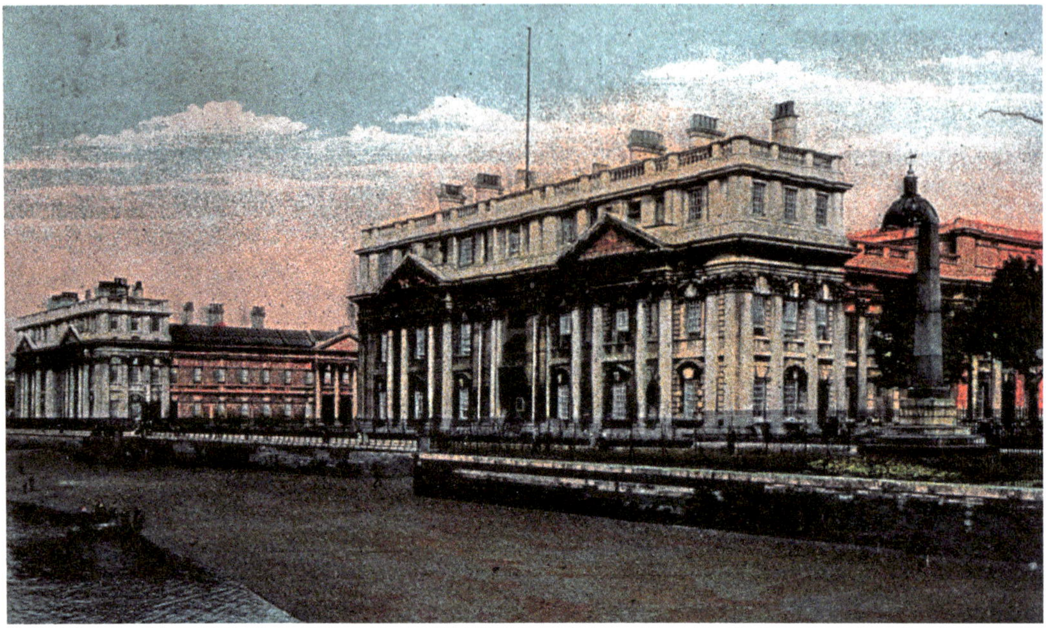

Foreshore of the Thames – Greenwich Hospital

Commissioned by Mary II and designed by Sir Christopher Wren the hospital for sick and injured seamen took more than fifty years to complete. Wren's contemporaries, Hawksmoor and Vanbrugh, would finish this magnificent project. To the west of these grand river front buildings stands a memorial to the French explorer Joseph-René Bellot who was killed on an expedition to the Arctic in 1853.

Inset. An inscribed contemporary stone laid between the east and west wings of the buildings commemorate the site of the original Greenwich Palace.

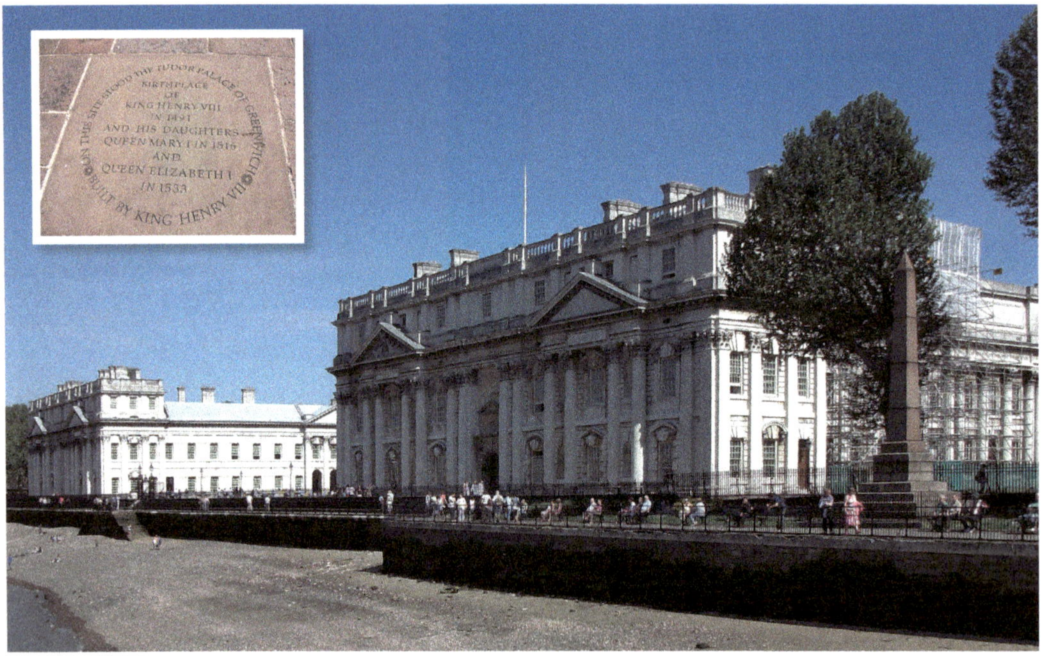

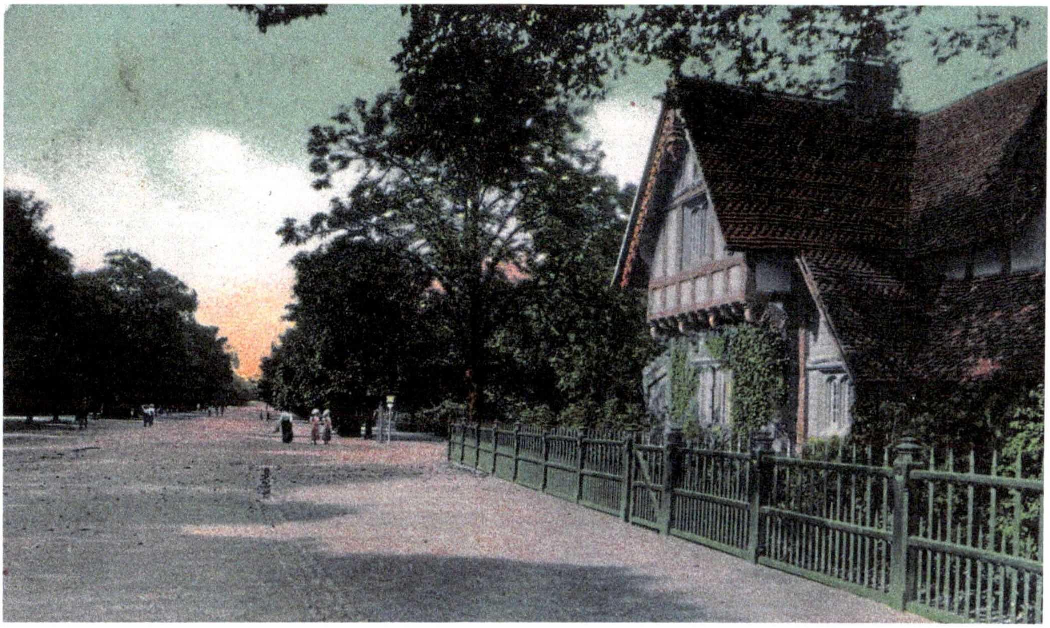

Gate Lodge – Greenwich Park

The Keeper of the Park's lodge was built in 1852 to the designs of architect John Phipps. The mock-Tudor style lodge replaced a seventeenth-century keeper's lodge at the park's centre. Greenwich Park Keeper Mr A. D. Webster, who lived in the lodge during the late 1800s, wrote a comprehensive history of Greenwich Park published in 1902. After a succession of park keepers occupied the lodge the building eventually fell into disuse. Recently refurbished the three bedroom lodge which has private parking and access to the park is available for private rent.

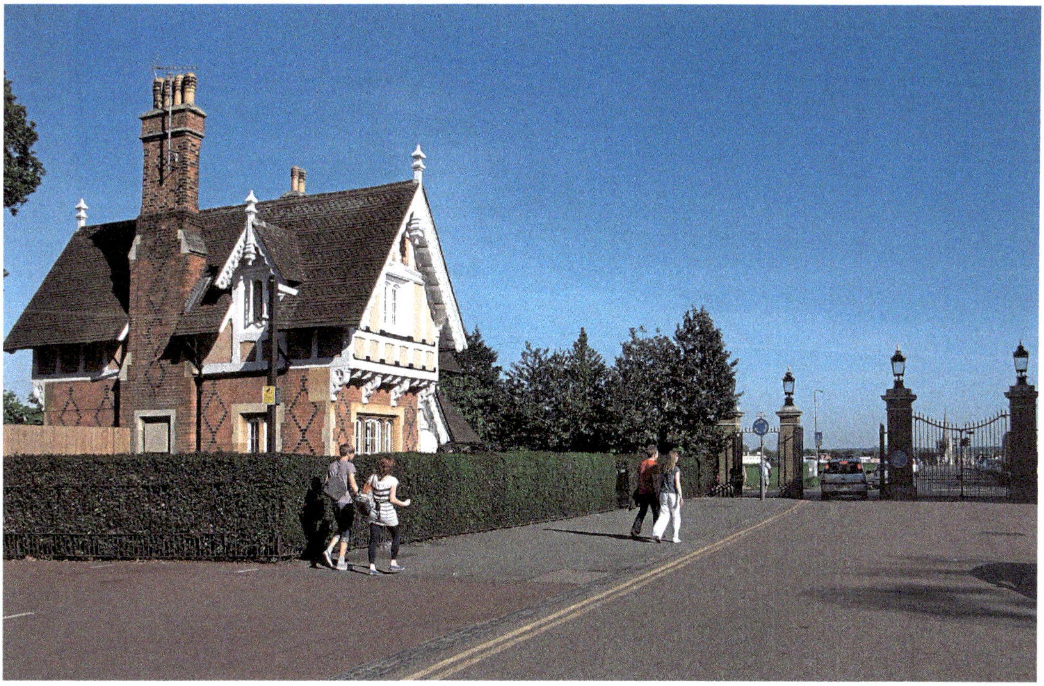

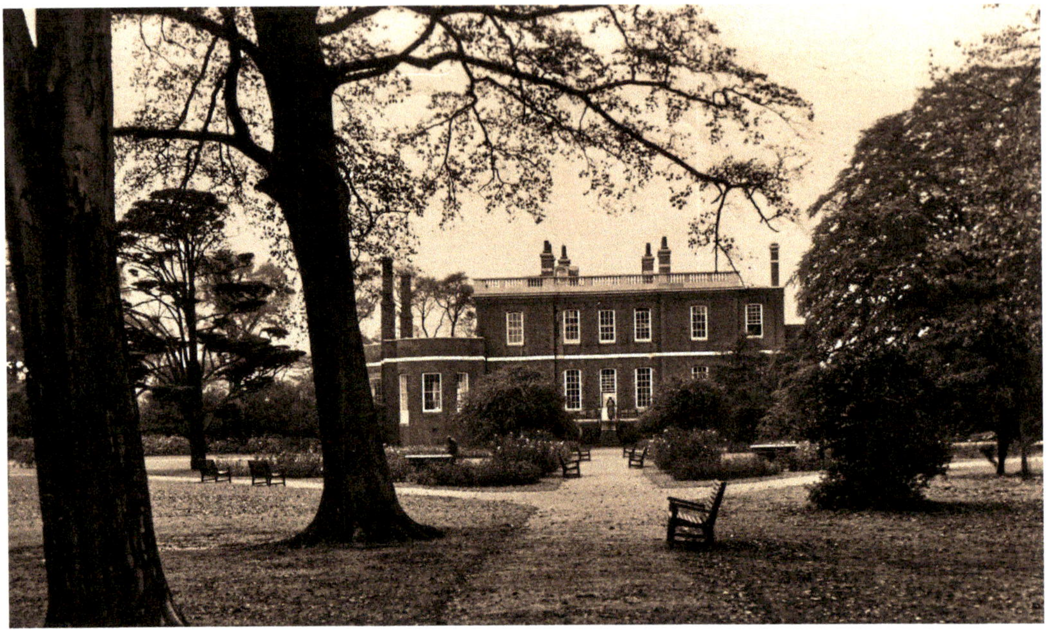

The Ranger's House

To the western edge of Greenwich Park is the Ranger's House, a Georgian villa built by seafarer Admiral Francis Hosier during the early 1700s. The house was later occupied by the sister of George III and by the early 1800s became the official residence of the Royal Park's Ranger. The house is now in the care of English Heritage for the exhibiting of traditional and contemporary art. To the rear of the house are the impressive Greenwich Park Rose Gardens, but at the front of the house the driveway has become a car park area.

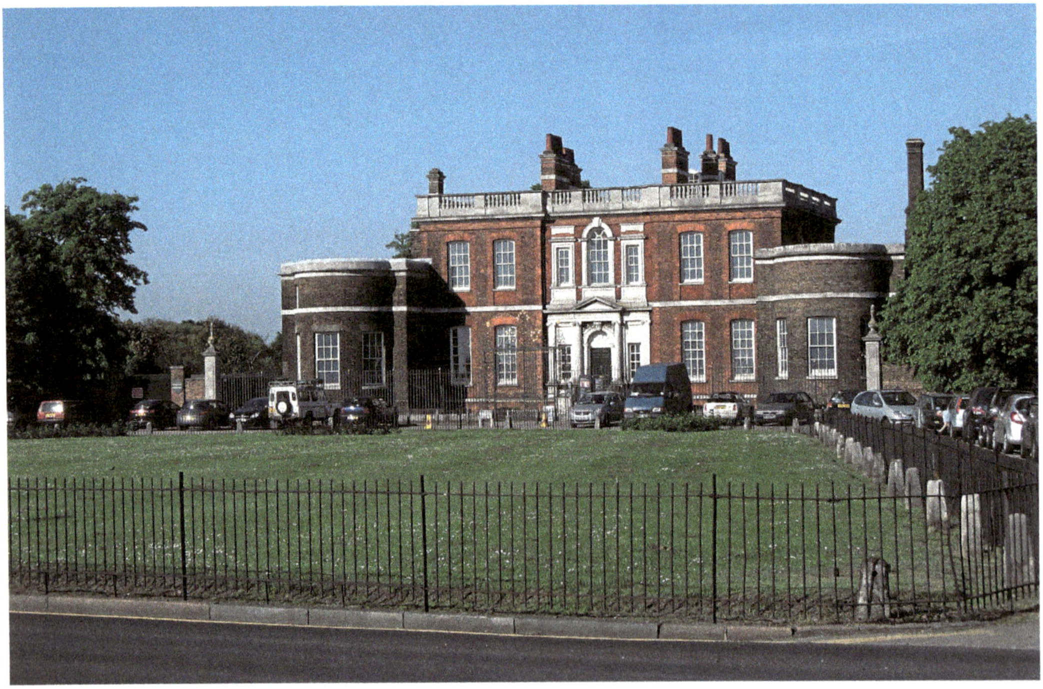

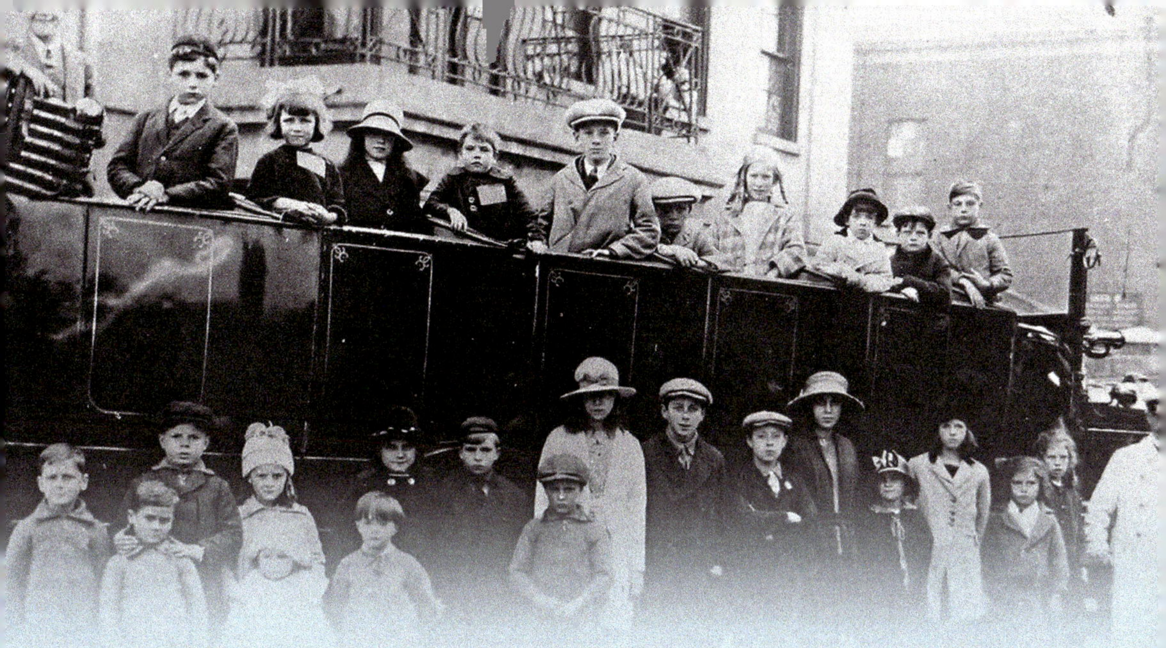

CHAPTER 2

In the Community

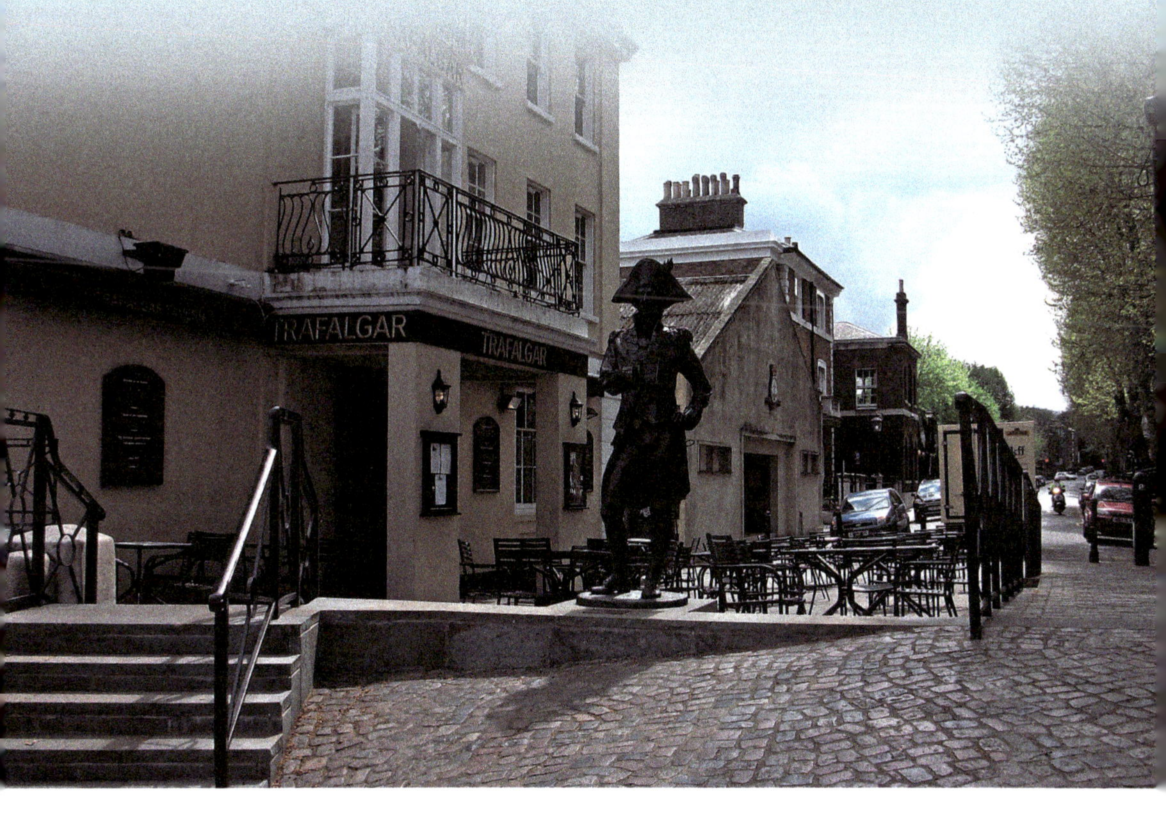

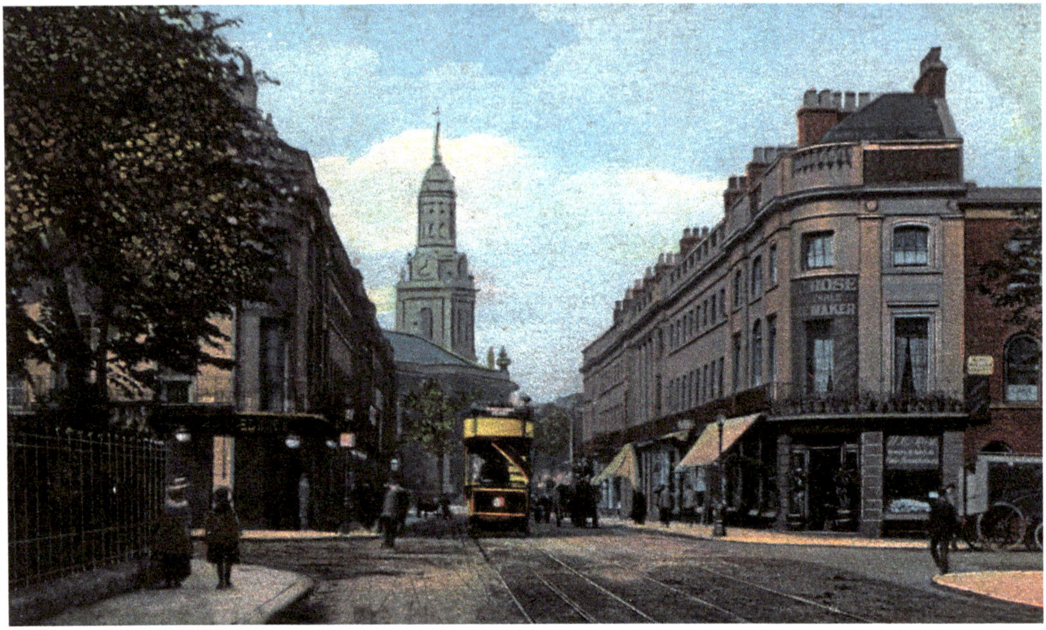

Nelson Road

Built as part of a new town development by Greenwich Hospital Estates in 1829, Nelson Road was named after hero of the Battle of Trafalgar Lord Horatio Nelson. During the 1800s the elegant shops positioned each side of the road were one of the most fashionable places to shop in south London. This main road through the middle of Greenwich to the parish church of St Alfege at the centre of the town is an area which continues to go through series of regeneration projects, development and change.

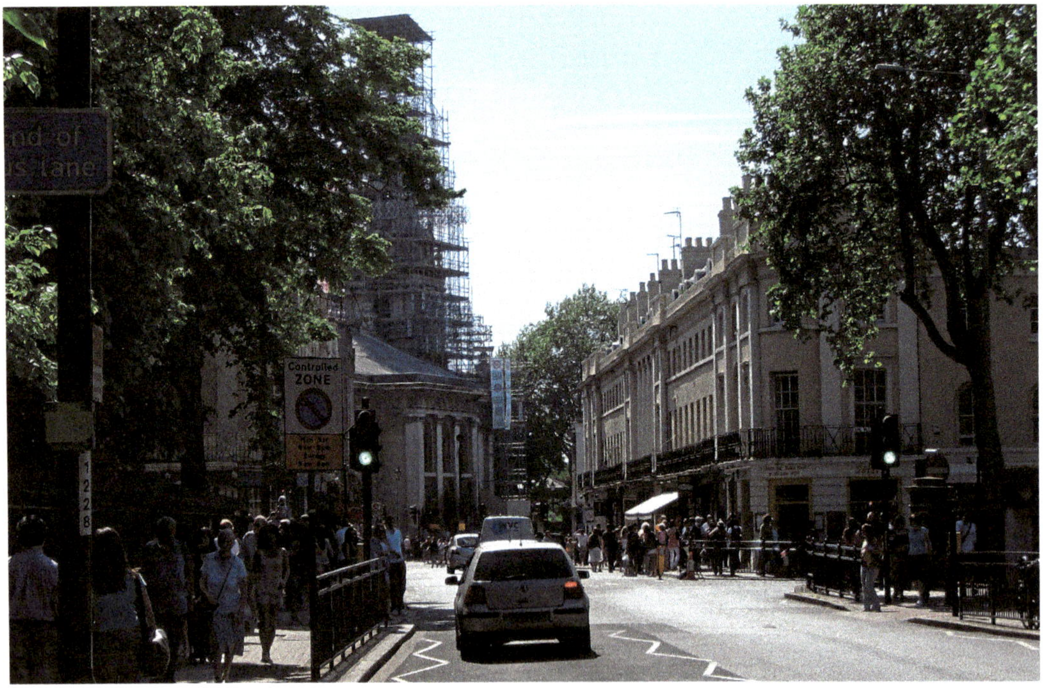

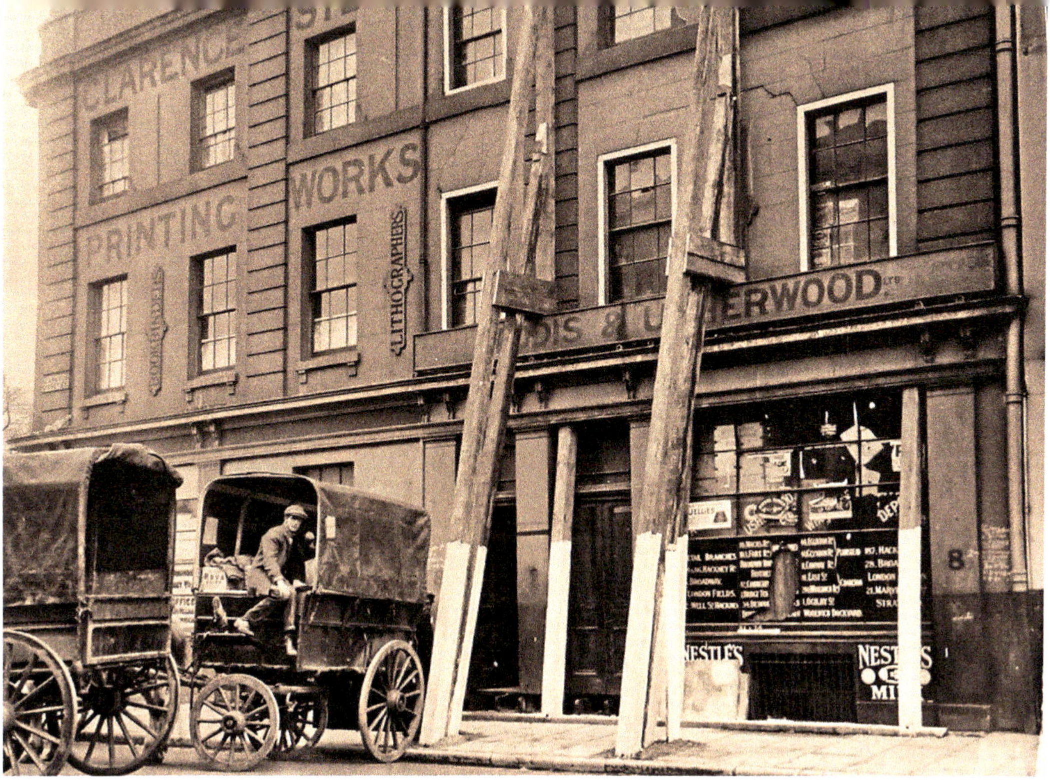

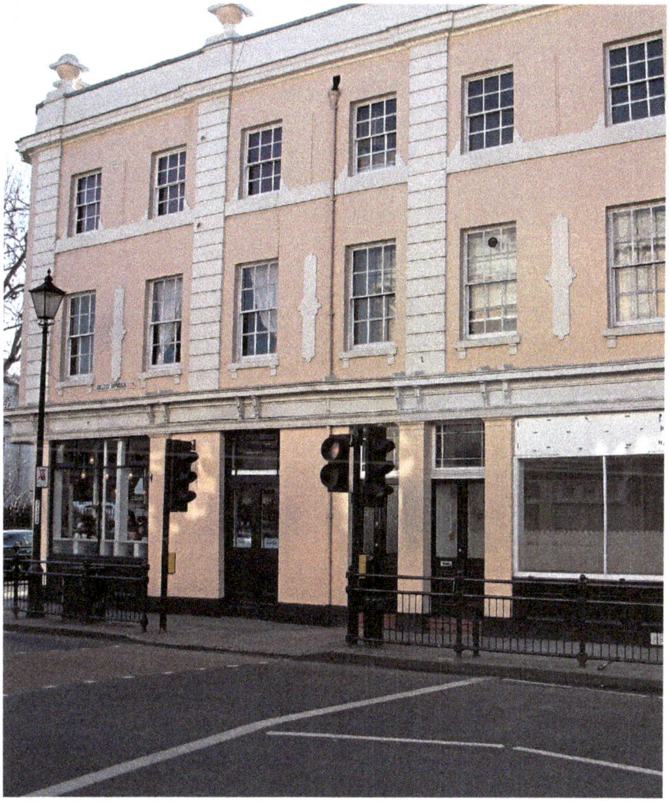

College Approach

In 1831 the area surrounding the present Greenwich Market had been full of narrow alleyways, lanes and courtyards, where some of the poorest Greenwich residents had been living. The Commissioners of the Royal Naval Hospital purchased these properties and their surveyor Joseph Kay transformed the whole area which incorporated Nelson Street, King William Street and Clarence Street, which is now College Approach. Although in need of a high level of repair by the turn of the twentieth century the buildings have been renovated and improved over the years and are now highly sought after period properties commanding high rental charges.

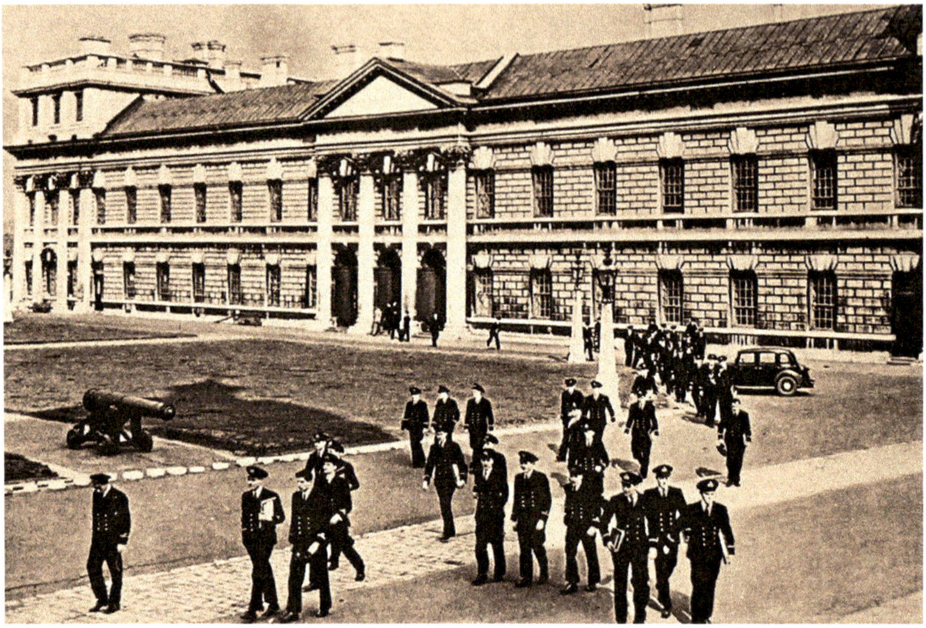

Royal Naval Officers – Royal Naval College

After the Royal Hospital closed down in 1869 the historical buildings were given over to the navy for the education of naval officers. The Royal Naval College incorporated the Naval Architectural College of Portsmouth and the Marine Engineering College of South Kensington. During the war years over 27,000 officers and 8,000 WRNS were trained at Greenwich. When the college moved in 1998 to larger premises in Suffolk, the University of Greenwich and Trinity School of Music acquired the buildings. The Royal Navy will often make a return to the old college to take part in historic events and festivals.

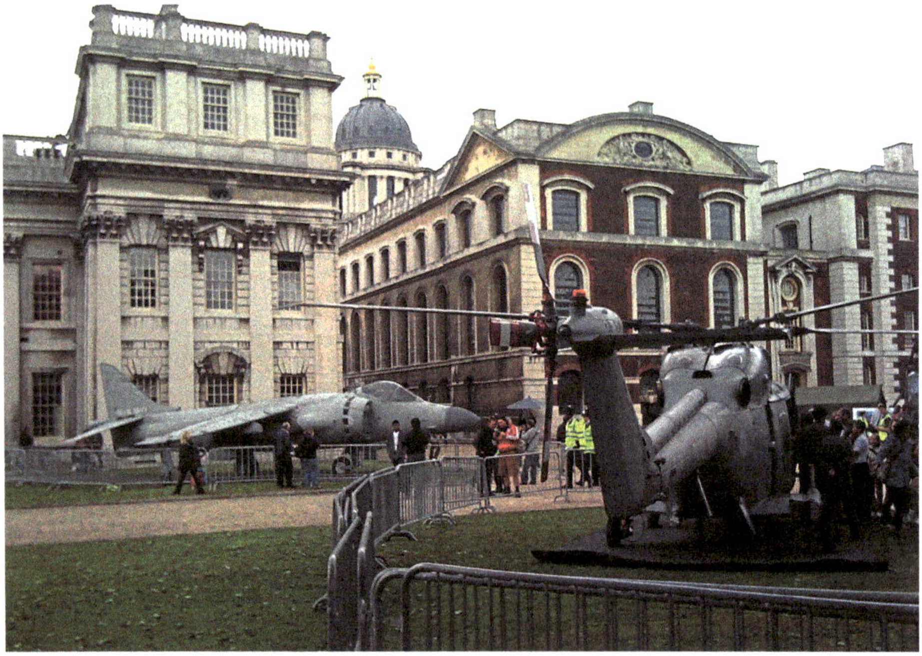

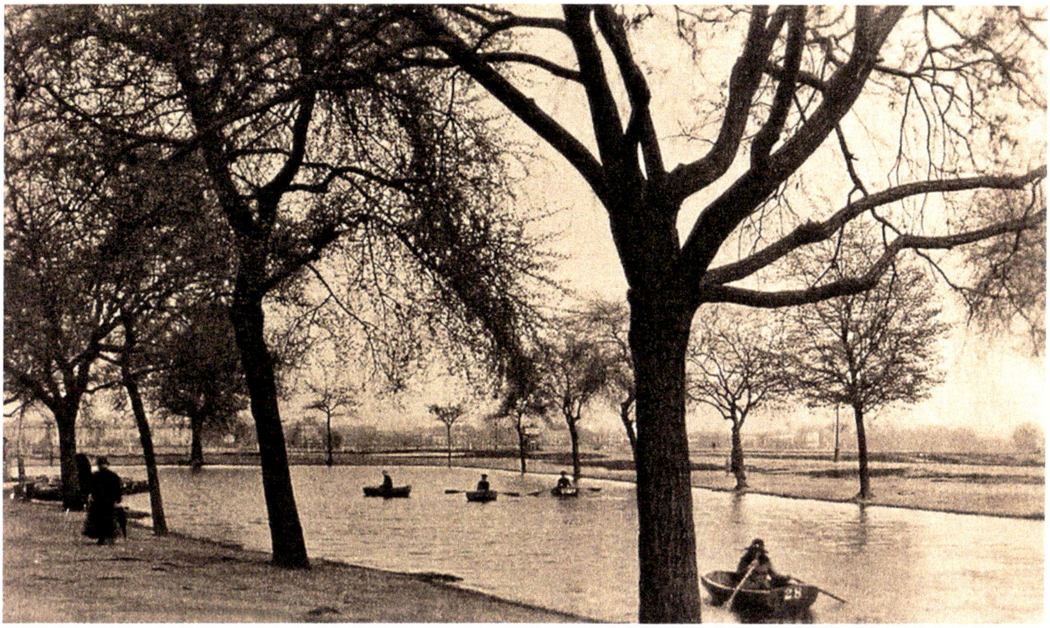

Boating – Blackheath

During the late 1800s Greenwich residents would go boating on a small lake on Blackheath opposite the park gates. Folly Pond, or Long Pond as it was also known, had origins as a gravel pit which was filled with water and used as a drinking source for cattle and horses travelling the Dover Road. The pond is no longer used for boating and the water source is supplied by a standpipe installed to stop the pond from drying out during the summer.

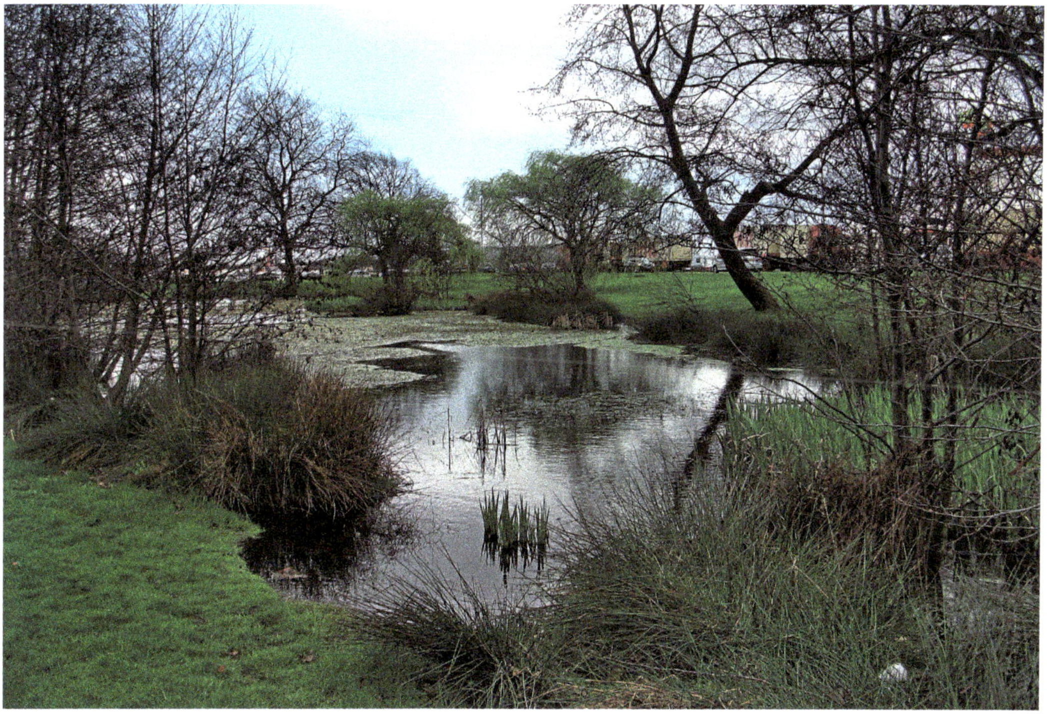

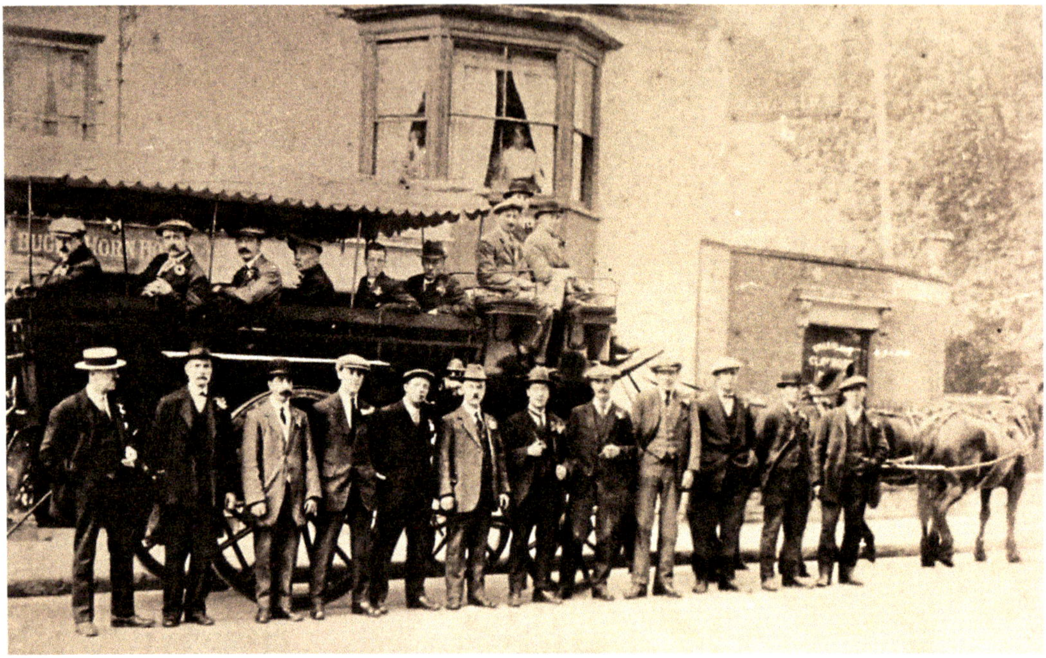

Public House Outing

The Bugle Horn in Charlton village east of Blackheath is one of the borough's oldest coaching inns. The inn was originally three eighteenth-century cottages knocked into one and was a popular meeting place for day trippers travelling out by horse-drawn carriage. In earlier times the Horn Fair was held near the Bugle Horn where Greenwich folk gathered in celebration of Herne the Hunter, also known as the Green Man, an ancient festival which had Celtic origins.

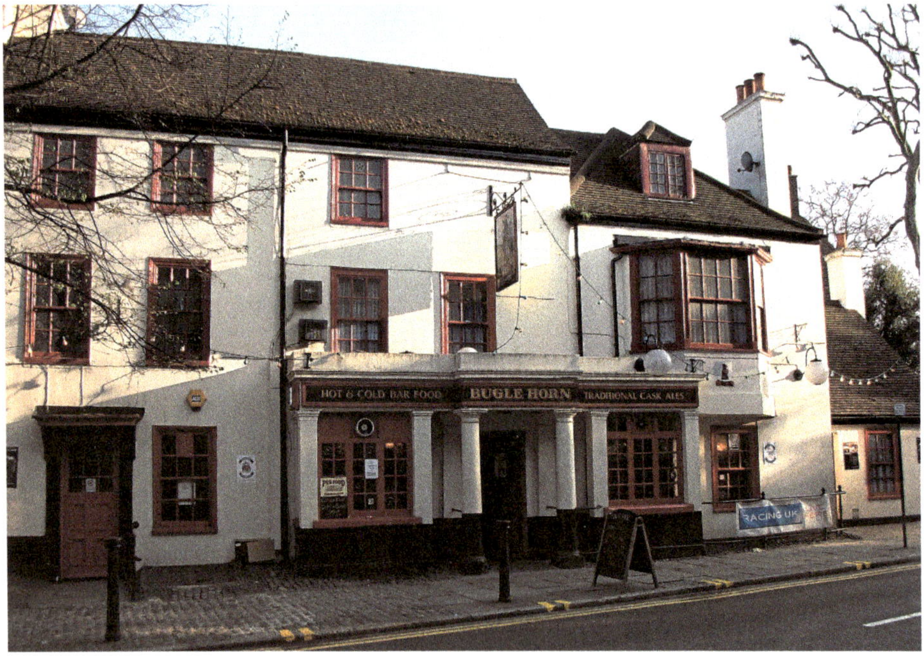

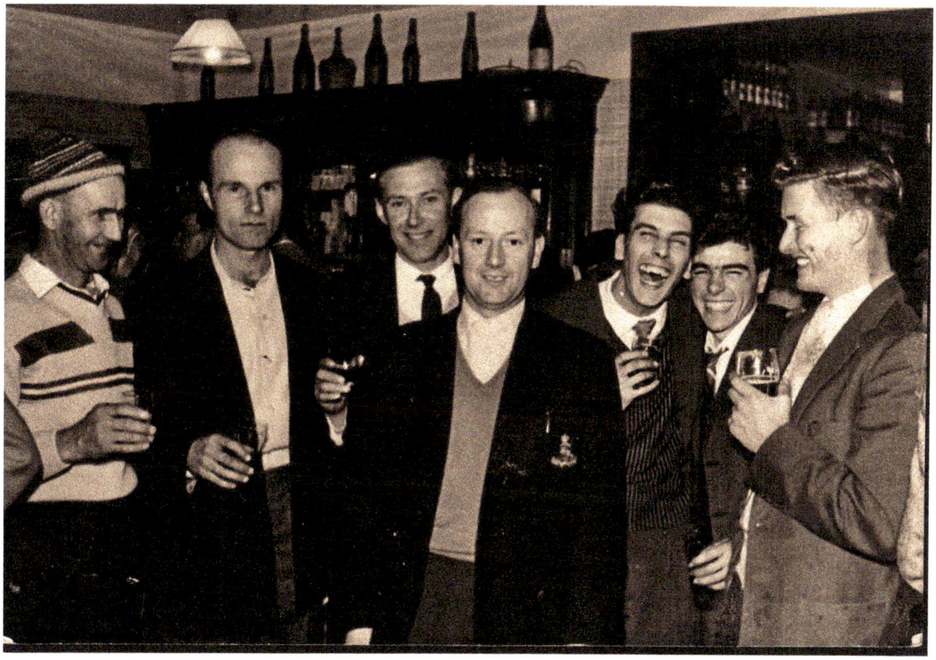

Local Drinking Companions

A group of regulars enjoying some local hospitality on a pub crawl during the late 1950s, with my father pictured third from the right of the group. The public houses of Greenwich were at one time an essential part of the local community where friends and relations would meet up socially for a pint after work and at weekends. This is a tradition which is carried on when I meet up with my own friends at the Bugle Horn after watching a match at our local football club Charlton Athletic.

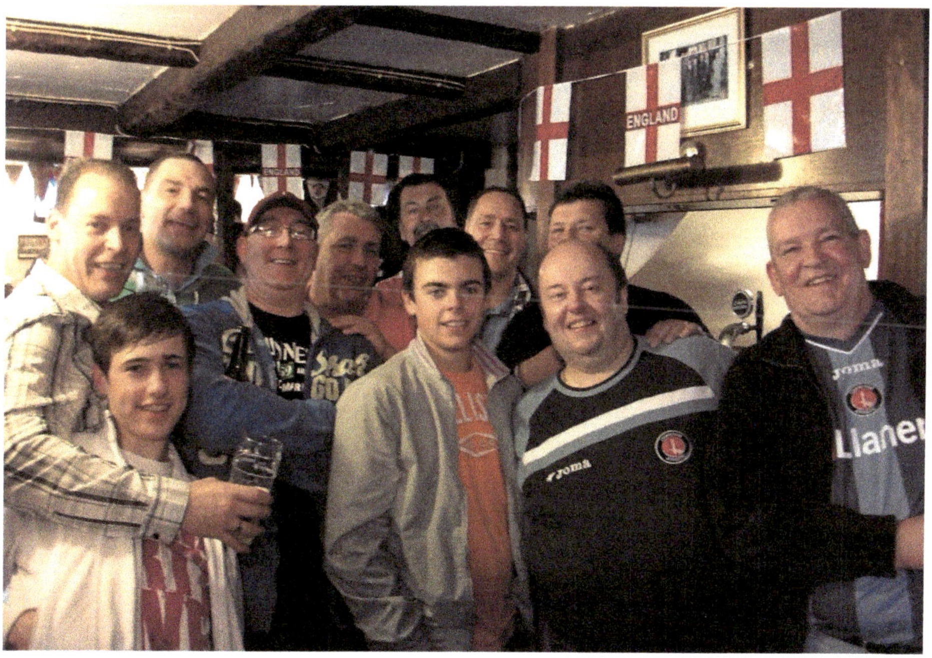

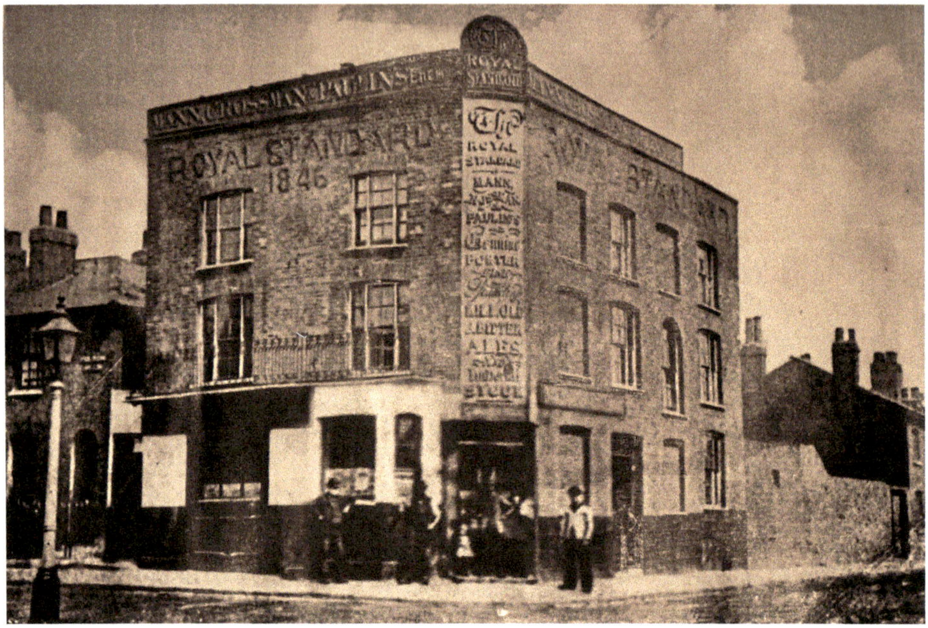

The Royal Standard – Pelton Road

Blocks of terraced houses built for Greenwich workers and their families during the Victorian period of the industrial revolution would include a public house on one of the corners of the block. The Royal Standard is one of the few surviving traditional pubs built during this time. Many of these locals have now gone, either bombed during the blitz or demolished to make way for new building developments, while others became wine bars, restaurants or private dwellings. The Royal Standard has so far remained true to the origins of local community public houses, where regulars still carry on the traditions of travelling by coach for a day out at the races or a weekend away to the coast.

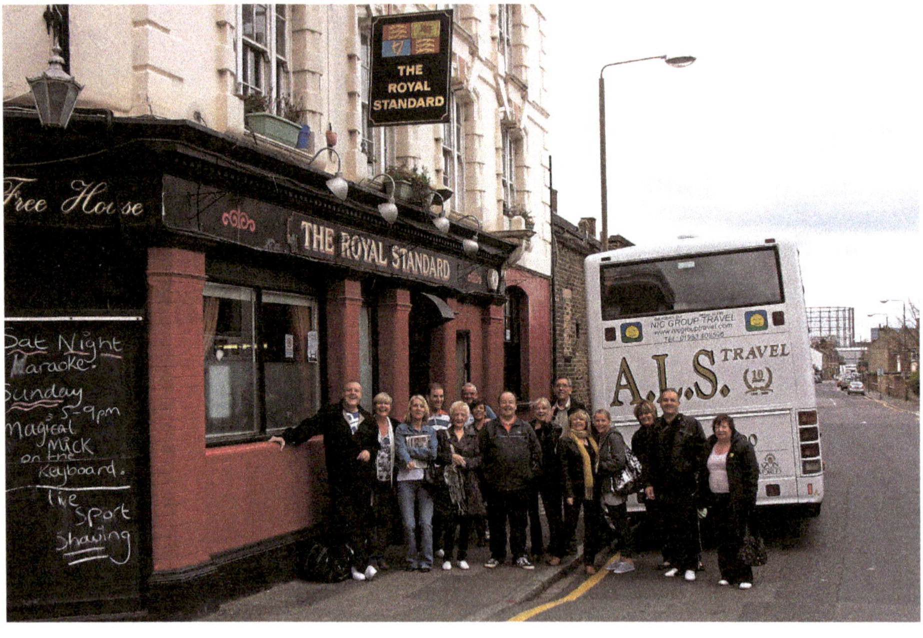

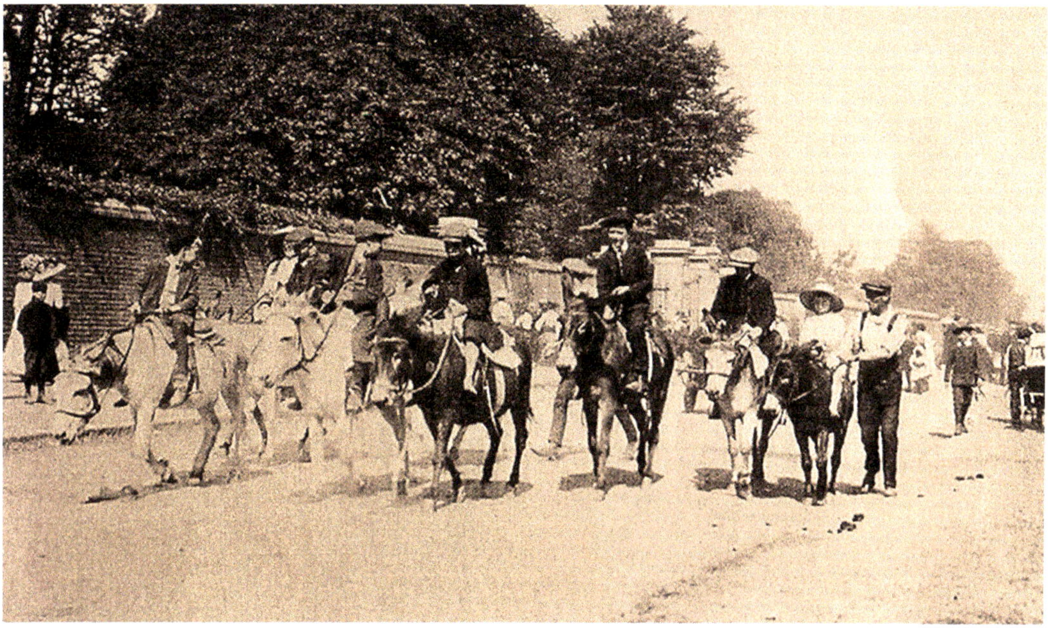

Donkey Rides – Blackheath

Children have been riding on Blackheath's famous donkeys for generations. Under the ownership of the same family since the rides began in the early 1900s, Len Thorn is the latest family member to preside over the rides and has been involved in the business for more than sixty years. The donkeys were stabled near Greenwich Marsh and would be led in single file through Greenwich up to Blackheath. On Sundays during the summer months, bank holidays and school term breaks children continue to take donkey rides along the well-trodden path of Duke Humphrey Way opposite Blackheath Gate at Greenwich Park.

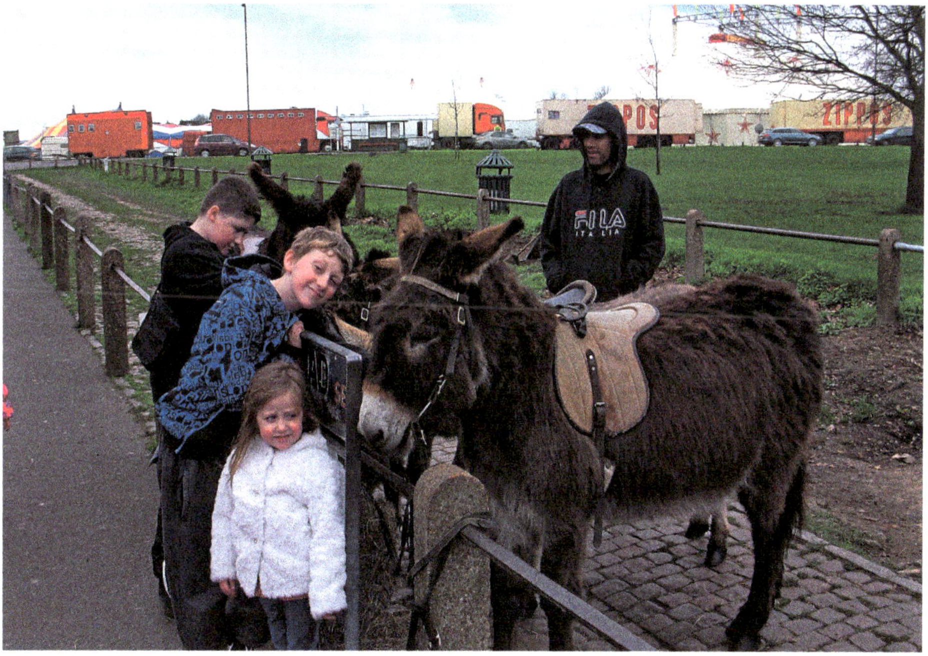

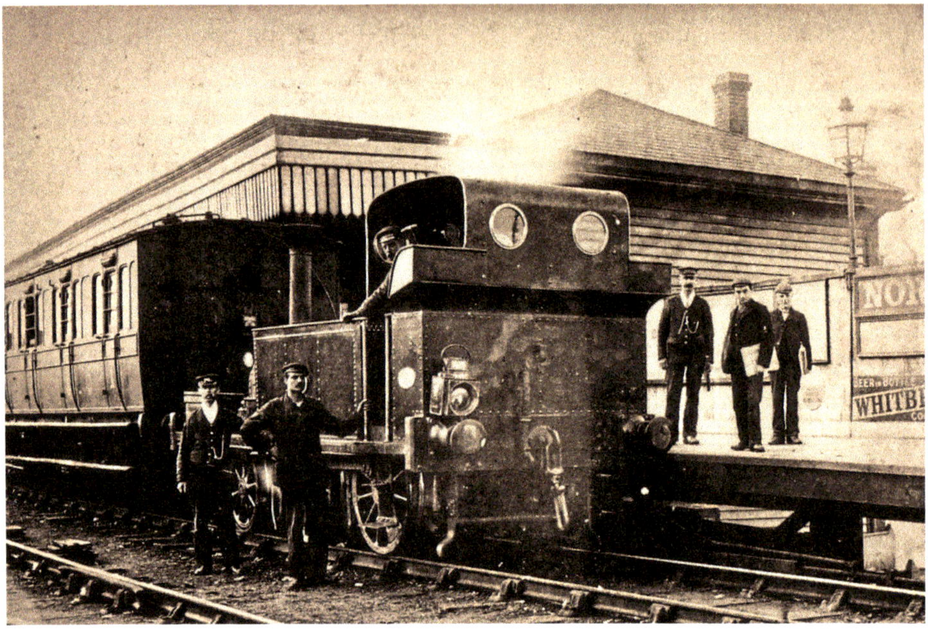

Greenwich Railway

The Greenwich to London railway line was the first passenger service to open in the city. In 1833 the railway received parliamentary approval and work began on building the line from Greenwich Station to London Bridge Station. Trains from Greenwich began transporting passengers in 1836 and within ten years the service was carrying 2 million people a year. The London Light Railway now runs through the station taking commuters under the river to the new business centre of Canary Wharf.

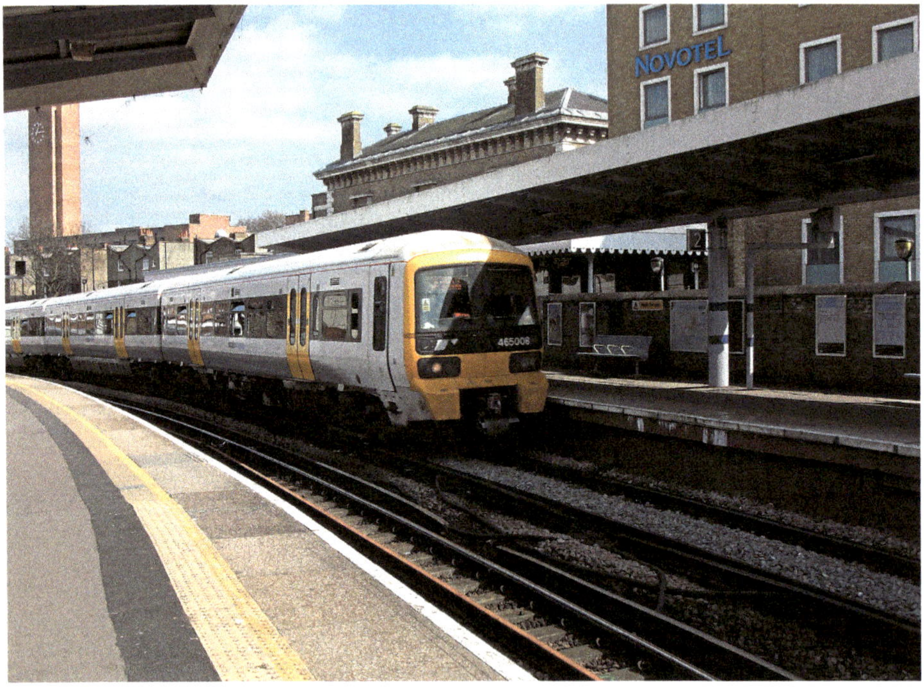

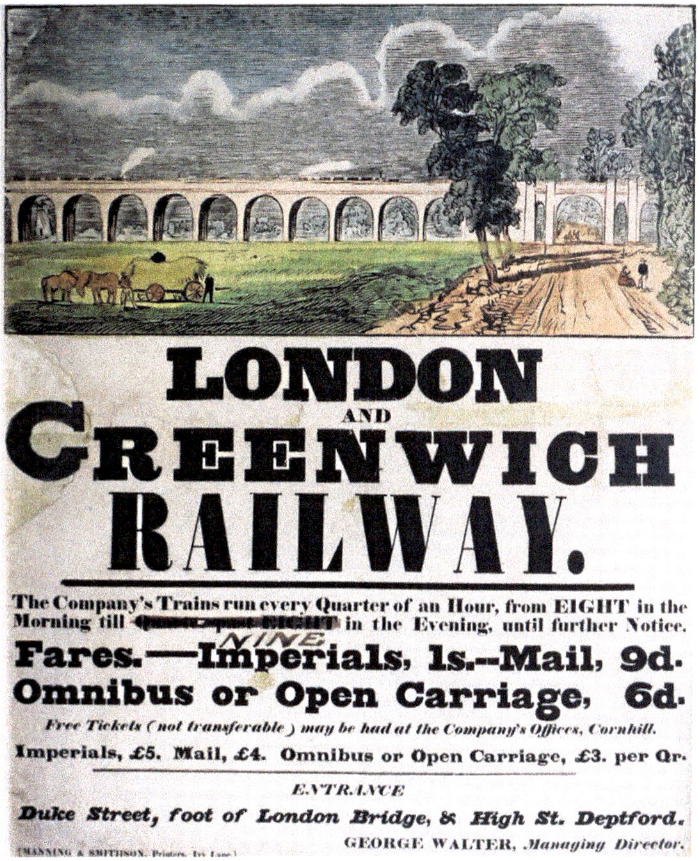

Greenwich Station

The impressive station building, designed by local architect George Smith, is one of the oldest railway buildings in the world. An illustration on a poster from the late 1800s depicts an image of the viaduct carrying the line out of Greenwich towards Deptford. The viaduct was built by over 400 navvies laying 100,000 bricks a day which caused a national shortage of bricks throughout the country.

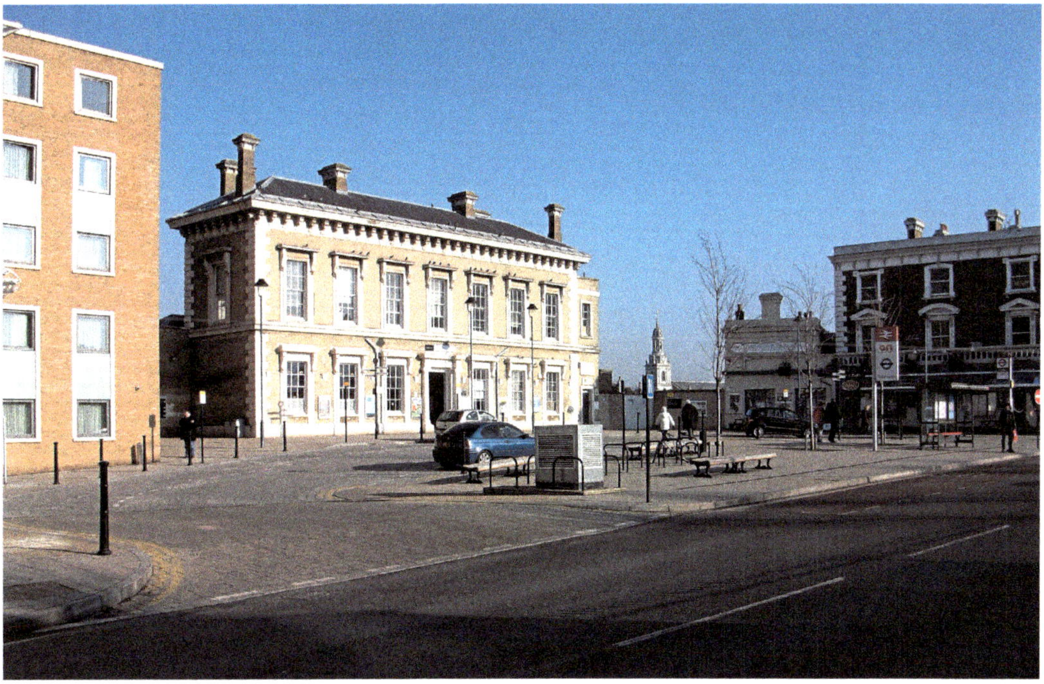

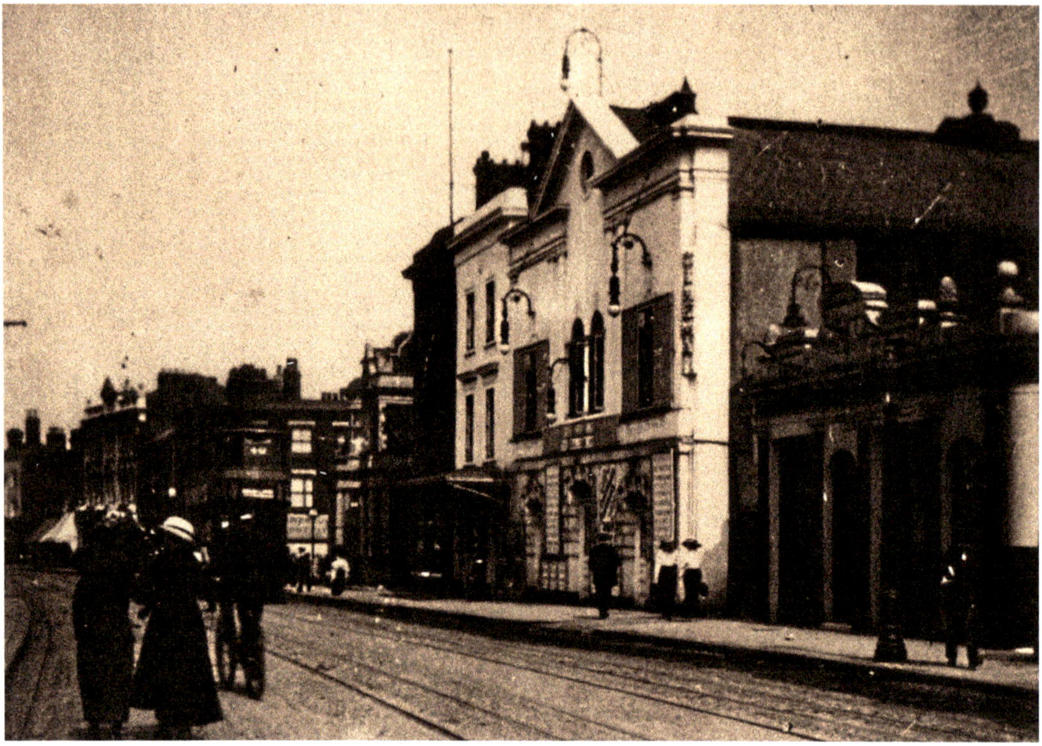

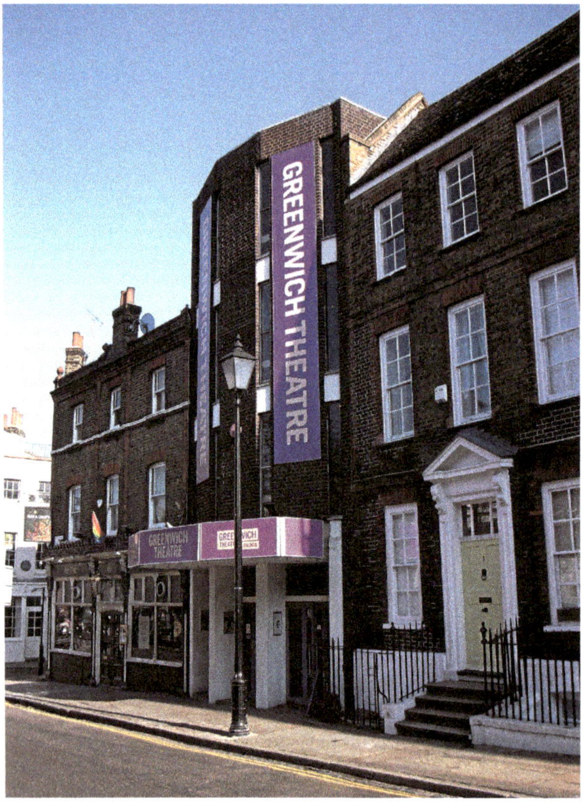

Greenwich Theatres

The Carlton Theatre on London Street, built in 1864, was one of several theatres and music halls in Greenwich. By 1937 the theatre had been converted into a cinema prior to its demolition to make way for the New Greenwich Town Hall. The Rose & Crown public house, a short walk from where Morton's Theatre stood, was built on the site of a music hall bearing same name. The music hall was rebuilt in 1871 as Crowder's Music Hall and was later renamed the Hippodrome. The Rose & Crown public house was rebuilt in 1888 and is to the left of Greenwich Theatre entrance.

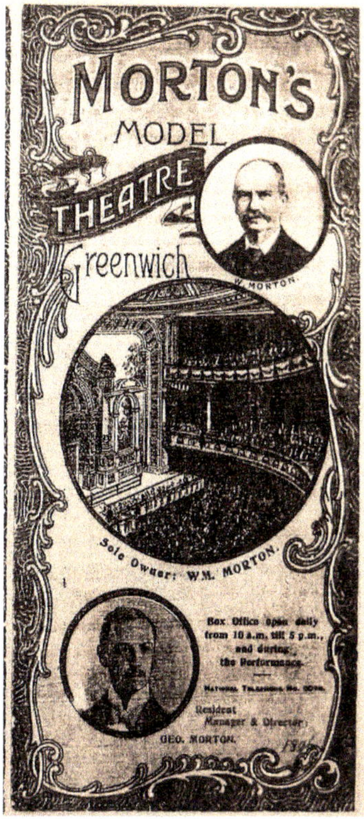

Old and New Theatrical Entertainment

Some of Britain's most popular artists of the day performed at Morton's Music Hall including entertainer Arthur Lloyd, singer and dancer Kitty Fairdale and comedian Dan Leno. By the time Morton's closed the Hippodrome had also been turned into a cinema which was closed down after the war. The building was facing demolition until a successful campaign was fought to save the theatre. After extensive renovations were carried out to the theatre the doors were open to the public in 1969. The old stage door entrance on Nevada Street is much the same as it was during the late 1800s and the Greenwich Theatre is now a progressive entertainments venue producing a variety of modern and classical theatrical work.

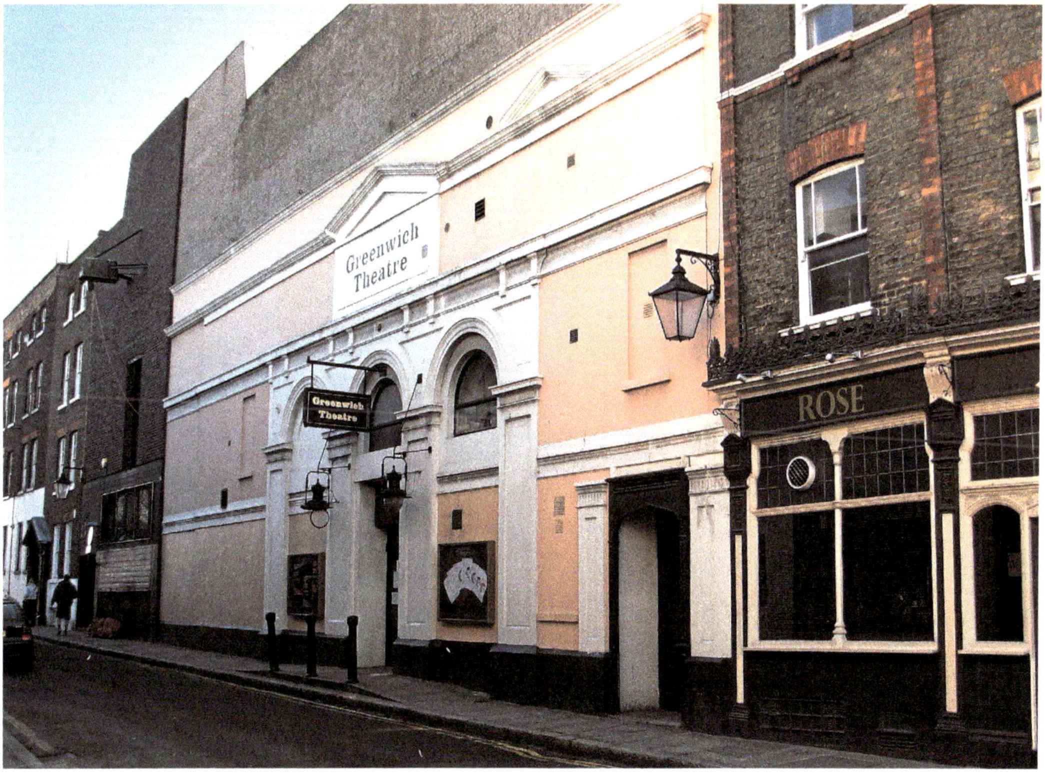

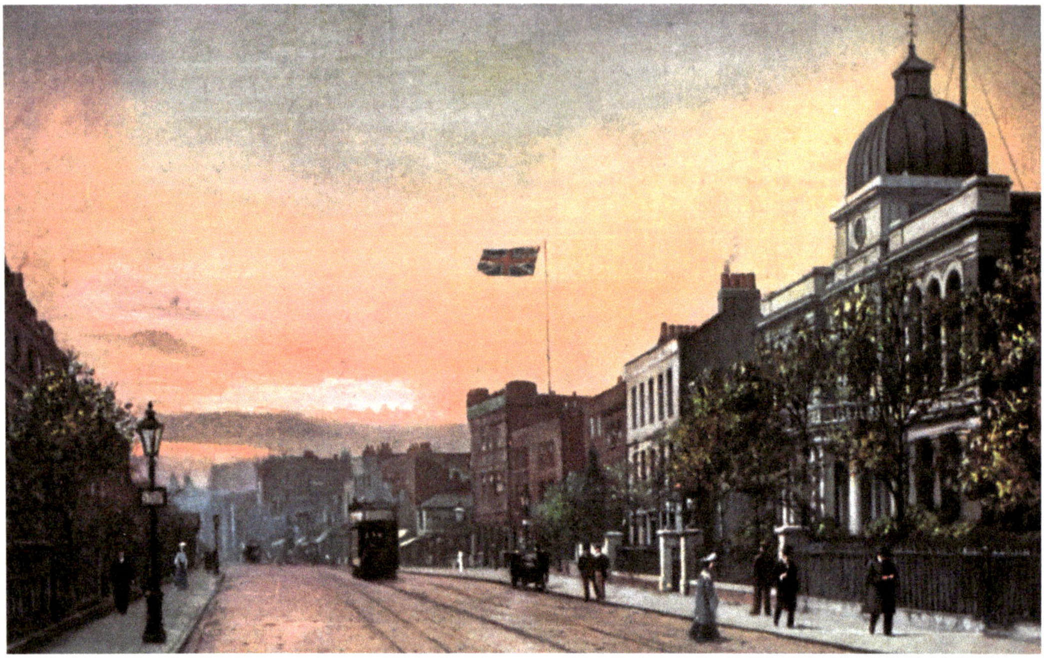

Greenwich Town Hall – Greenwich Road

The domed building, to the right of the picture, on Greenwich Road was officially opened in 1877 as the District Board of Works offices by chairman and local brewer Thomas Norfolk. In 1900 the Borough Council was formed and the building was used as the Council Town Hall until 1939. A V1 flying bomb landed on a row of houses next to the town hall causing extensive damage to the building. After the war the Town Hall was repaired and renamed West Greenwich House in 1958. The building is now the Greenwich West Community & Arts Centre.

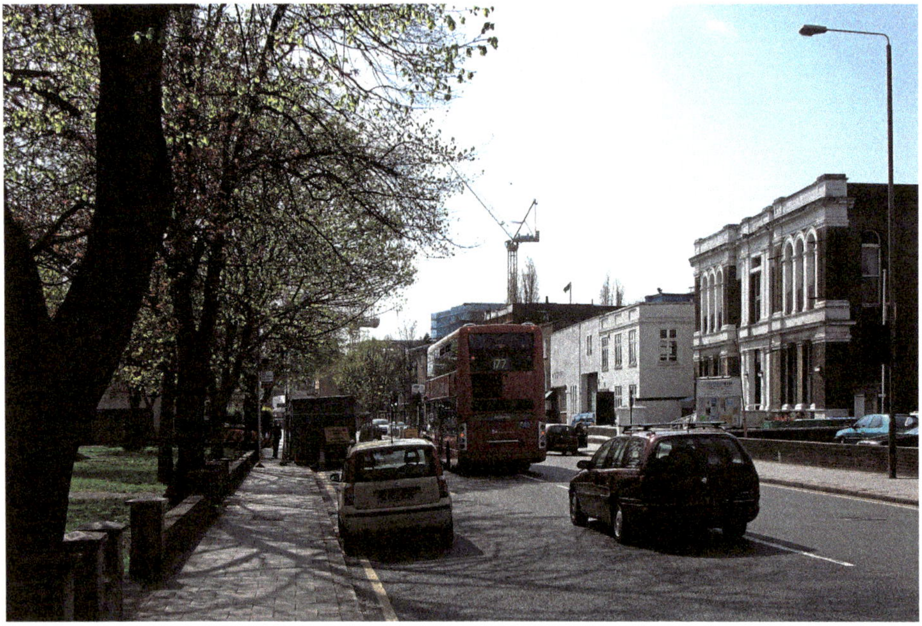

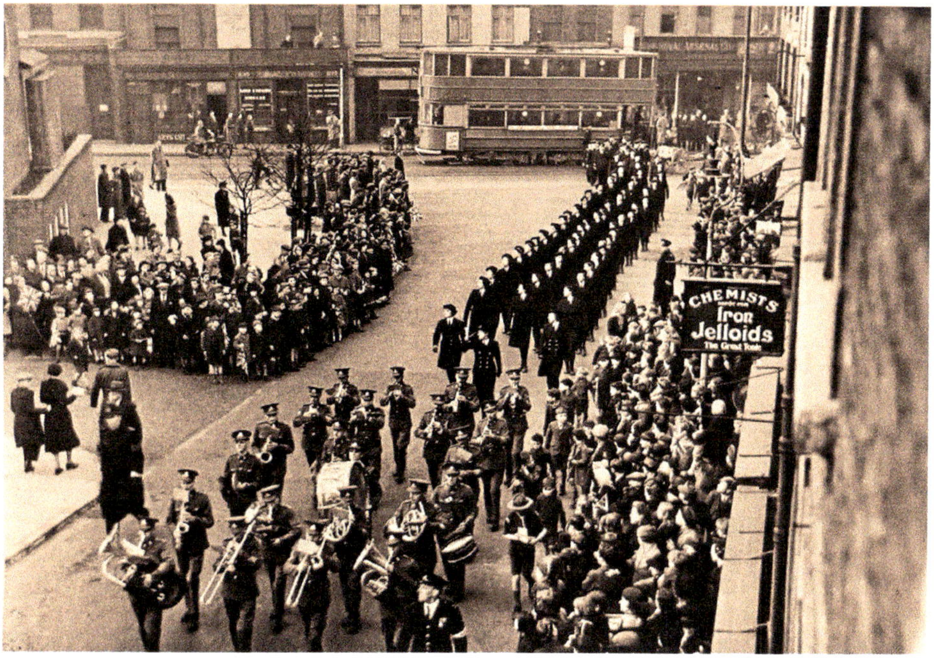

Borough Hall – Royal Hill

Members of the armed forces are on parade outside the main entrance of Borough Hall after the official opening in 1939. Designed by architect Clifford Culpin the council building was erected on the site of Morton's Music Hall. An enclosed observation platform at the top of the clock tower was once open to the public offering spectacular views over Greenwich and beyond. When the London Borough of Greenwich was formed in 1965 the Town Hall duties were transferred to Woolwich. In the early 1970s the building was converted into offices and the municipal halls are now home to the Greenwich Dance Academy.

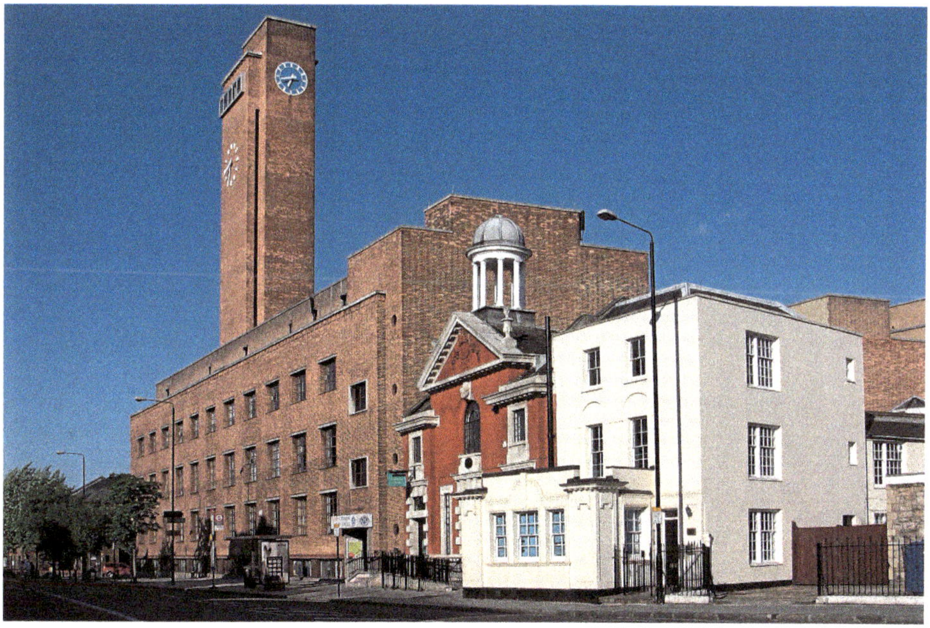

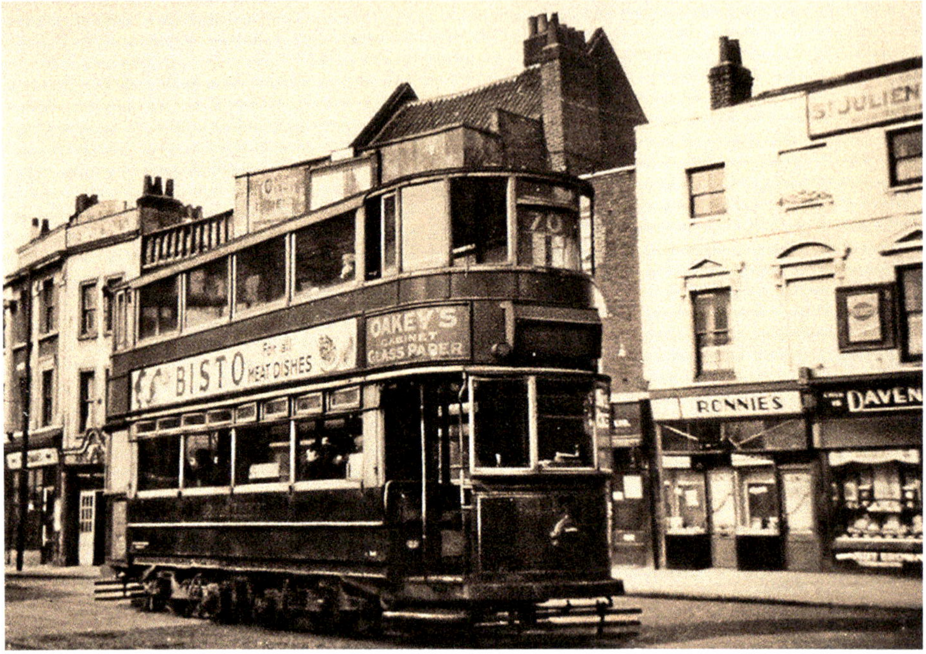

Public Transport – Greenwich Church Street

In 1904 London County Council took over the running of the city's transport system and began replacing the horse-drawn trams with modern electrified trams. These electric trams would run on London's streets for over fifty years and the tram in the picture above is passing a row of shops at the front of Greenwich Market at the centre of West Greenwich during the 1950s. There is now a one way system in operation around the market square where the latest ultra modern red buses now pass the shops in the opposite direction.

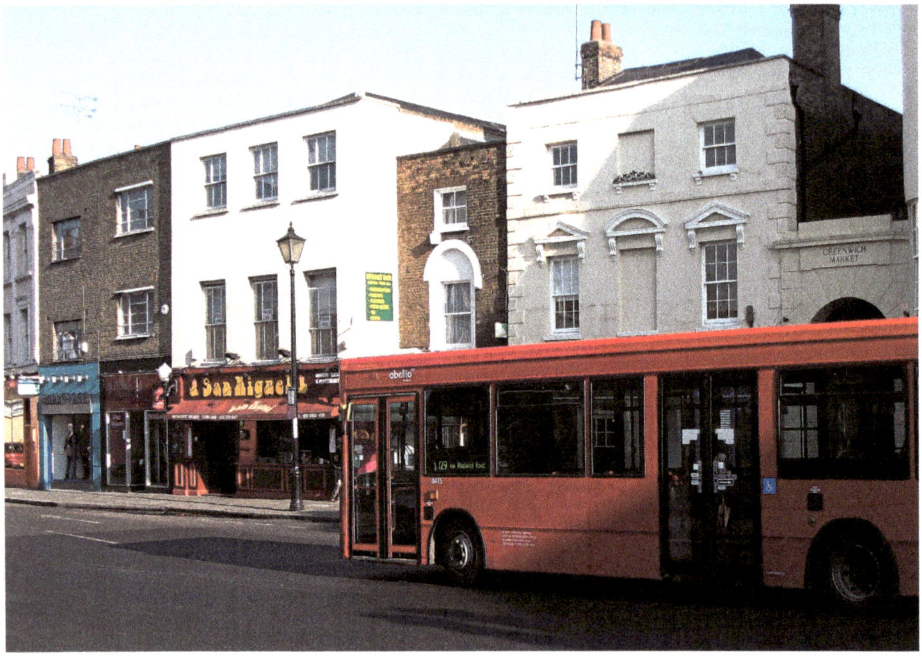

Greenwich Market Entrance

In between the fishmonger's on one corner and the greengrocer's and butcher's on the other is the west entrance of Greenwich Market square. The market transferred from the old Naval Hospital grounds in 1831 where the entrance on Church Street was erected as part of the areas redevelopment in 1829. Although awarded a Royal Charter in 1849, the market and surrounding properties are under constant threat of redevelopment through plans to turn this historic market into a modern shopping centre.

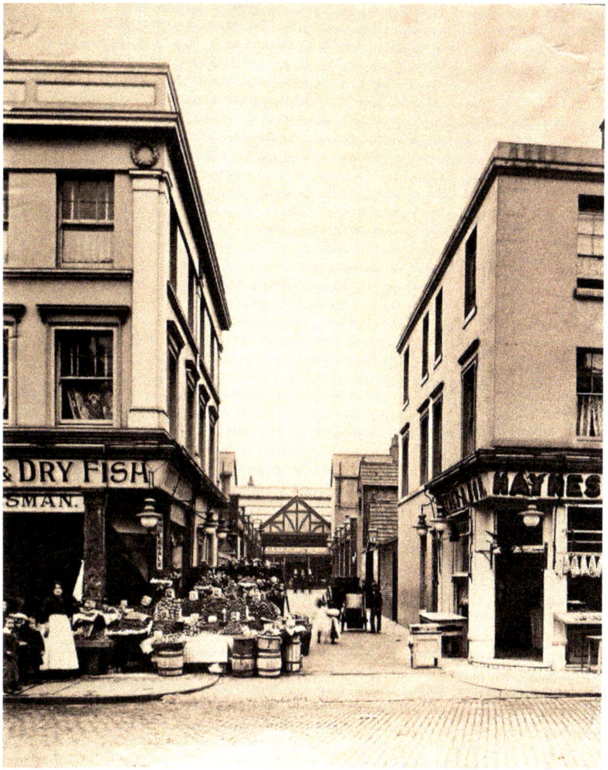

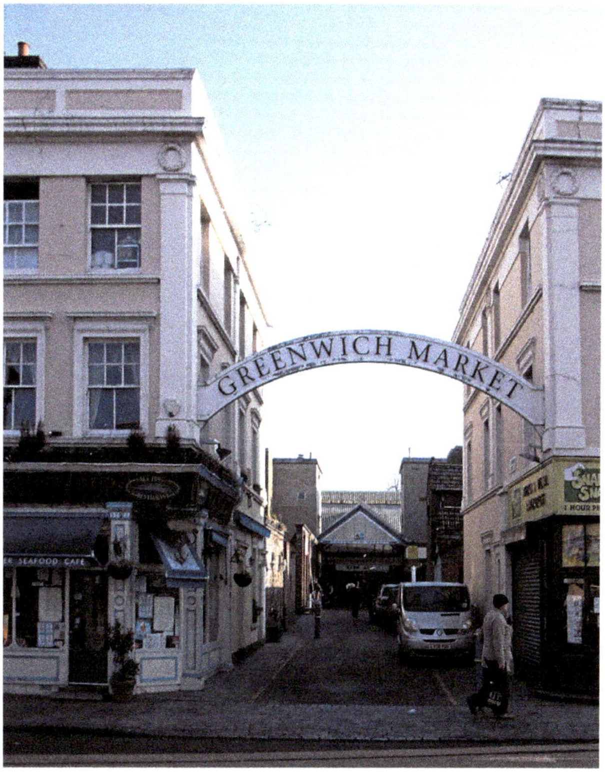

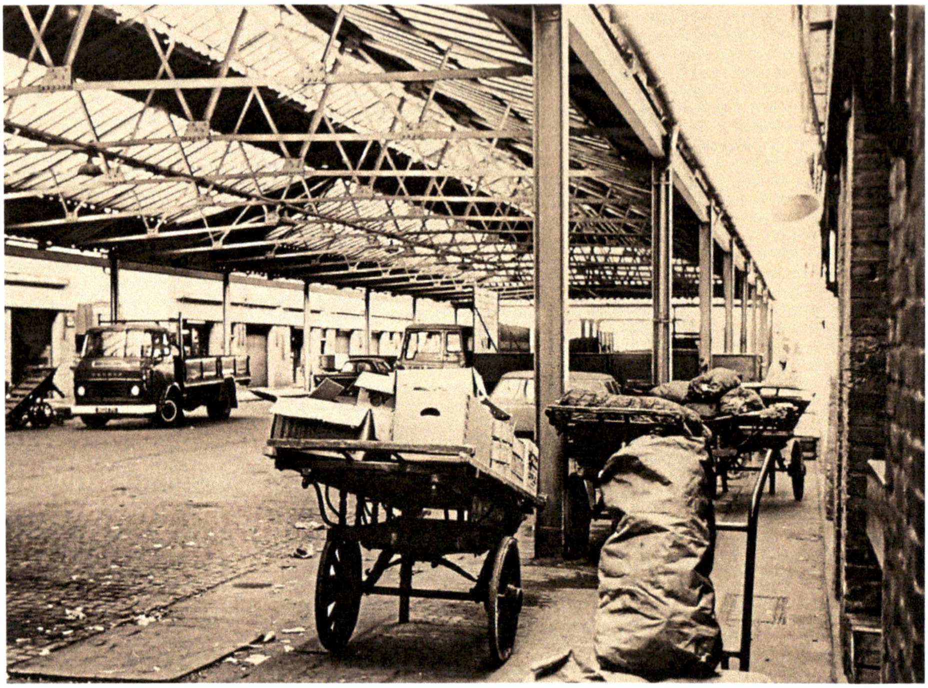

Greenwich Market

The market square in the centre of West Greenwich was built to include stores, a slaughterhouse, public houses, stables and a music hall. By the mid 1900s after over 100 years of trading the market began to go into decline. During 1958 a majority of the market interior was refurbished and the market was open for trading once more. Visitors to Greenwich will now find the market full of arts and craft stalls, shops, galleries, restaurants and wine bars.

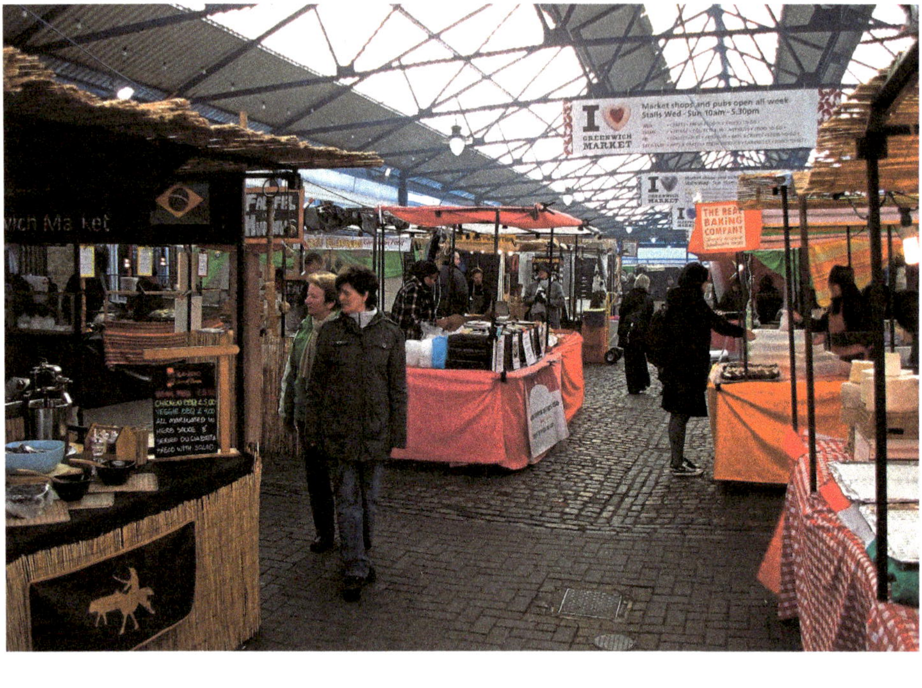

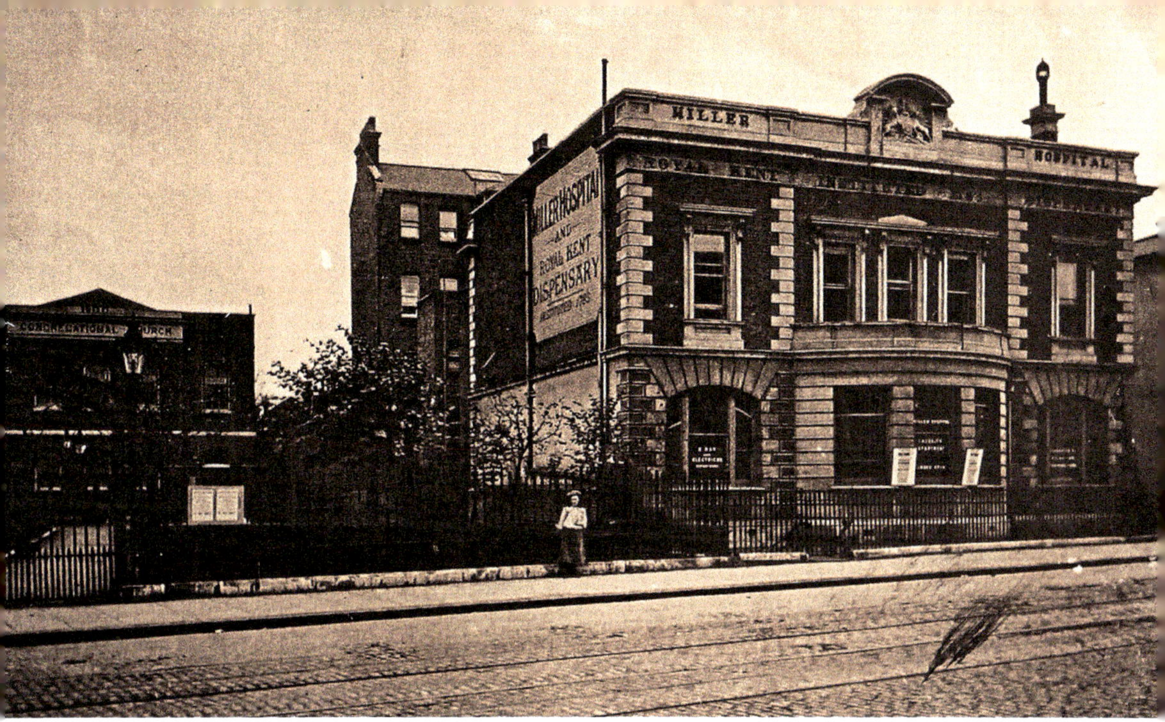

Miller Hospital – Greenwich South Street

Founded by Revd Canon Miller in 1783 the Royal Kent Dispensary, located in Deptford, moved to Greenwich South Street when a new building was commissioned in 1851. A charitable hospital was erected next to the dispensary in 1883 and named the Miller Hospital in honour of the dispensary's founder. The hospital was administered by the National Health Service between 1948 and 1974 and after closure a majority of the buildings were demolished to make way for housing. The listed Royal Dispensary remained, becoming a children's home and then housing.

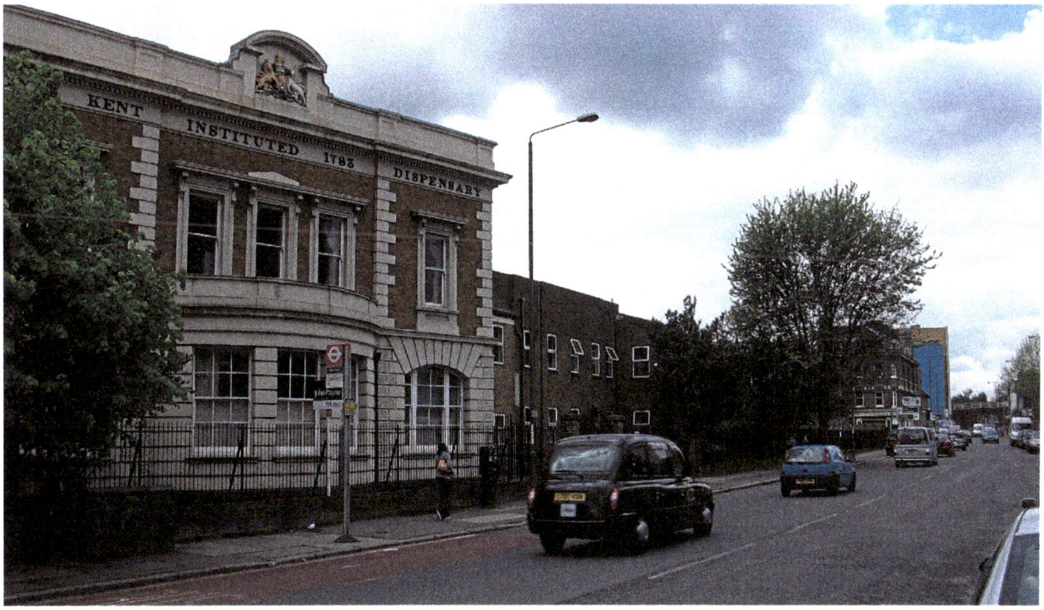

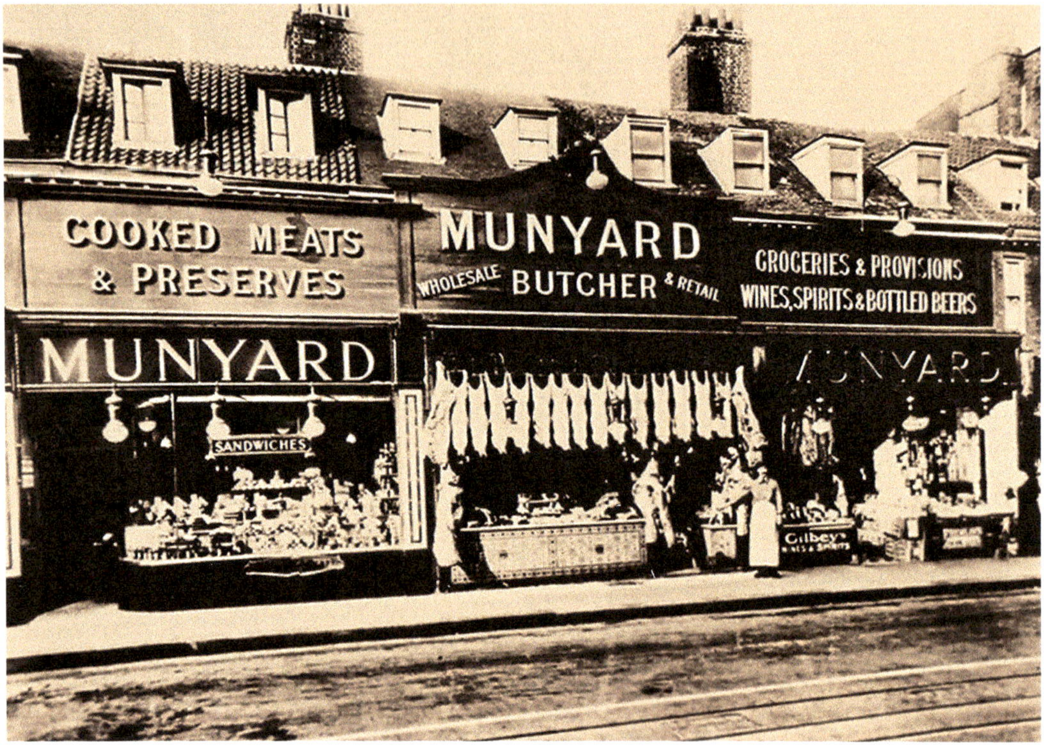

Munyard's Stores – London Street

The row of stores on London Street were all owned by a local grocery business Munyard's, who also ran other grocery stores located throughout the Greenwich area during the late 1800s and early 1900s. Many of the local stores like Munyard's would eventually close down as large supermarket chains bought up properties on the high streets. The stores on London Street, which is now Greenwich High Road, were all demolished and replaced by a modern shopping complex.

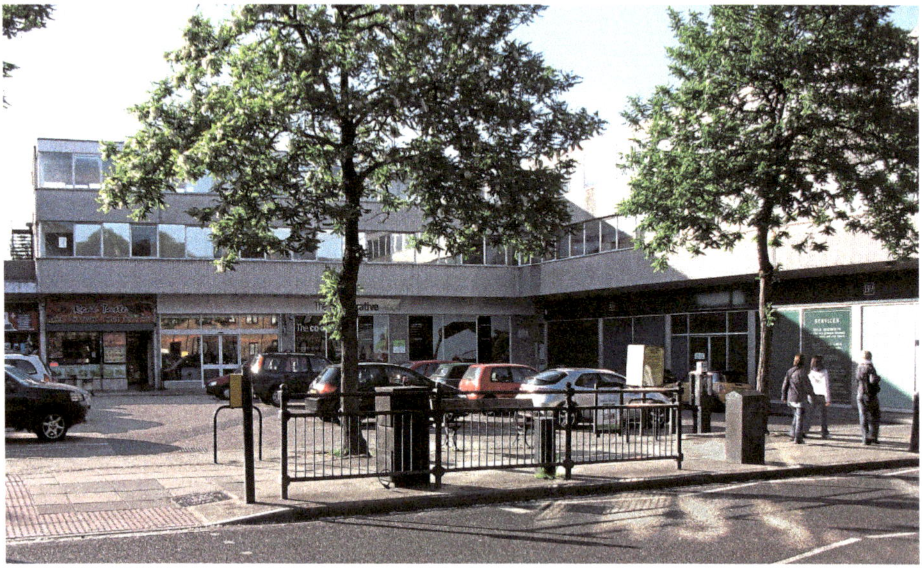

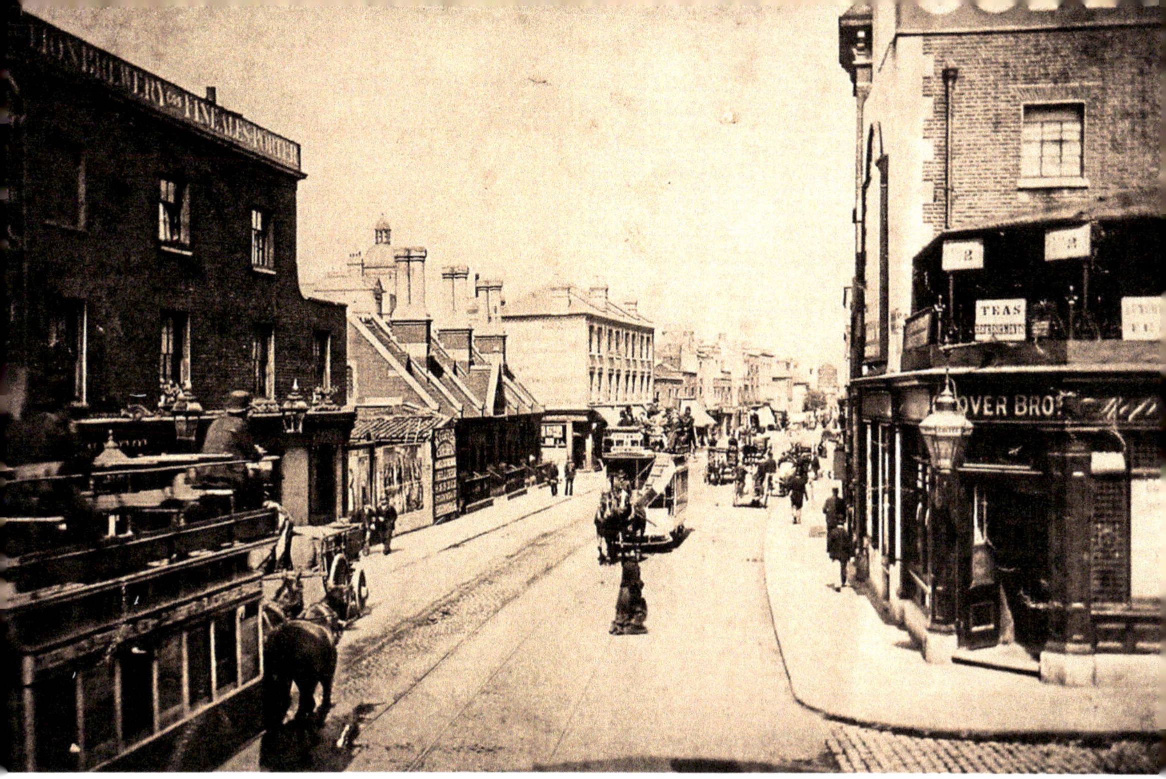

Good Duke Humphrey – Trafalgar Road

Situated at the junction of Trafalgar Road and Park Row the large nineteenth century coffee house was a popular centre of entertainment. The Good Duke Humphrey, named after the younger brother of Henry V, also served as a music hall, hotel and restaurant. The building was knocked down in the early 1900s and the public house and almshouses to the left of the picture were destroyed in a bombing raid during the war. The buildings each side of the road were replaced by new flats, houses, a car park and petrol station.

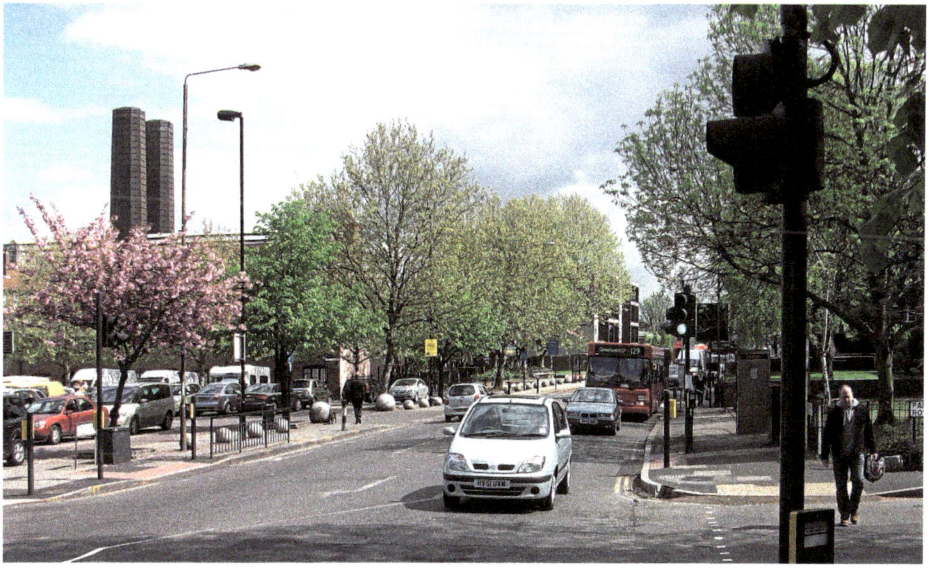

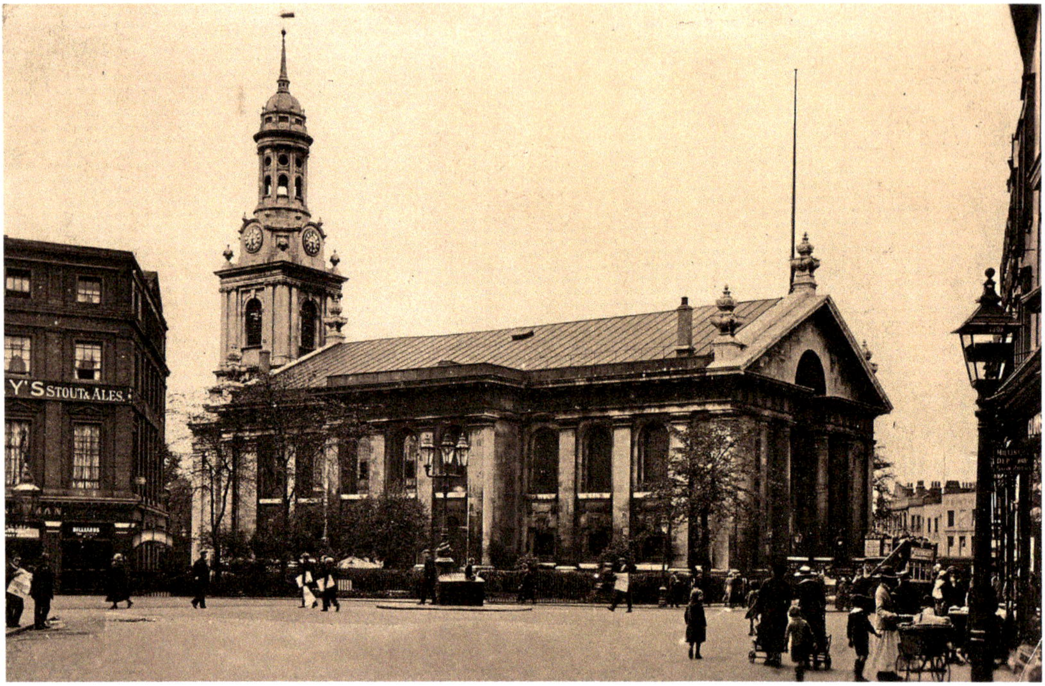

St Alfege Parish Church

The present church is the third place of worship built on the site to commemorate Arch Bishop of Canterbury Alfege, stoned to death rather than be ransomed by his Danish captors in 1012. The eleventh-century church, erected on the spot where the Bishop had died, was replaced in the thirteenth century by a larger church which collapsed during a great storm in 1710. Nicholas Hawksmoor designed the current eighteenth-century parish church which was dedicated to St Alfege in 1718.

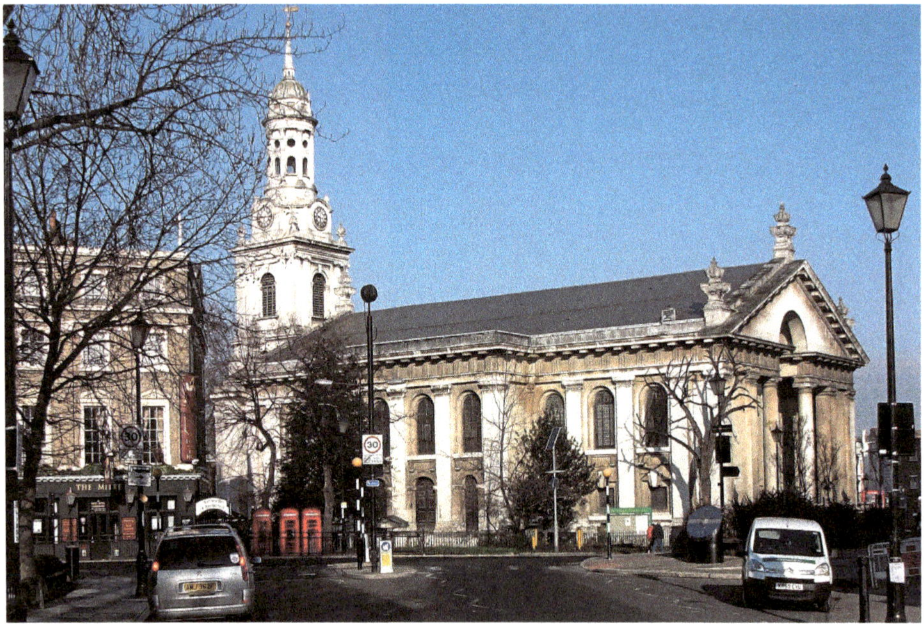

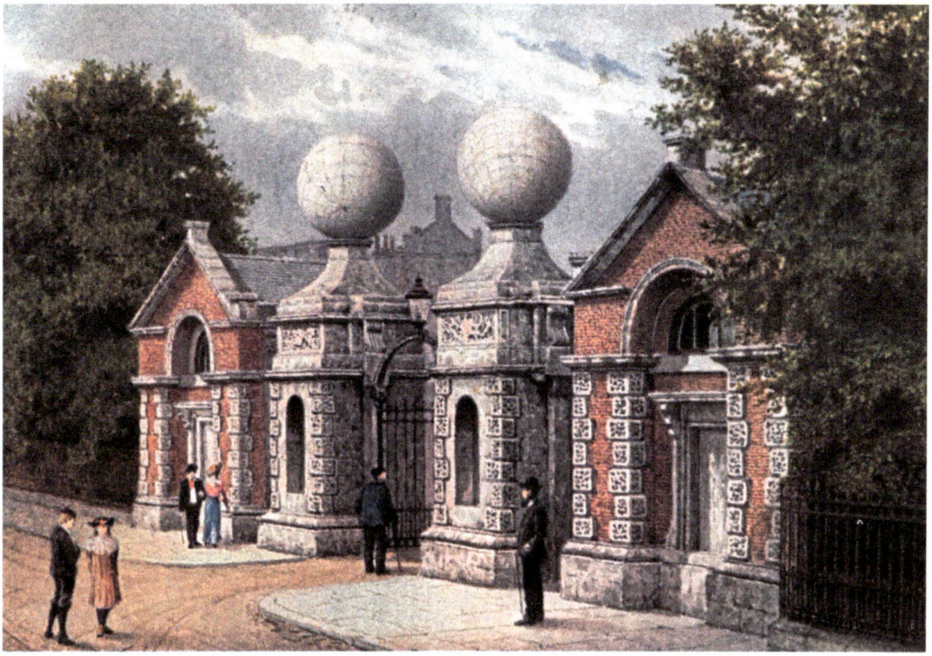

Royal Naval College West Gate – King William Street

Dating from 1752 the stone- and brick-built entrance and porter's lodges were moved from their original position within the Royal Naval College and erected on the site of the old Greenwich Market during the mid 1800s. The pillars support large stone globes, one celestial one terrestrial, each one measuring six feet in diameter and weighing seven tons. The celestial globe on the left is laid with copper bands depicting the twenty-four meridians, the equinoxial, the ecliptic, tropics and circles; the terrestrial globe on the right showing the parallels of latitude.

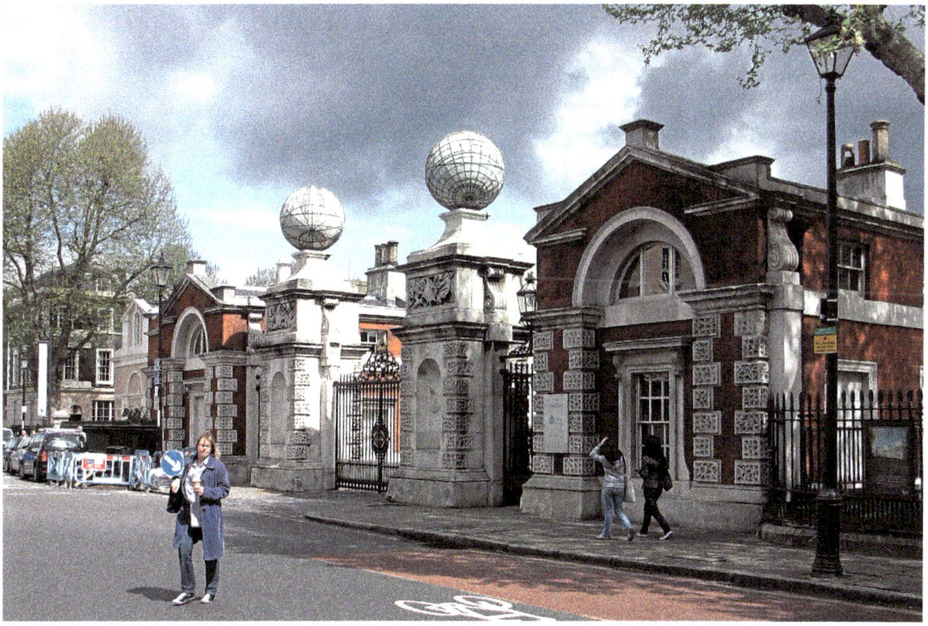

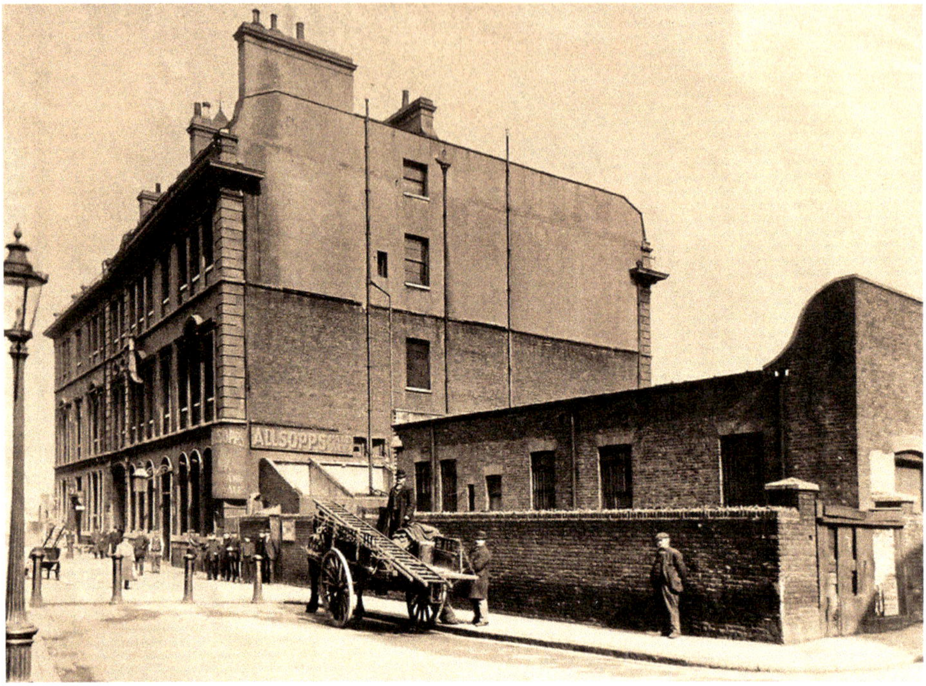

The Ship Tavern – Billingsgate Dock

The Ship Tavern, made famous by its parliamentary whitebait dinners, was an imposing old building and the fourth of a succession of inns which had stood on the site since the early seventeenth century. In 1941 the tavern and the surrounding houses were severely damaged in an air raid which resulted in the whole area undergoing redevelopment after the war. In the 1950s a dry dock was built on the site of the old tavern for the clipper ship *Cutty Sark*. During seasonal events and bank holiday festivities international food stalls selling their own traditional fare can be found lined up in a row next to where the tavern once stood.

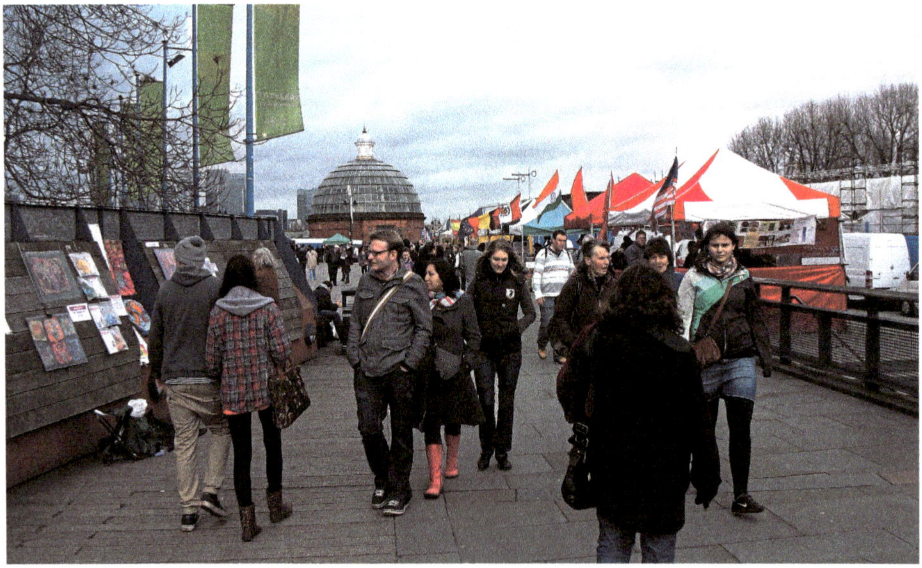

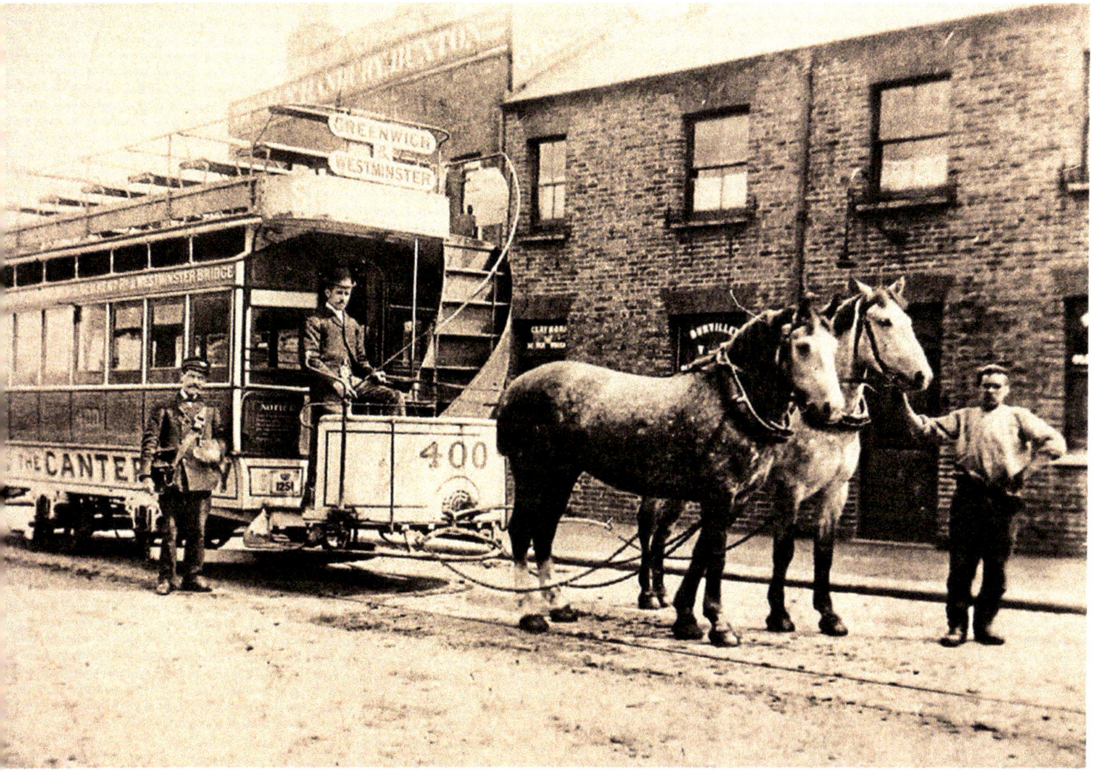

Star & Garter – Lower Park Street

A horse-drawn tram running from Greenwich to Westminster waits for passengers outside the Star & Garter on Lower Park Street. Independent operators ran the tram routes until London County Council bought out the tram services in the 1930s. Behind the public house is the imposing Greenwich Power Station built to provide power for the electric trams which eventually replaced these horse-drawn vehicles. The power station now produces electricity as a back up for the London Underground system.

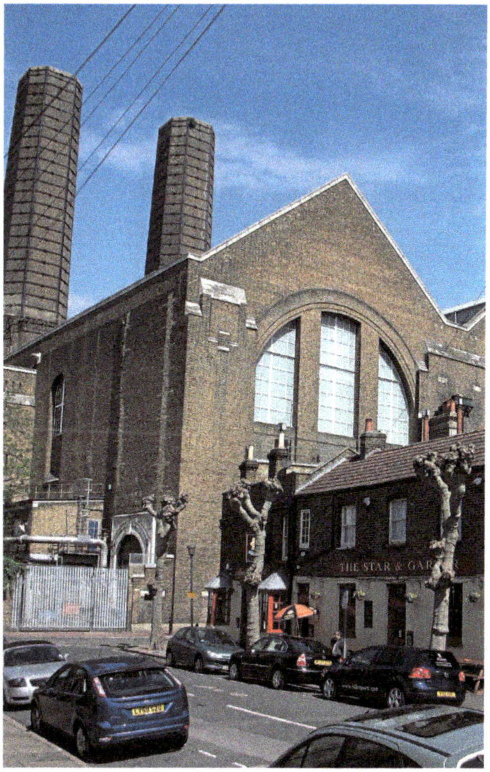

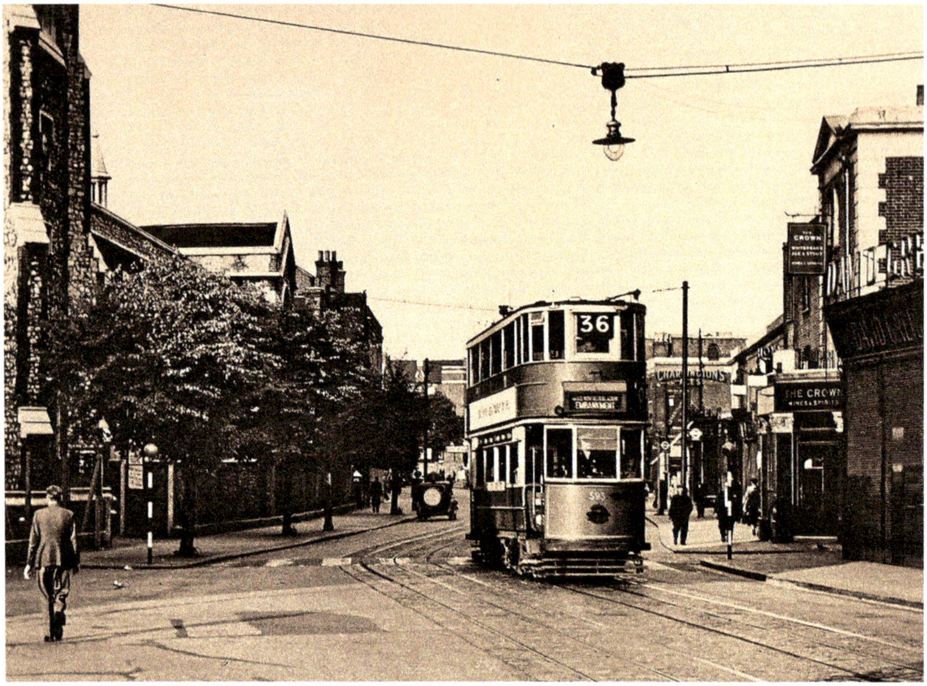

Electric Tram – East Greenwich

Tram 36 running on the last of the city's tram routes in 1952. To the left of Trafalgar Road is the Victorian-built Christ Church, to the right a row of local shops including a baker's, greengrocer's, hardware store, butcher's, fish monger's and two public houses the Crown and the British Queen. Through the 1960s and 1970s many of these shops were replaced by fast food outlets and supermarkets. As East Greenwich has become a more fashionable place to live, some independent shops selling specialist goods are making a comeback.

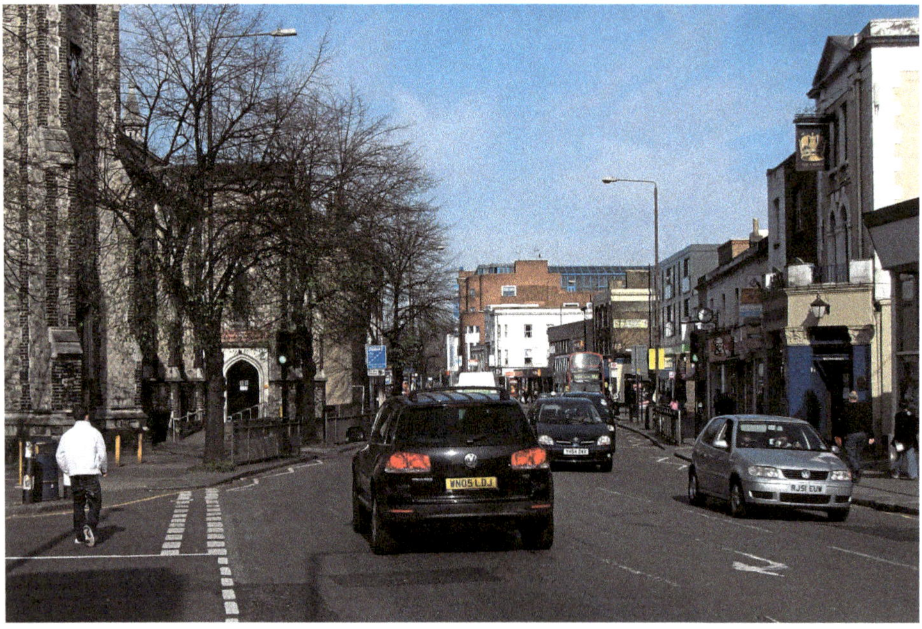

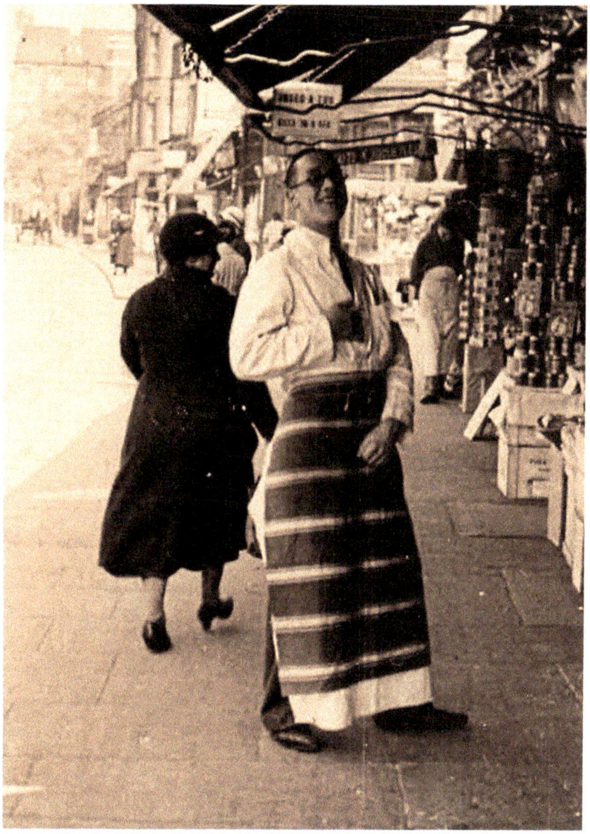

Local Shop Keeper – Trafalgar Road

Friend of the family Sid Gallagher outside Francis & Campion on Trafalgar Road where he worked in the grocery trade. The shop was bombed out during the war and many of the shop workers were killed or injured; Sid was one of the lucky ones to survive. The shops were rebuilt after the war but changes in people's shopping habits saw an end of the local independent stores as high street supermarkets took over their trade. After retirement Sid became a resident of Trinity Hospital.

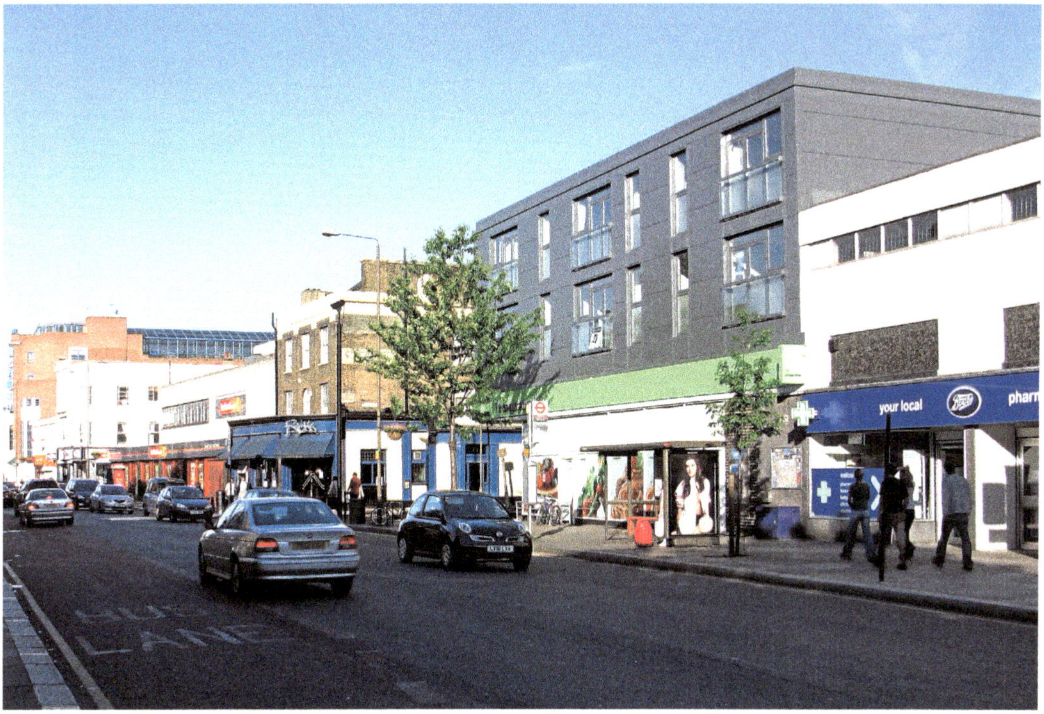

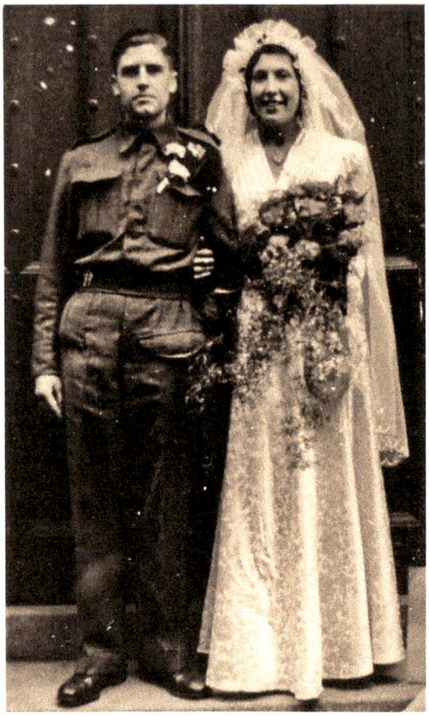

Weddings – Christ Church

The wedding of my Aunt Marrian and her husband-to-be George took place at Christ Church during the war while George was home on leave. Many other family members and friends have been married at our local parish church. One ceremony I attended in 1995 was the wedding of my old school friend Geoff and wife-to-be Barbara, thirty-five years after we had met on our first day at Christ Church Primary School, which was next to the church.

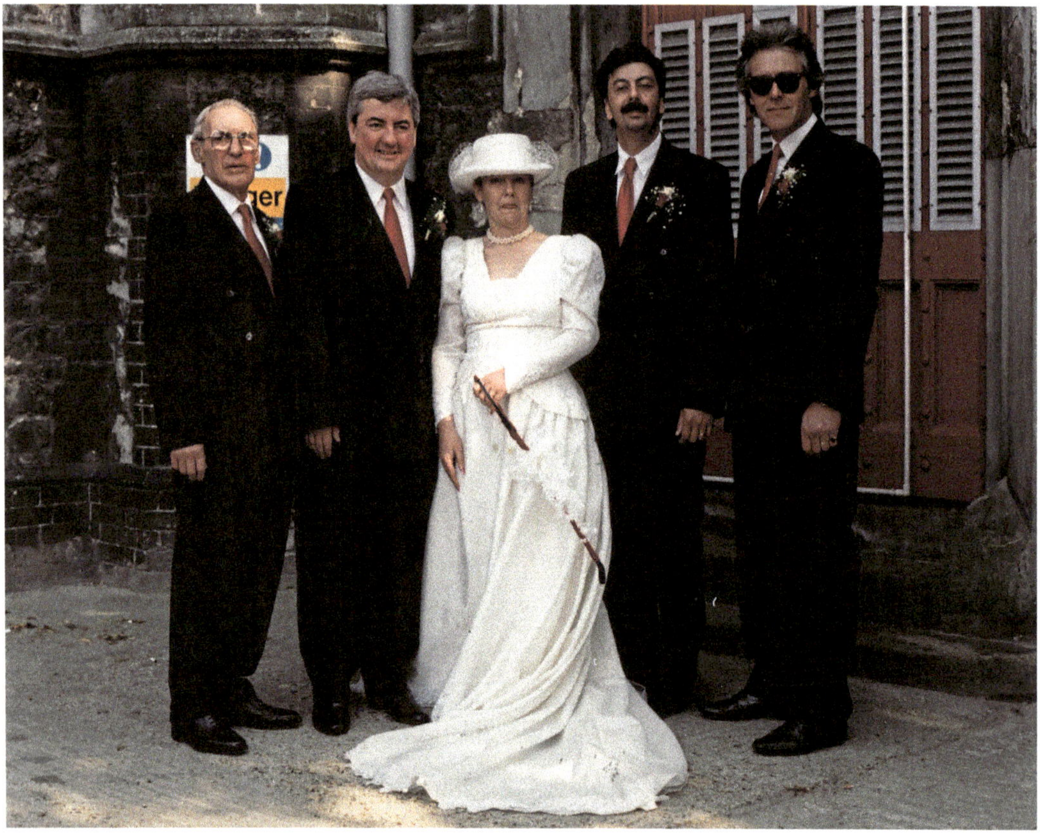

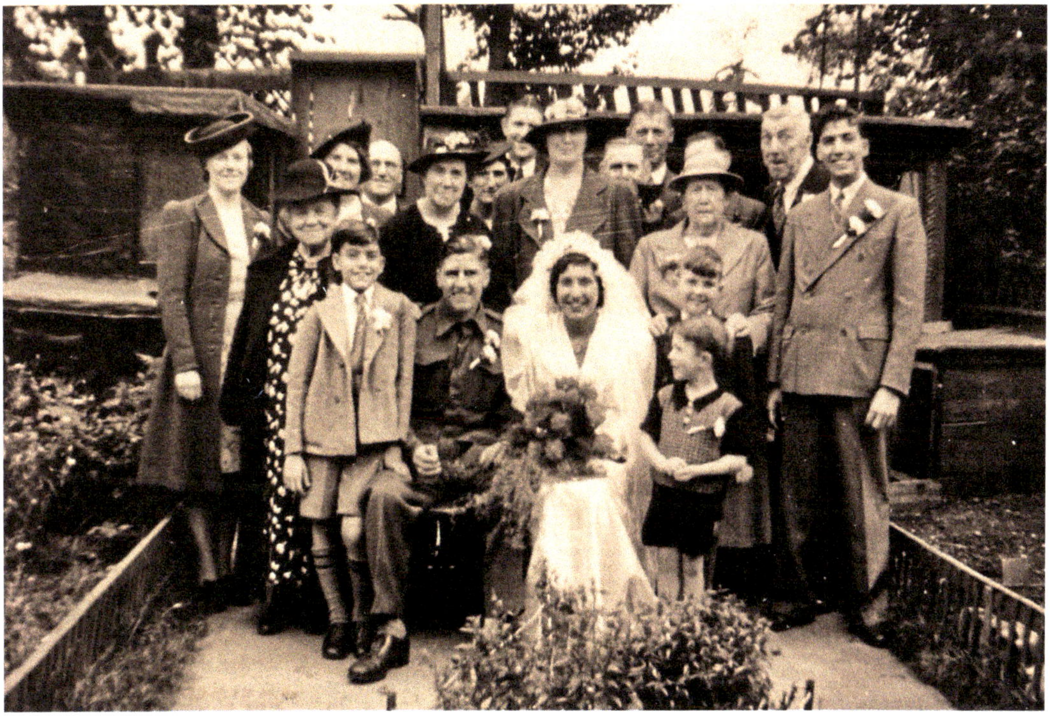

Wedding Portraits

A family wedding photograph taken in the back garden of our home in East Greenwich after my uncle and aunt's wedding at Christ Church. My father who was around ten at the time is standing to the left of the groom and my grandmother is standing behind the bride. In the 1995 wedding photograph below I am standing to the right of the groom who is behind his new bride. The bridesmaids and pageboy are all dressed in the colours of Charlton Athletic football club, the team my friend and I have supported since we were both schoolboys.

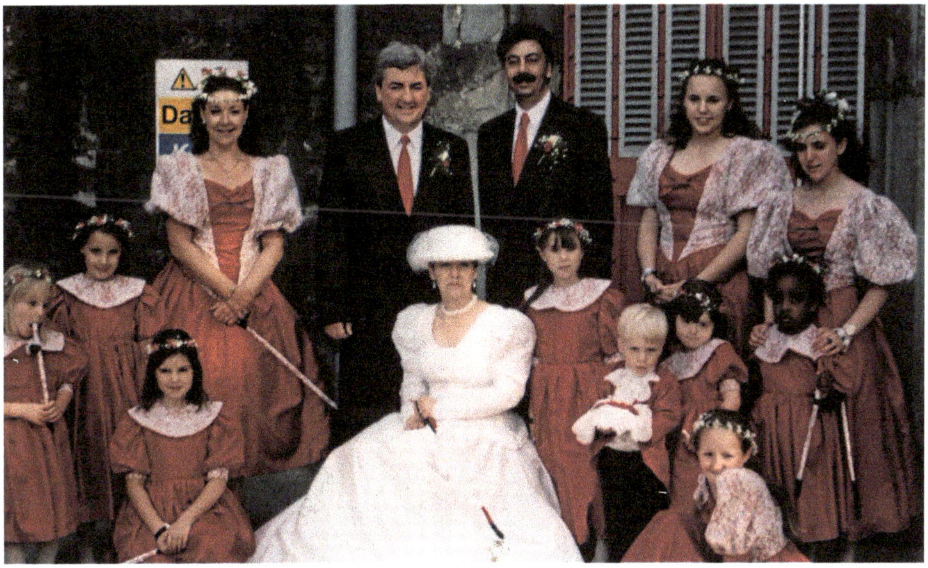

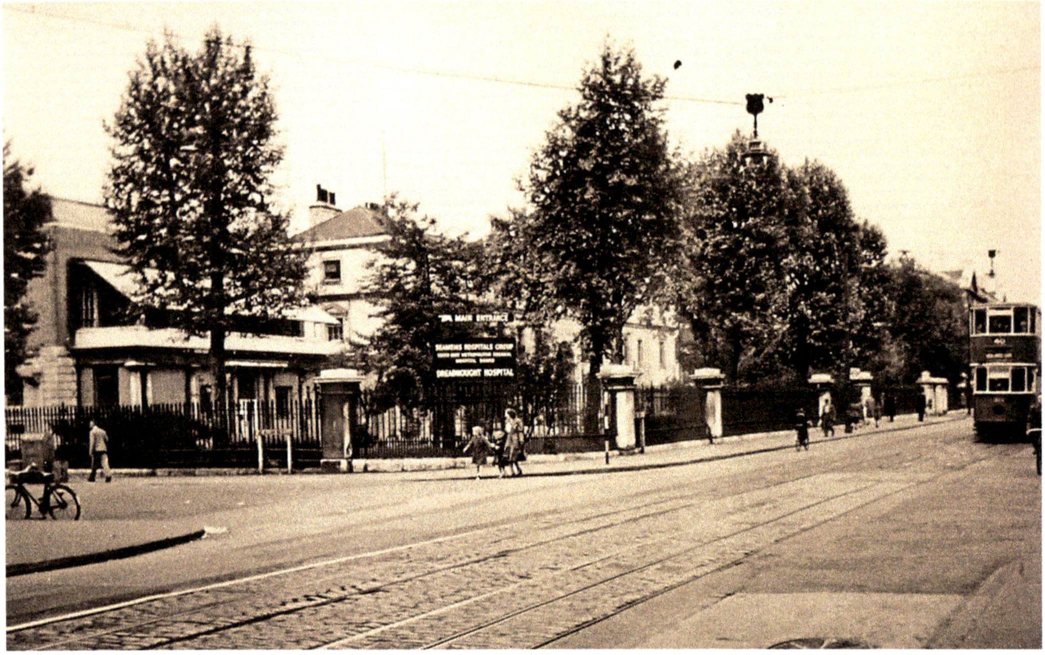

The Dreadnought Seamen's Hospital – Romney Road

The hospital was named after the man-of-war hulks moored at Greenwich Reach during the nineteenth century which were used as hospital ships for sick and injured seamen. The last of these dreadnoughts were broken up in 1872 and the patients moved on shore to be cared for at the vacated infirmary of the Royal Hospital. The Dreadnought Seamen's Hospital became a specialist unit of the National Health Service until its closure in 1986. The Regency building stood empty for over ten years before conversion into the library of the University of Greenwich.

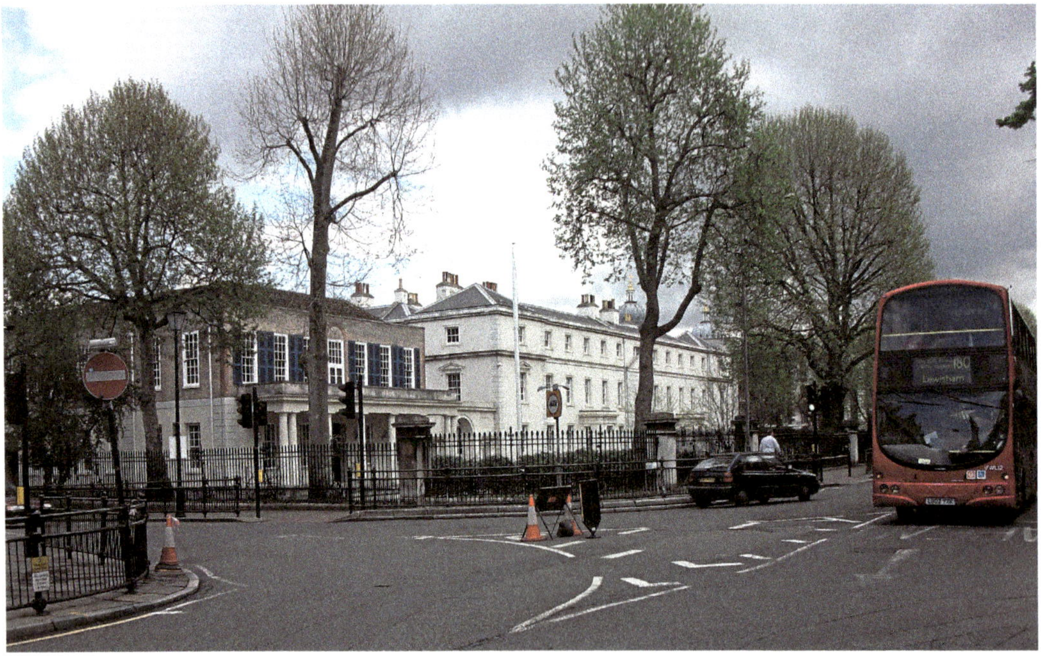

The Yacht – Crane Street

A riverside tavern had been in existence on the site for over 300 years and up until the eighteenth century was known as the Barley Mow. The Yacht is situated half way down Crane Street, a narrow walkway with terraced cottages on one side and riverside workshops and wharfs on the other, which leads from the Royal Naval College to Highbridge Wharf. After a series of alterations and renovations the interior of the Yacht Tavern has been modelled on one of the lounge bars of the ocean liner *Queen Mary*.

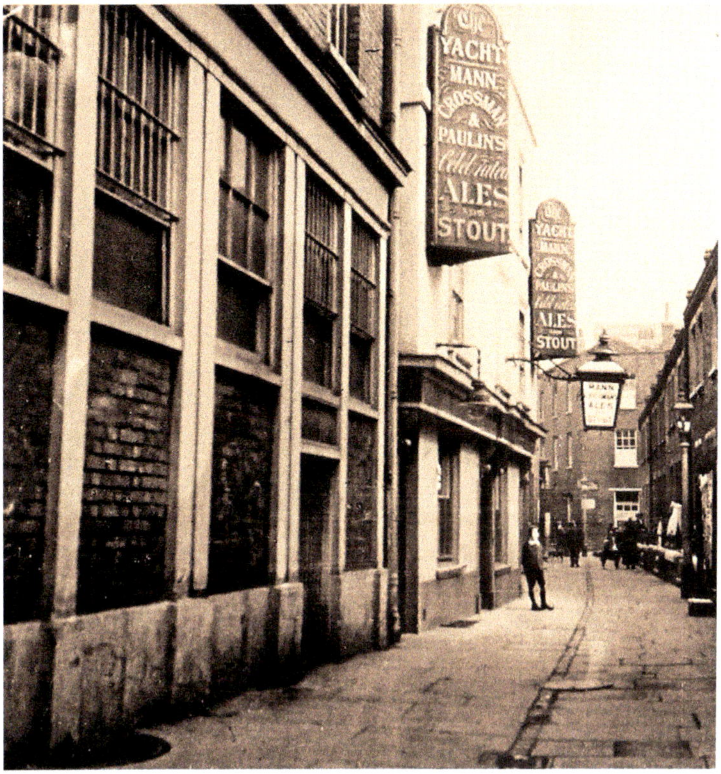

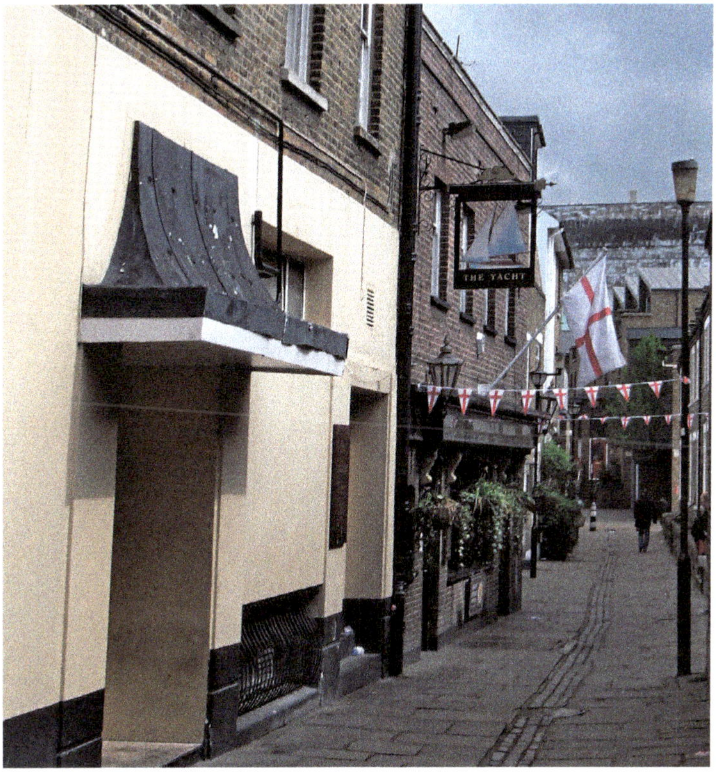

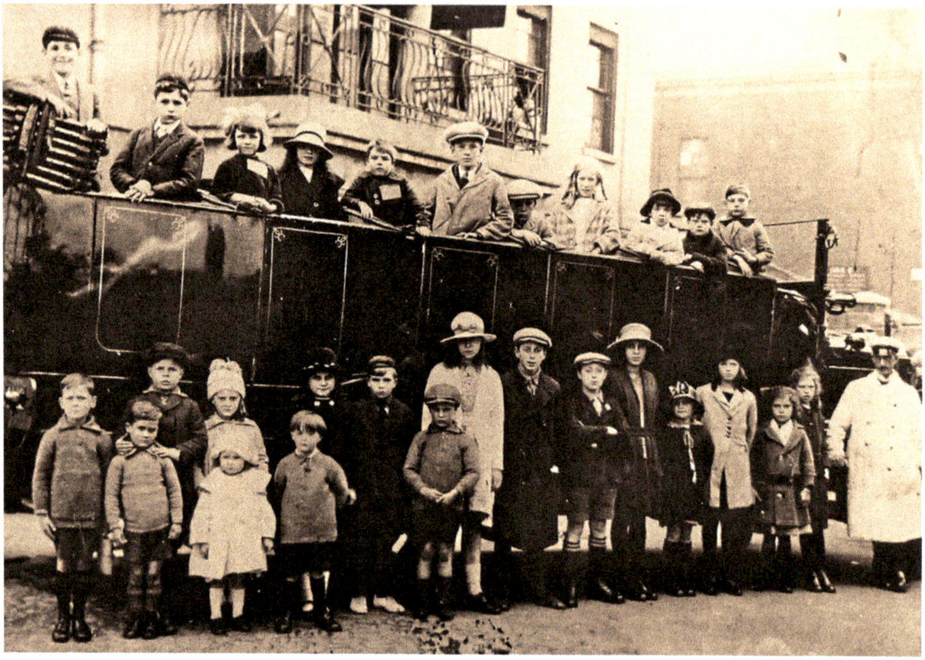

Children's Sunday School Outing – Park Row

A charabanc outside the Trafalgar Tavern in 1922 taking a group of Greenwich youngsters off on a day's outing. The Trafalgar was a rival to the Ship at Greenwich Pier and served whitebait dinners to members of parliament. The Ship Tavern has since gone while the Trafalgar Tavern remains a popular attraction for tourists who come to try out the tavern's fish dinners. Outside the main entrance of the tavern stands a bronze statue of Admiral Lord Nelson waiting to welcome visitors on a day's outing to Greenwich.

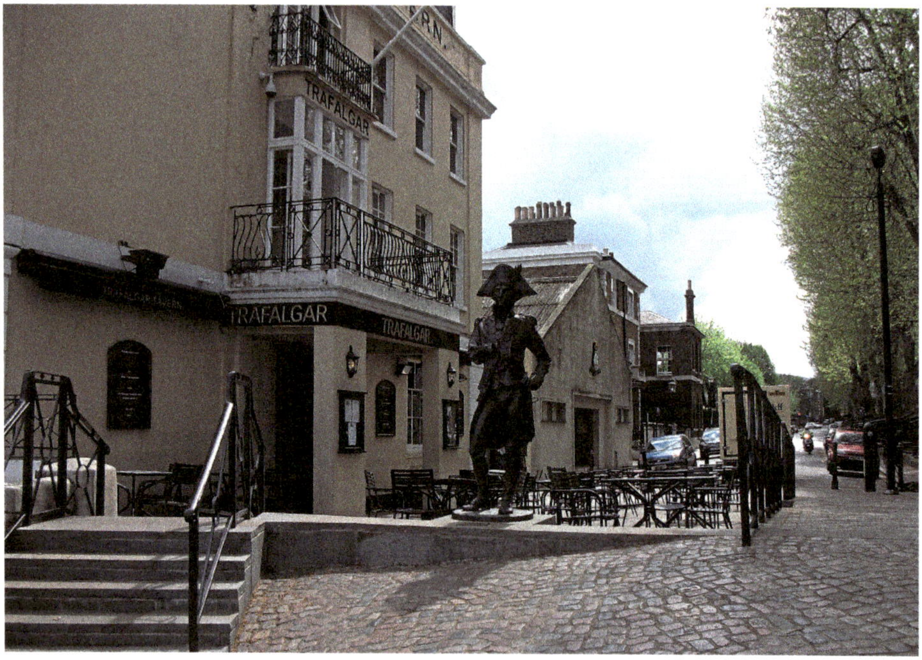

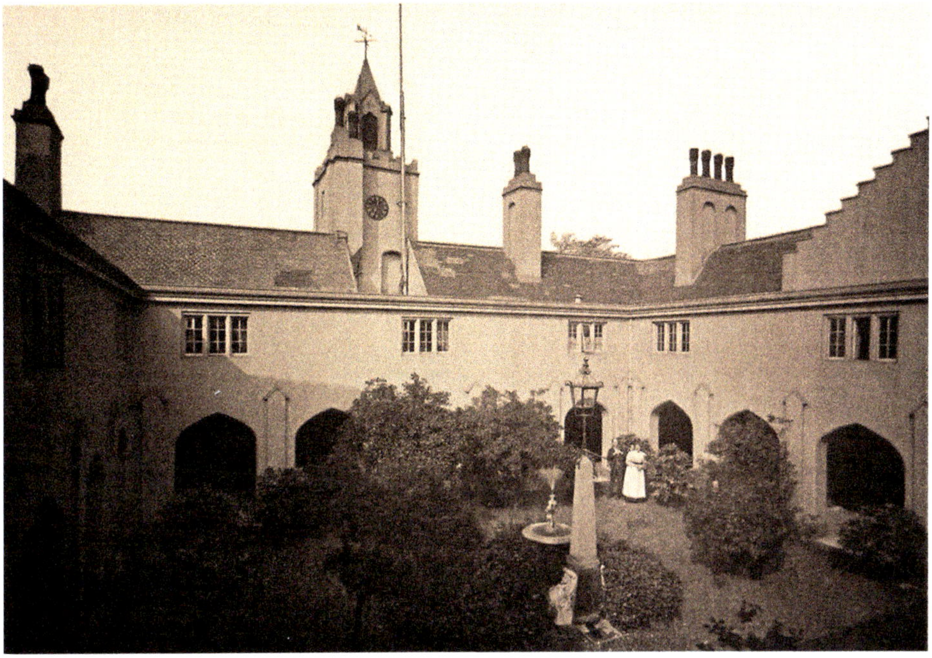

Trinity Hospital Almshouses – Anchor Iron Wharf

Founded in 1613 by the Earl of Northampton, Trinity Almshouses provided accommodation for retired gentlemen of Greenwich. The hospital, the oldest building in the centre of Greenwich, is run as a charity by the Mercers' company who provide care for elderly residents. The attractive and historic hospital and almshouses are overshadowed by Greenwich Power Station erected next to the hospital on Anchor Iron Wharf.

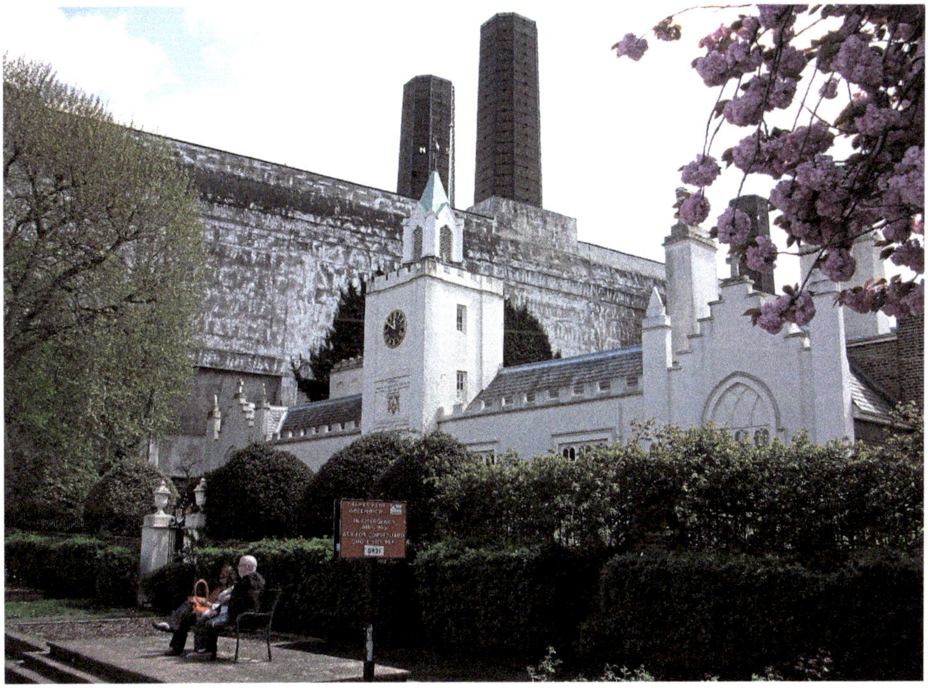

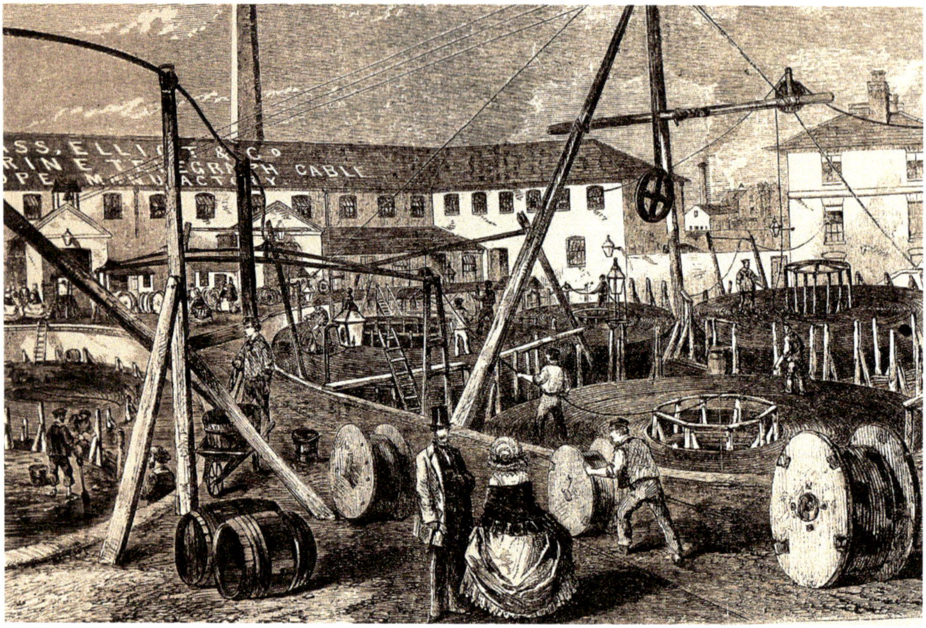

Glass Elliot – Enderby's Wharf

One of the main employers in Greenwich during the mid 1800s were Glass Elliot & Co telegraph cable manufacturers. Originally the site was owned by the Enderbys a family of whaling entrepreneurs. The transatlantic submarine telegraph cable laid by Brunel's Great Eastern in 1866 was manufactured on the site, where cables were made until the late 1900s. A large area of the site towards the river has now become derelict, one building which remains is the 1830s listed Enderby House on the river front once the residence of the Enderby family.

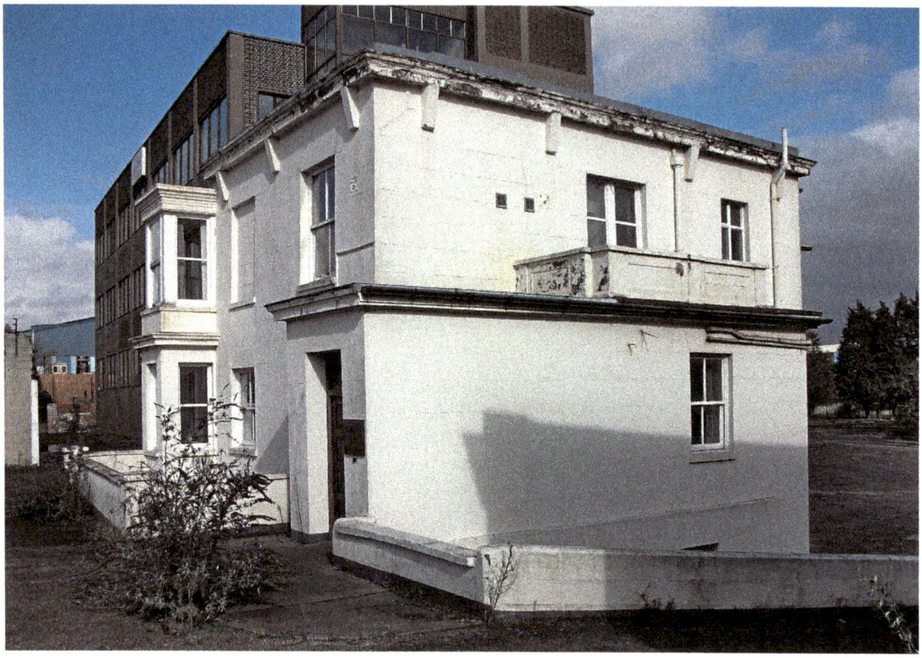

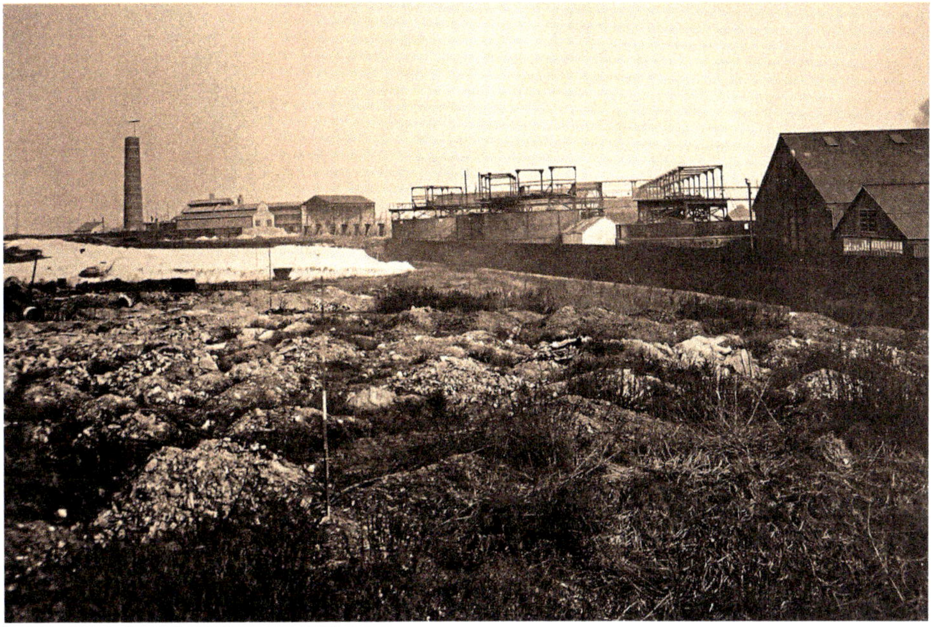

Greenwich Marsh – Greenwich Peninsula

Between the eighteenth and nineteenth centuries Greenwich Marsh had become a huge centre of industry and manufacturing. After the war as the industries went into decline and the communities moved out the marsh became a vast wasteland. When a location was needed for the millennium celebrations Greenwich Marsh was chosen as the area for regeneration. Developments on the Peninsula included homes, schools, shops, businesses and a massive circular exhibition centre, the Millennium Dome. When the year-long celebrations came to a close the Dome almost became a great white elephant, but has recently been voted the best entertainment venue in the world.

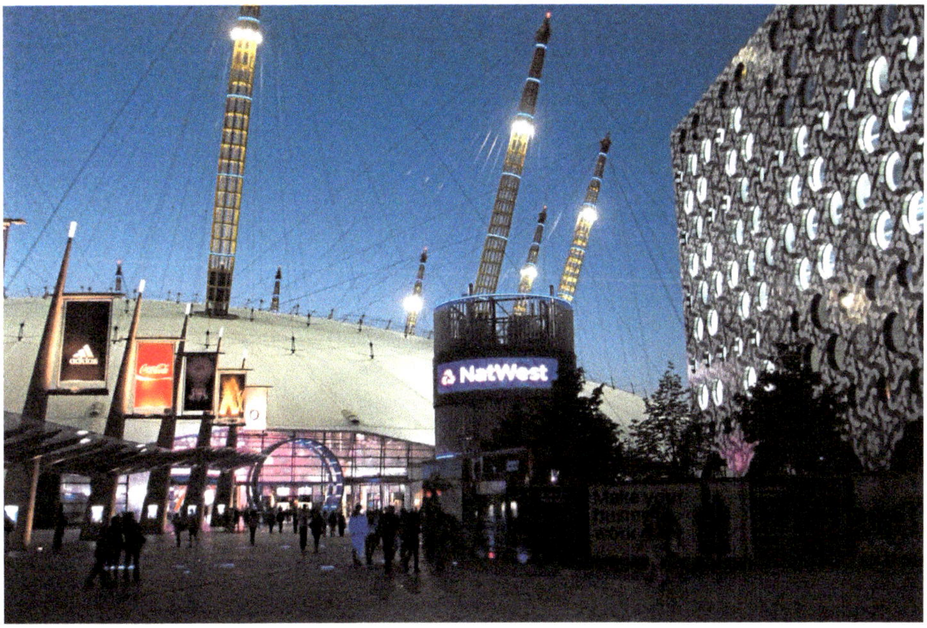

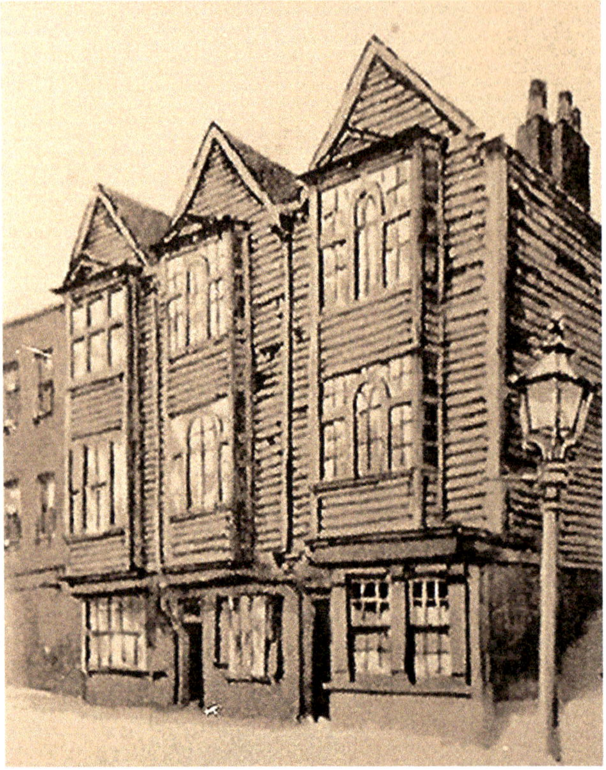

Medieval Greenwich – Church Street

The historic medieval centre of Greenwich covered an area from the south bank of the Thames to Stockwell Street, a warren of narrow streets and alleyways made up from timber buildings erected between the fourth and fifteenth centuries. The medieval properties were in need of constant repair and alteration which resulted in the centre of Greenwich becoming a jumble of hovels and squalid housing. In 1830 Greenwich Hospital Clerk of Works and architect Joseph Kay was given the task of redeveloping the whole town centre. All of the medieval buildings were torn down with only a few of the original medieval street lines retained in the new Greenwich centre development.

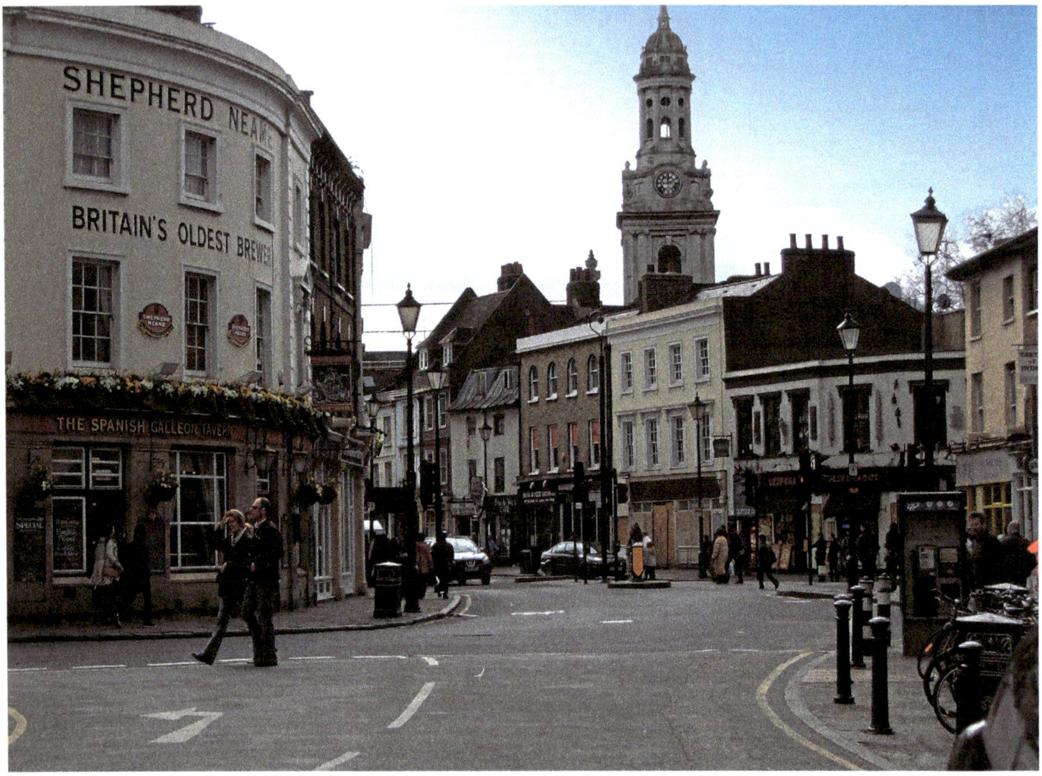

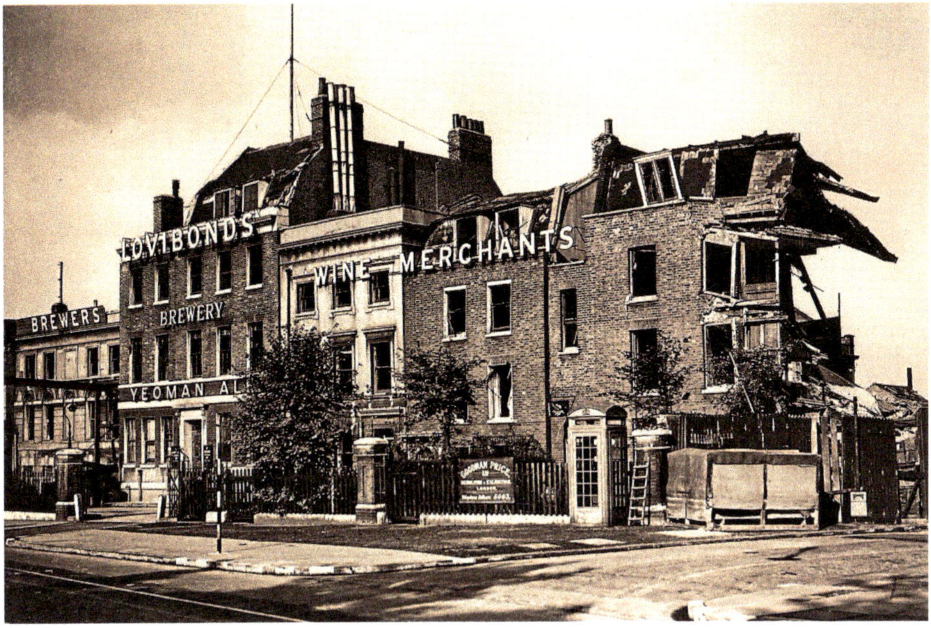

Lovibonds Brewery – Greenwich High Road

West Country brewers, Lovibonds, moved into the Greenwich area in 1847 and built a new brewery on Greenwich High Road in 1865. The brewery was damaged by a doodlebug in 1944, which stopped production for a short period. Although Lovibonds had opened branches and depots throughout London the brewery eventually closed when the brewers were bought out in 1968. John Davy & Co purchased the buildings for use as a wine vault and wine bar. In 2005 an independent brewer moved into the old Lovibonds depot at Henley-on-Thames to reform the Lovibonds Brewery.

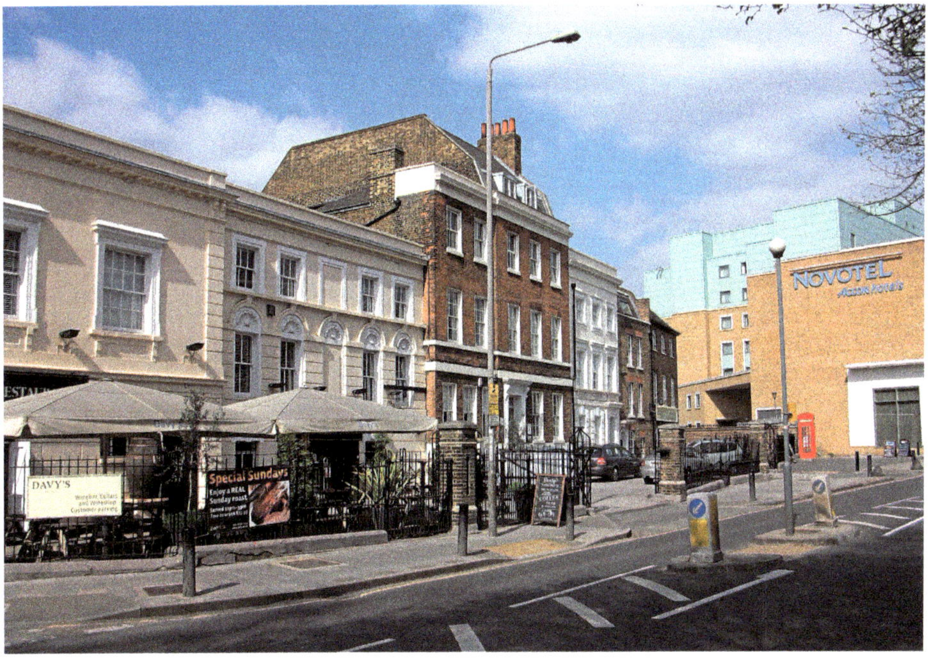

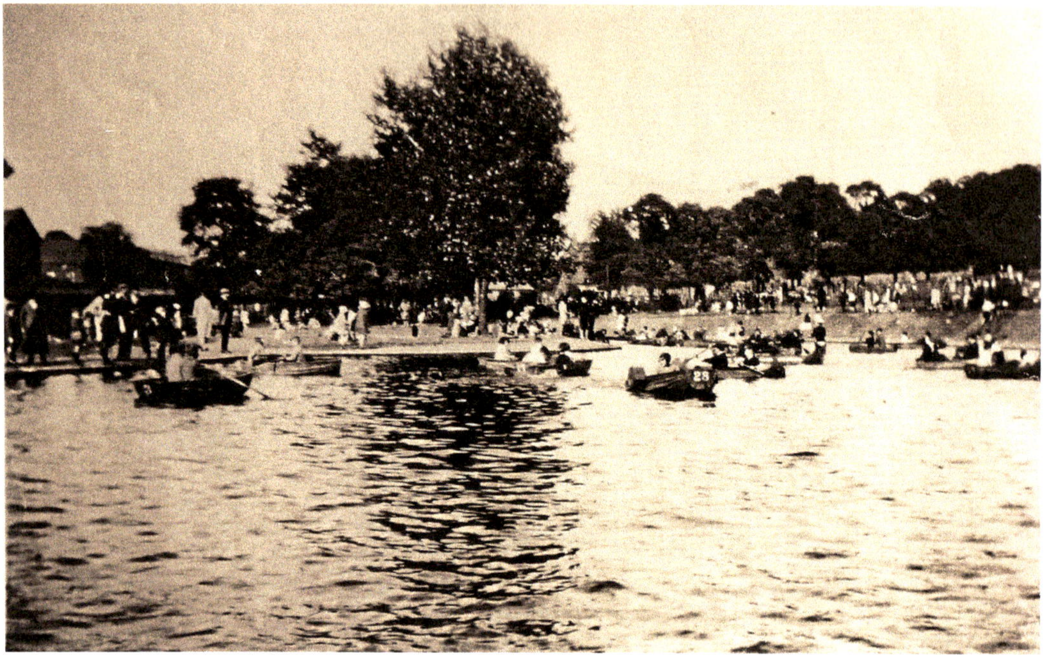

Boating – Greenwich Park

Children have been boating on a small lake in Greenwich Park in all types of craft from Canadian canoes to pedalos since the early 1950s. The meridian line passes directly through the middle of the lake where you can row or peddle a boat from one side of the hemisphere to the other. The large sundial seen in the picture below was intended to have been positioned directly on the meridian line, but due to a miscalculation is two metres out of alignment.

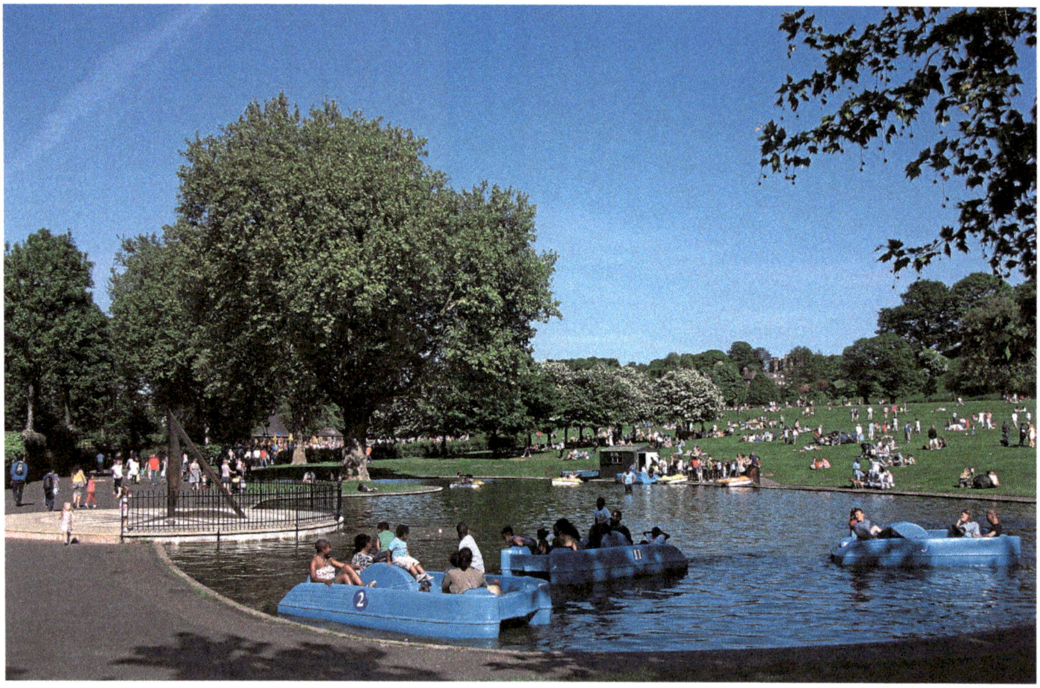

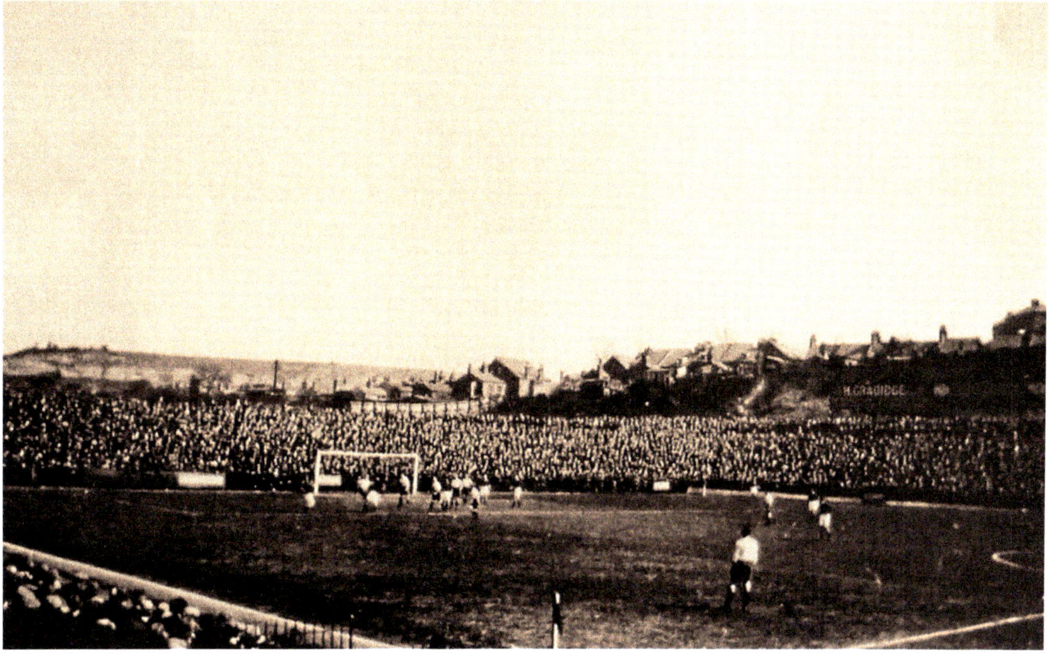

Charlton Athletic Football Club

Formed in 1905 Charlton Athletic played at various locations in the local area until moving to The Valley in 1919. During the early 1920s crowds of over 7,000 were attending matches played in the Third Division South. My family and friends have supported the 'Addicks' through all the years the club has progressed up the football league. The Valley became an all seated stadium with a capacity of just over 27,000 during Charlton's most successful years playing in the Premier League.

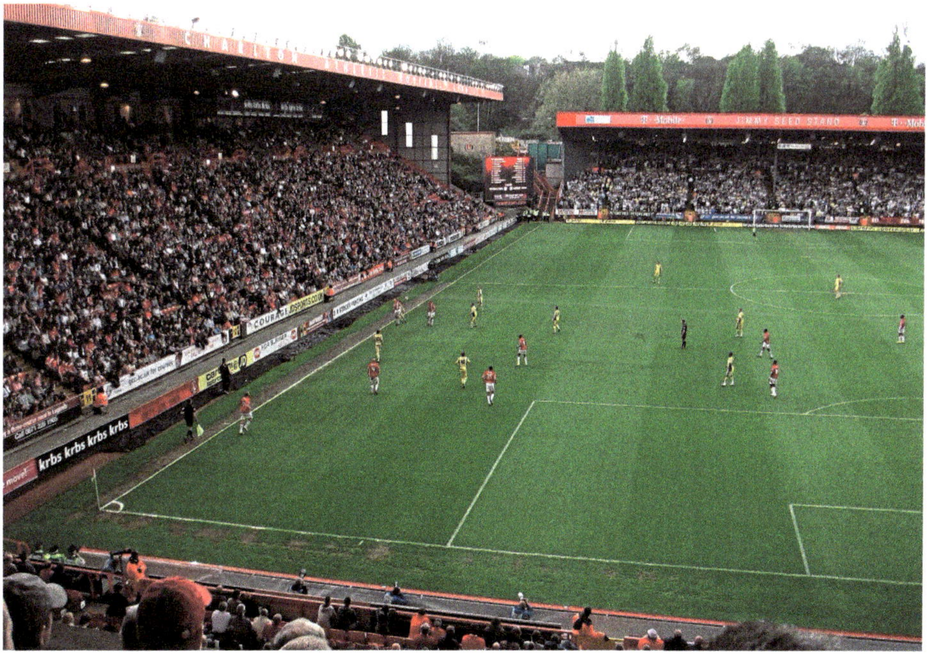

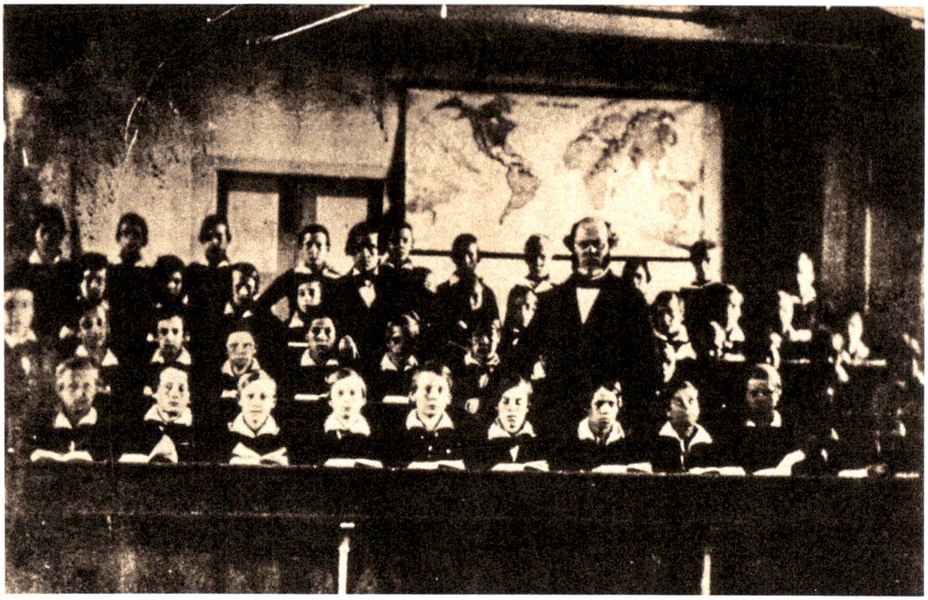

Royal Hospital School – Maritime Museum

Headmaster John Riddle and a class of school boys from 1855. Over 10,000 boys educated at the school between 1874 and 1930 joined the navy as able seamen, five becoming Admirals. When the Royal Hospital School moved to Suffolk the National Maritime Museum took over the building and opened the doors to the public in 1937. Thousands of youngsters now come to visit this historic museum including the 2nd Long Stratton Brownies from Norfolk who were enjoying their day at the museum on the group's visit to Greenwich in 2010.

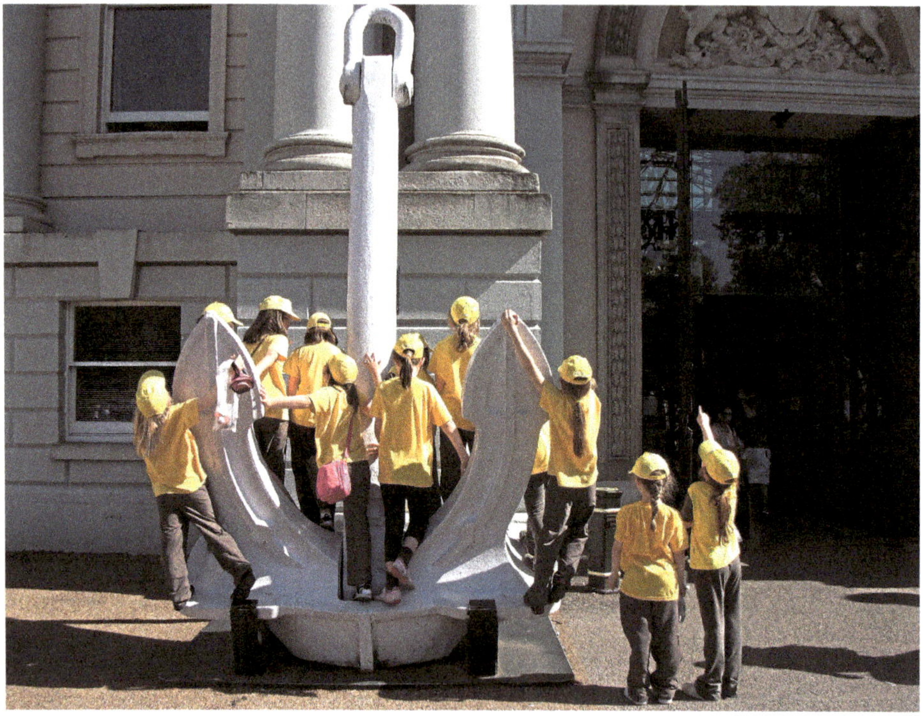

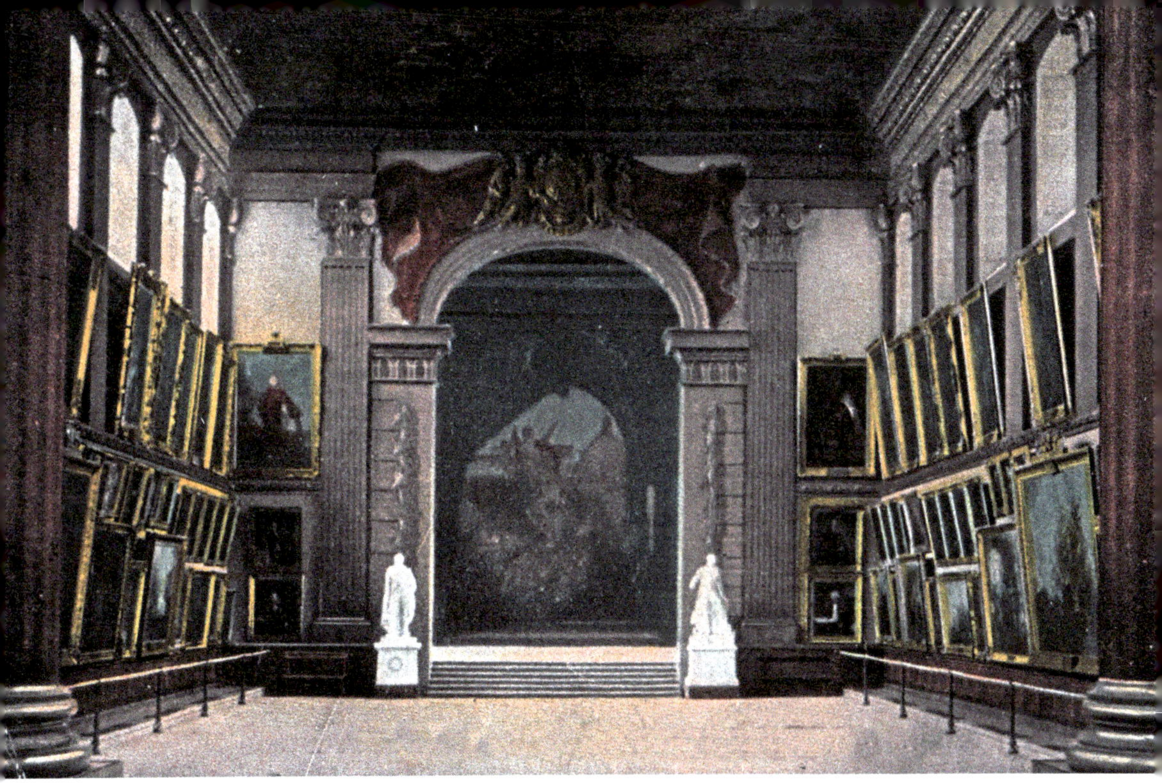

Painted Hall – Royal Naval College

British artist Sir James Thornhill was commissioned to decorate the dining hall at the Seaman's Hospital in 1709, which took the artist nineteen years to complete. The Pensioners ate in vaulted undercrofts while the work was being carried out and when the hall was finally finished it was too grand for its purpose and became something of a money-making tourist attraction where Pensioners ran tours. The body of Lord Nelson was laid in state at the hall in 1806 and in 1824 it became the National Gallery of Naval Art. The Painted Hall is considered to be one of the finest in the western world and is still a popular tourist attraction today.

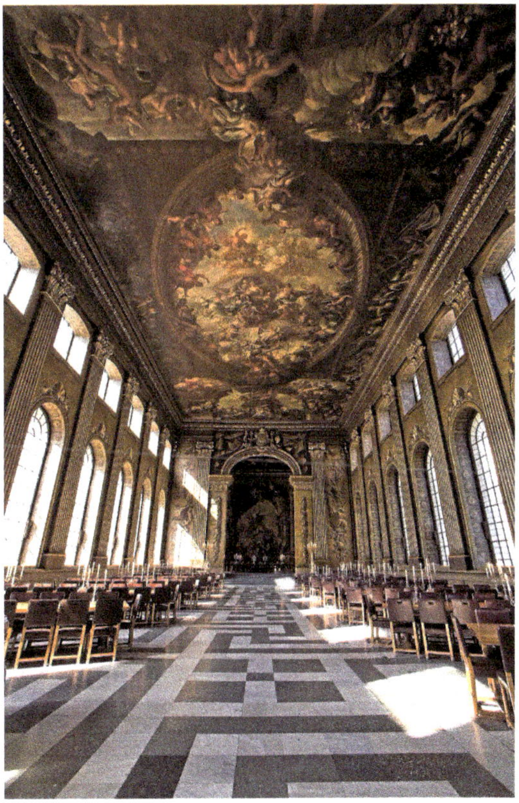

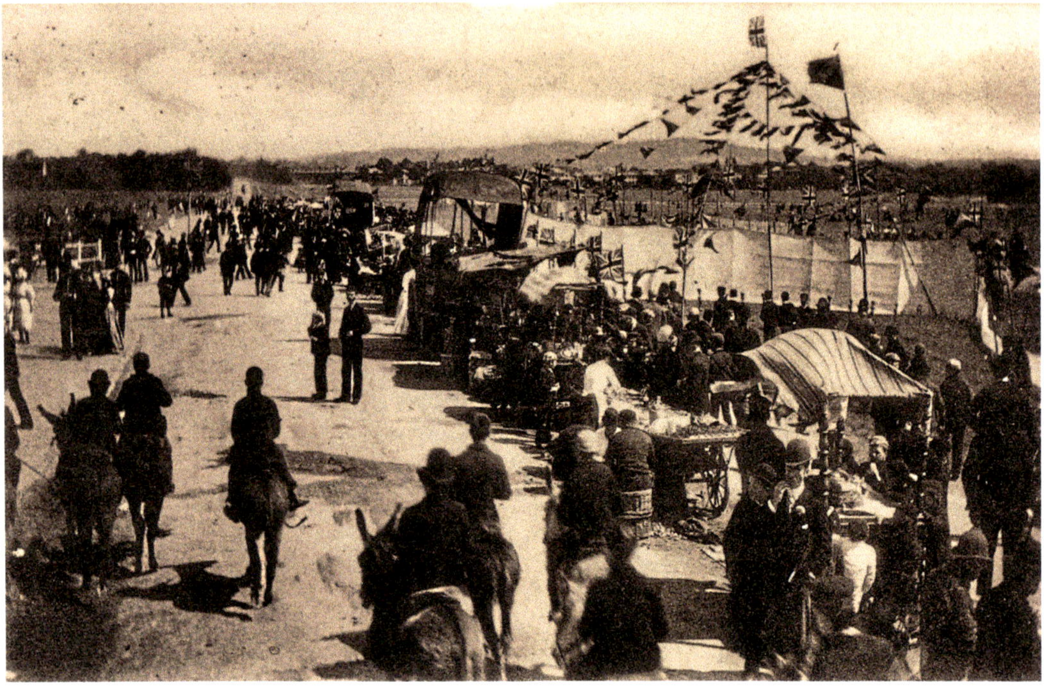

Fun Fair – Blackheath

Community fairs had been held on the heath ever since the mid 1600s. Military parades, hog roasts, sporting events and freak shows were popular attractions for thousands of visitors attending the fairs during May and October. The fairs were held outside Blackheath Park Gate, as seen in the image from the 1900s above. Suppressed by government order in 1872 the fairs were later reinstated by popular demand. During public holidays and bank holiday weekends the fair arrives on Blackheath with traditional and modern rides to entertain the public.

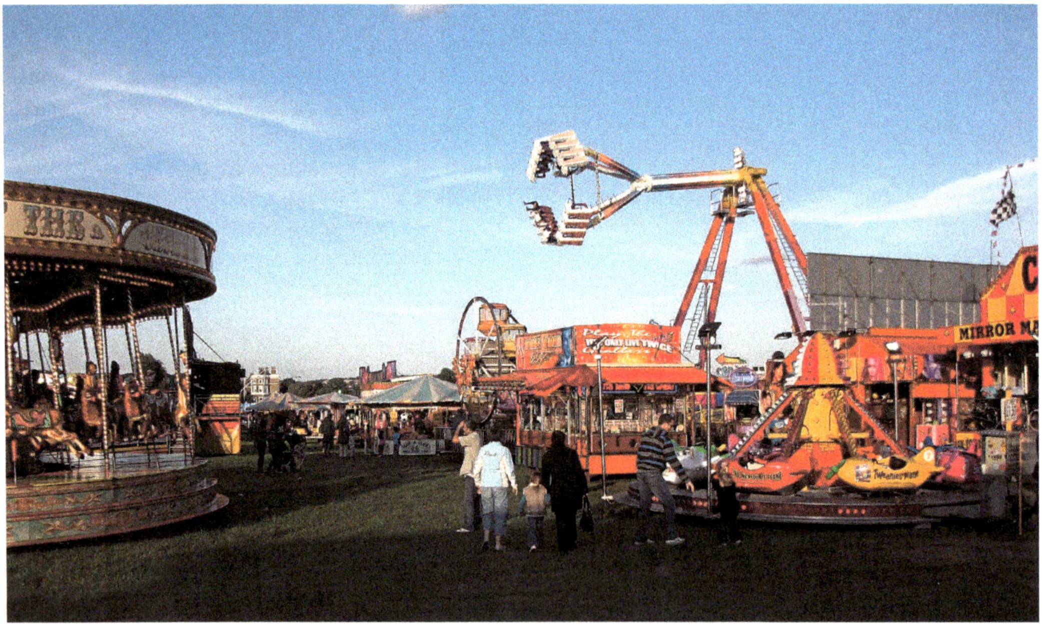

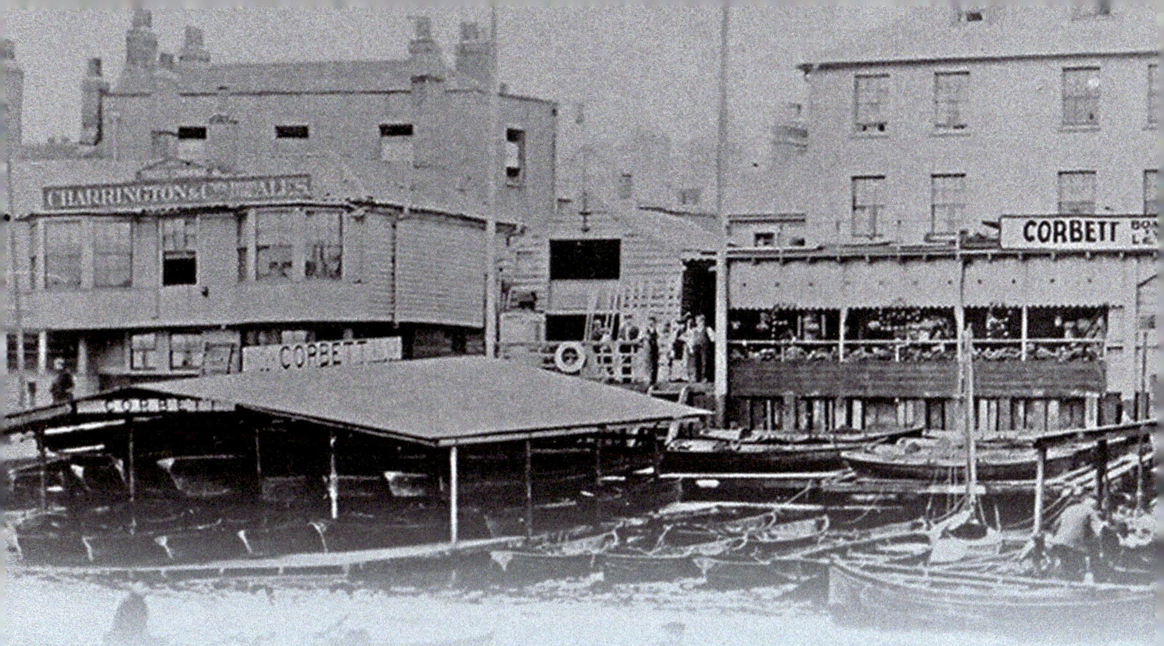

CHAPTER 3

On the Waterfront

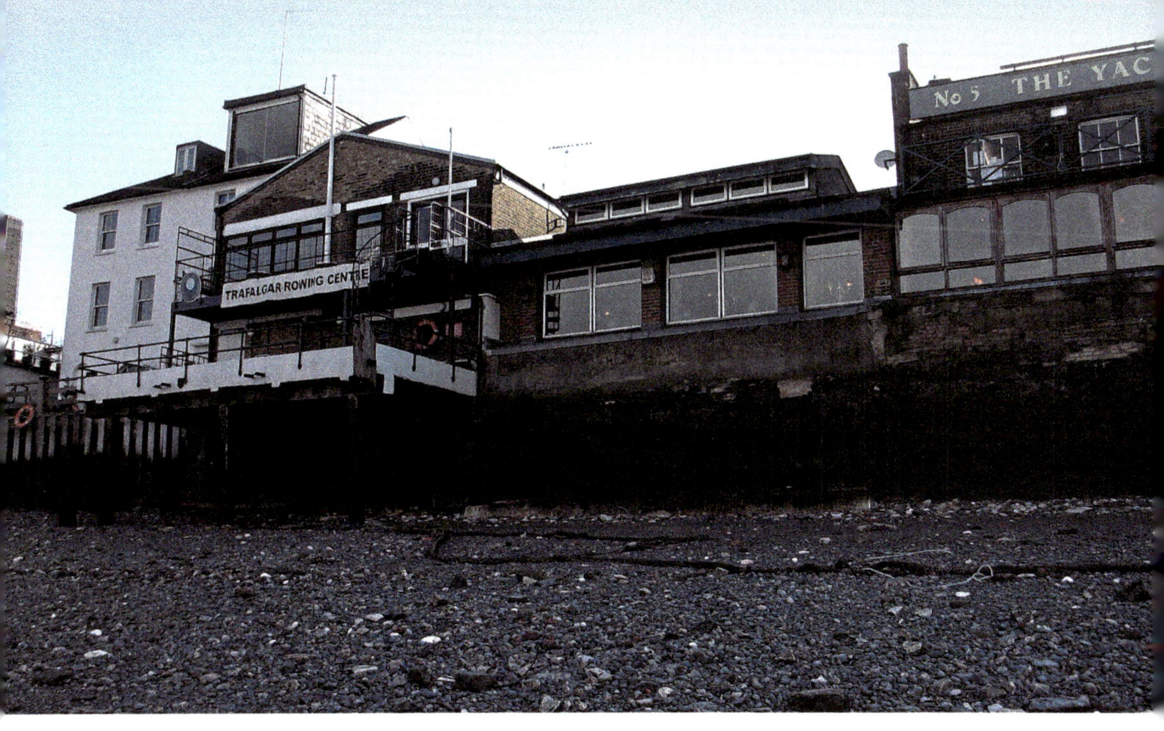

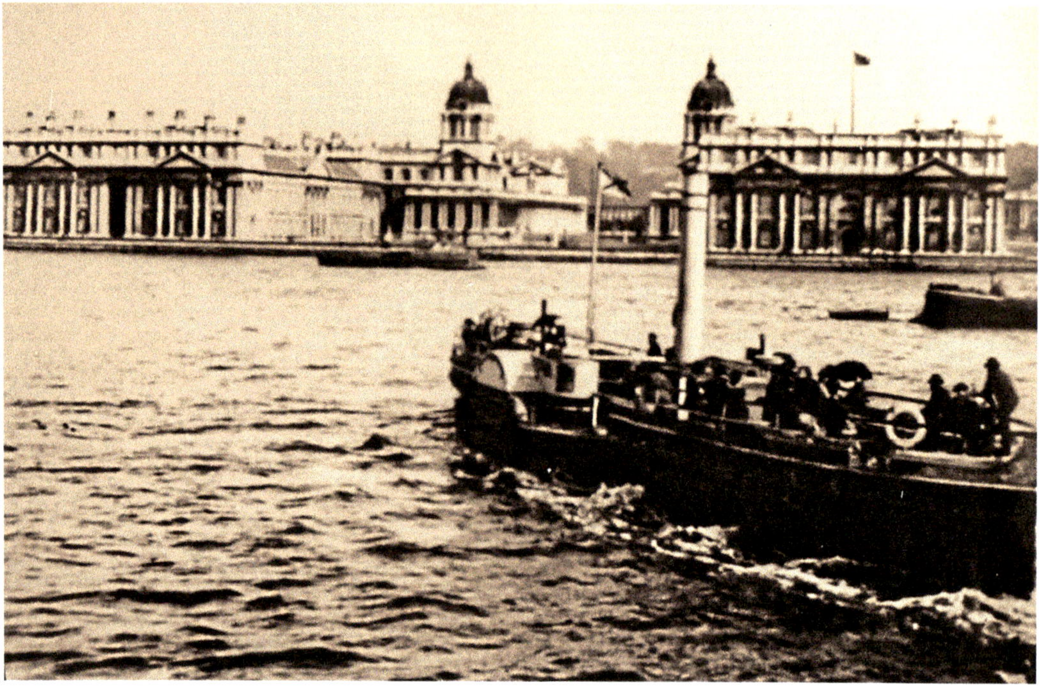

Royal Naval College

River boats on the Thames have taken travellers back and forth past these buildings for over 300 years, in galleys, sail boats, paddle steamers and now sleek modern river ferries. Sir Christopher Wren's grand architectural masterpiece is best viewed from Island Gardens across the river on the Isle of Dogs; the gardens can be reached through the Greenwich foot tunnel.

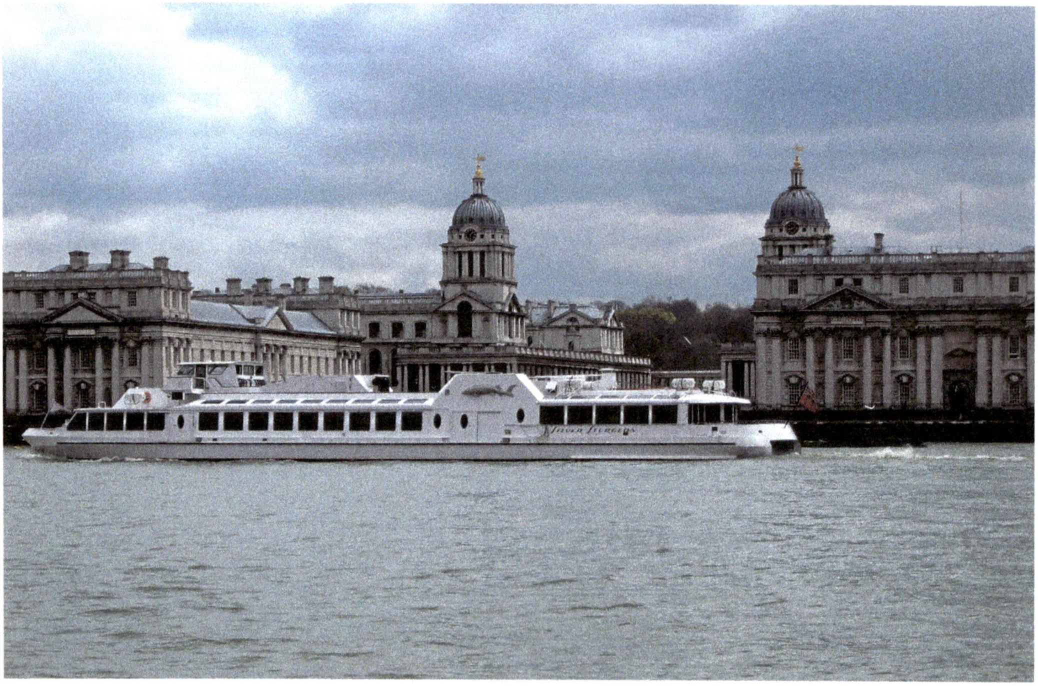

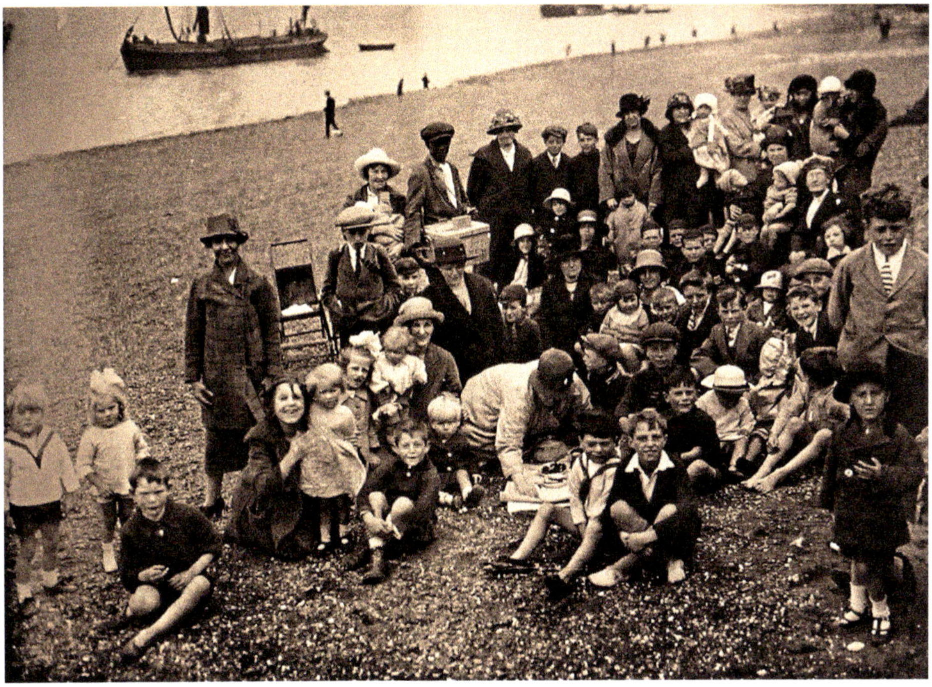

Greenwich Beach

A day out to Greenwich Beach during the 1930s. This strip of sand and shingle had been a popular place for families to visit since the early 1800s. Victorians came to the beach to paddle and play in the river even though the Thames was heavily polluted from industrial waste. The beach is reached by the Queen's Steps in front of the Royal Naval College, on sunny summer days when the tide is out people can relax on the beach next to a much cleaner River Thames.

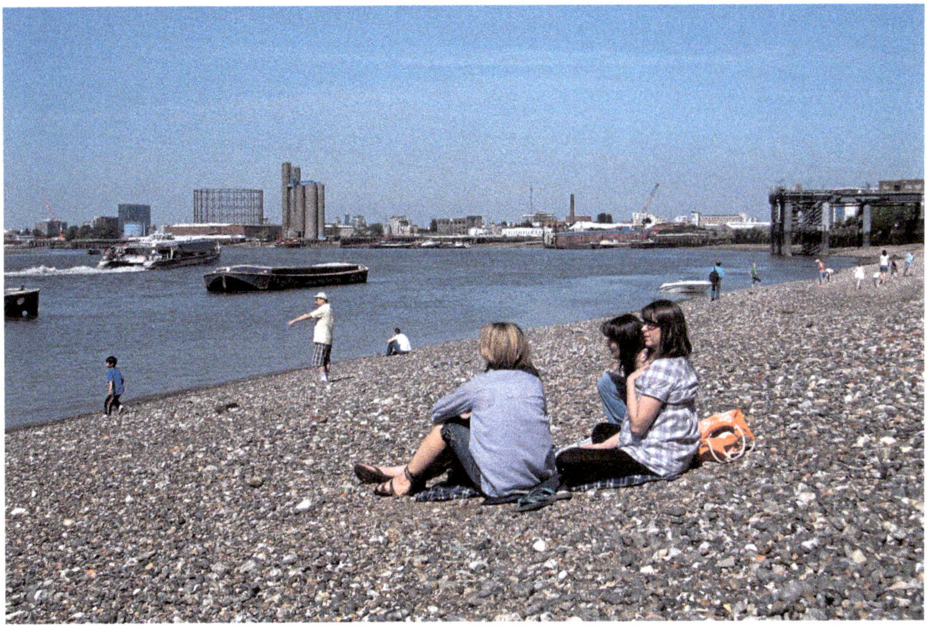

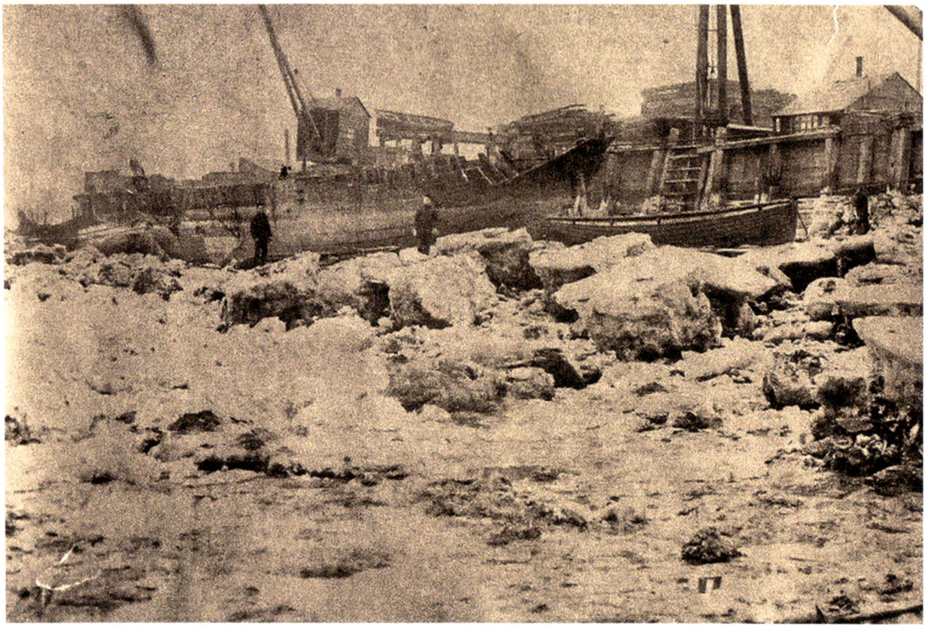

Frozen Thames – Greenwich Reach

A huge ice flow brought river traffic to a standstill near Greenwich Reach in 1895. Records of these freezes date back to AD250 when the Thames froze solid for nine weeks. Henry VIII travelled by sleigh on the Thames from Greenwich to London in the winter of 1536 and Queen Elizabeth practiced her archery on a frozen Thames. The last time the river froze solid was during the winter of 1814 which is unlikely to occur again although heavy snowfalls during the early part 2010 made Ballast Quay at Greenwich Reach an icy place to walk.

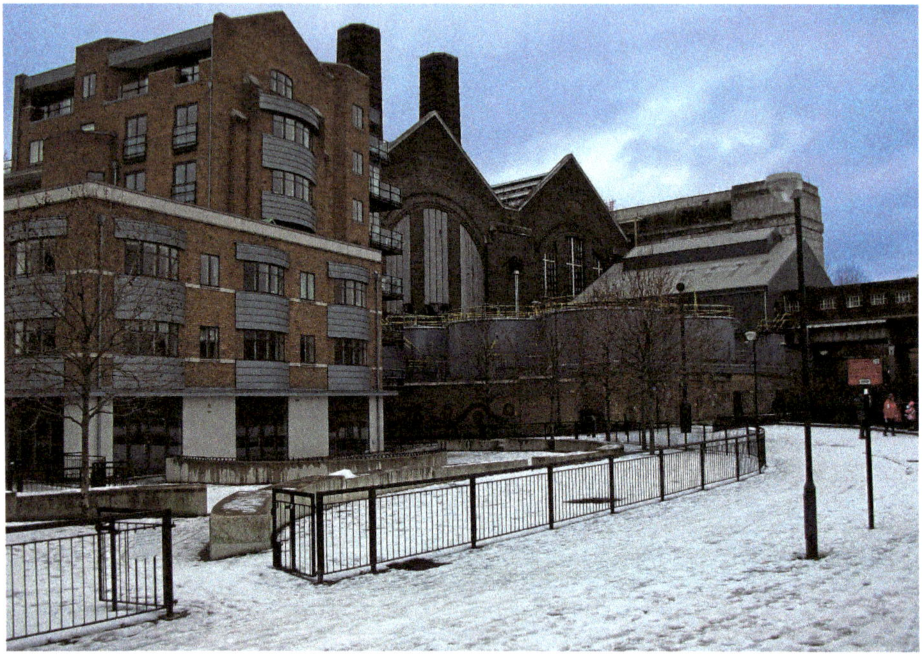

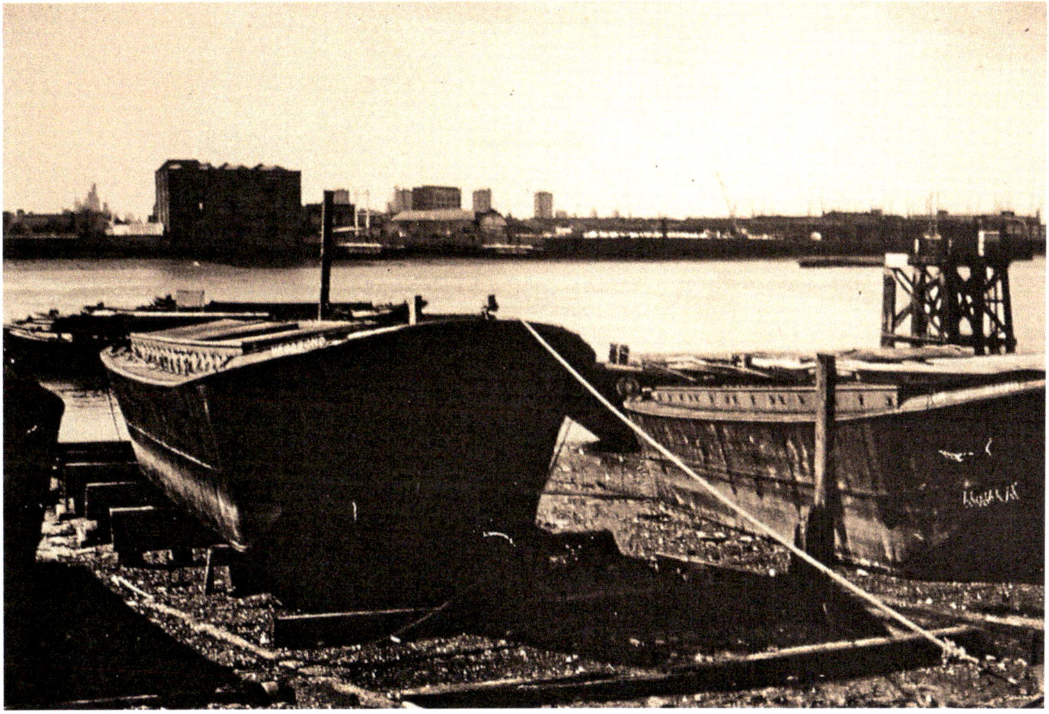

Barge Builders – Piper's Wharf

These container barges at Piper's Wharf were used to transport cargo up and down the river during the 1950s. The yards were rented by James Piper in the late 1890s for building sailing barges and lighters, container barges. Boats and barges are still repaired at Piper's Wharf the last link to boat building in Greenwich.

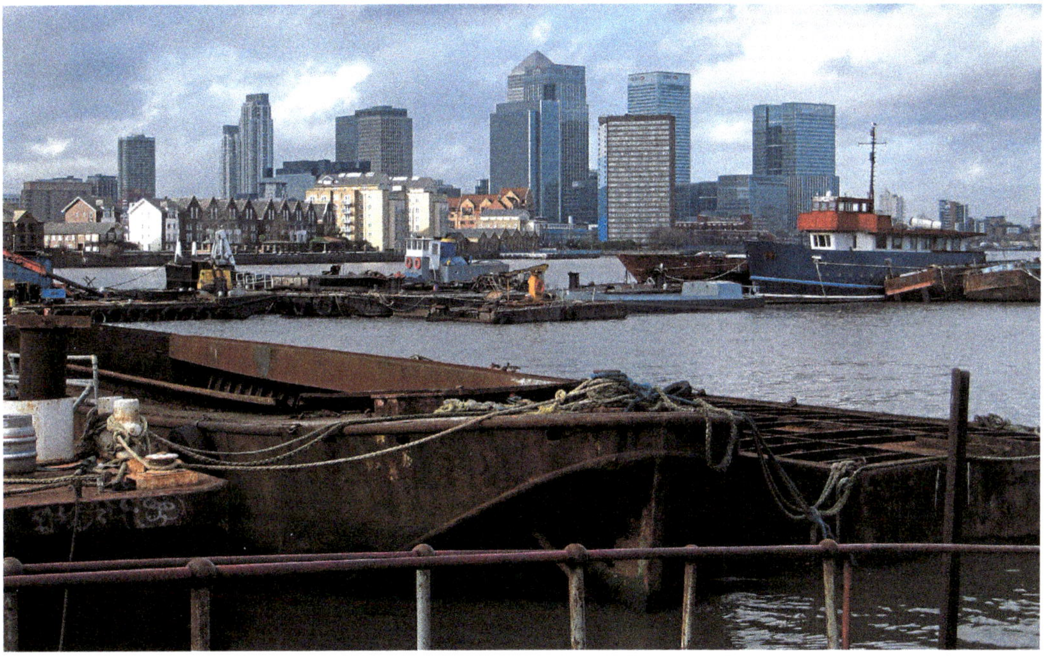

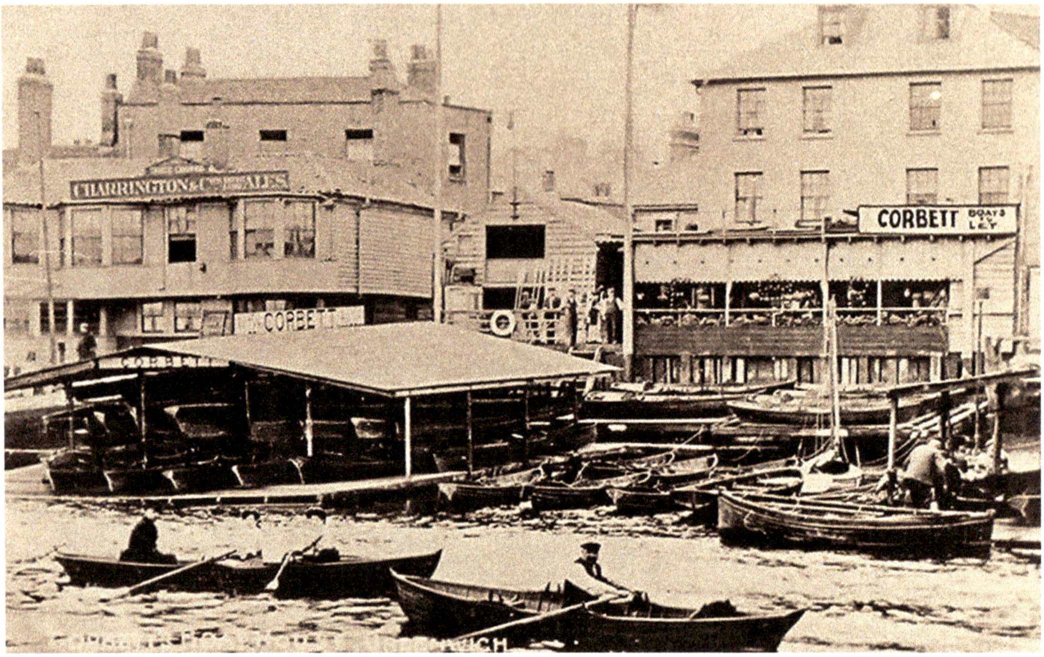

Corbett's Boats – Crane Street

Rowing boats of all types could be hired at Corbett's boat builder's pontoon to the rear of the riverside properties on Crane Street. J. Corbett & Sons had been building boats at Wood Wharf, close to Deptford Creek since the mid 1800s. The pontoon was used for storing their own boats and the boats of local rowing clubs. The house behind Corbett's pontoon still exists which is next to the Trafalgar Rowing Club. Further to the right is the Yacht Tavern where you can watch the rowers from one of the bars overlooking the river.

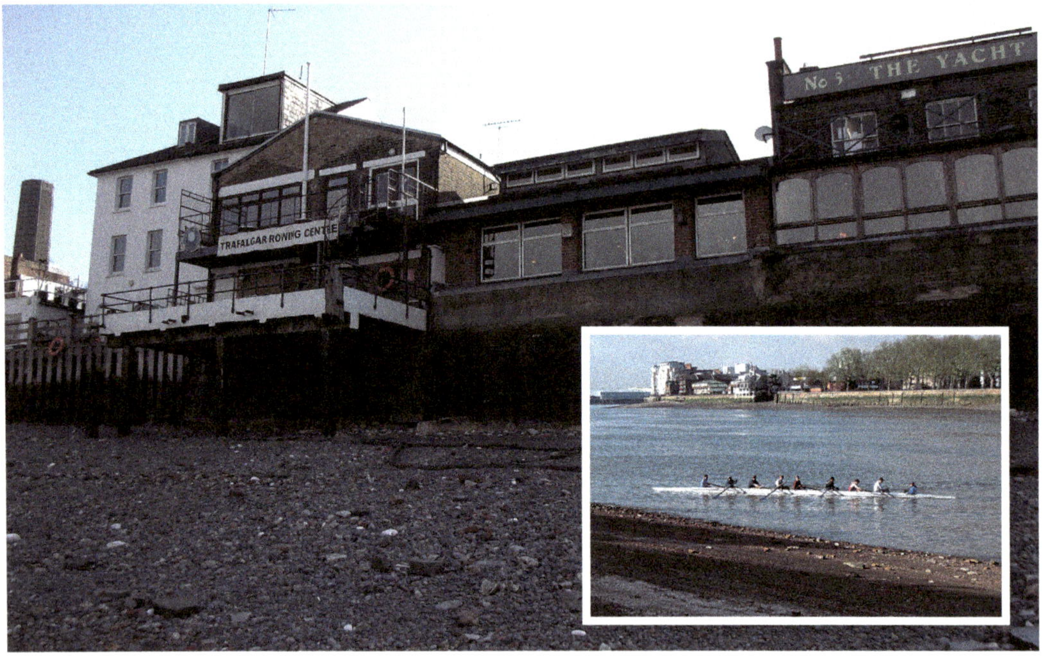

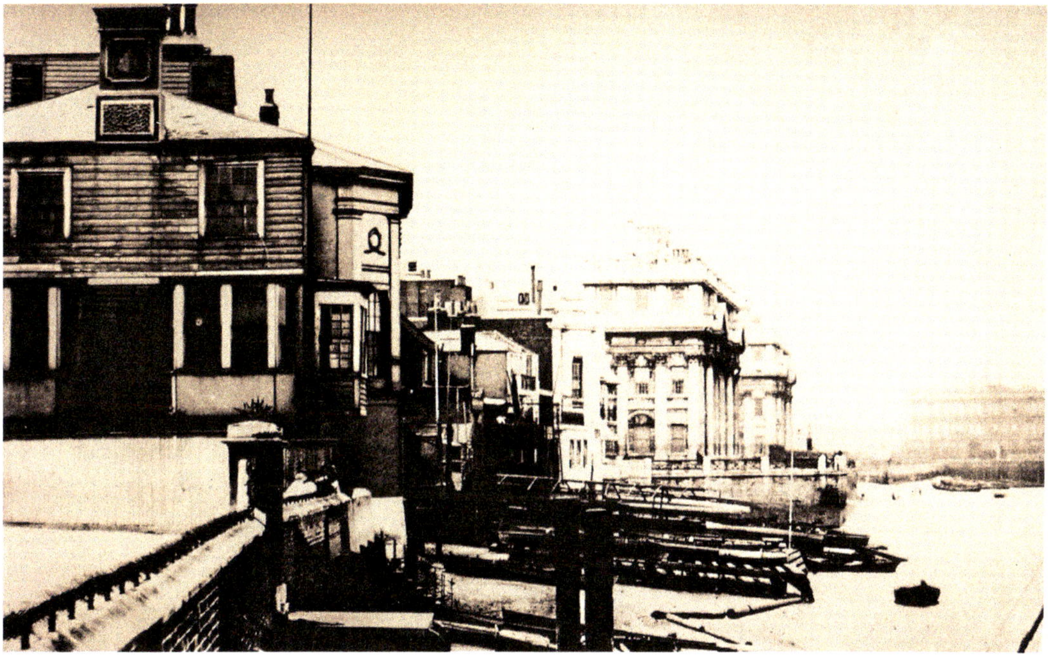

Highbridge Wharf

A view looking west towards the Royal Naval College shows the riverfront properties at the turn of the nineteenth century. The name Highbridge comes from a fifteenth century bridge situated at the site used to move goods back and forth from ship to shore. In the sixteenth century it was forbidden for Venetian galleys to sail upstream beyond Highbridge for fear of piracy. The working riverfront buildings at Highbridge have now been replaced by residential properties.

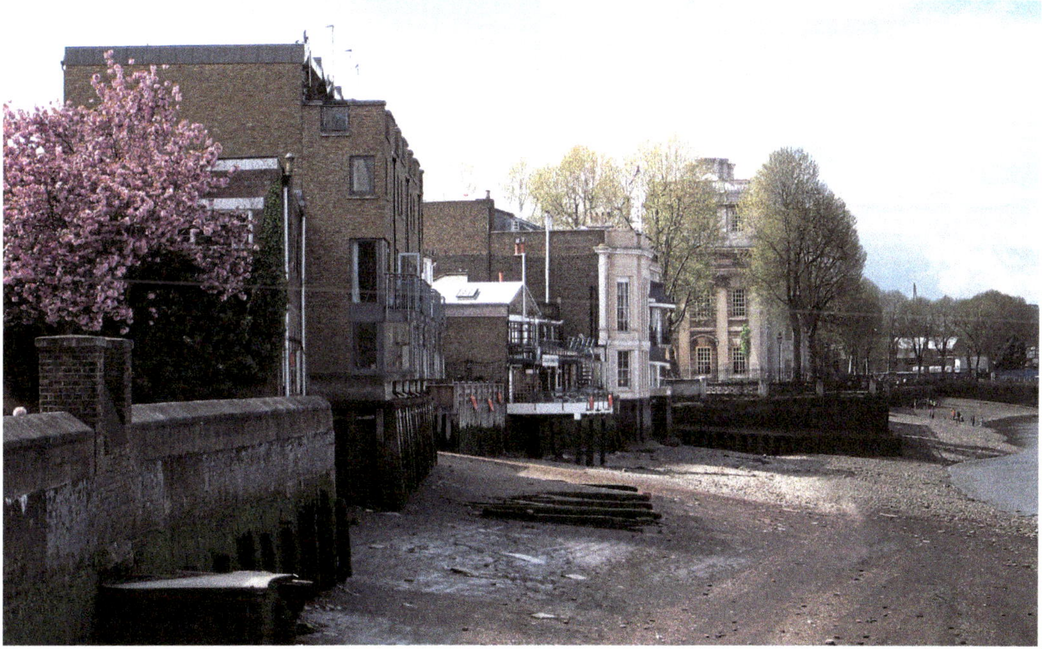

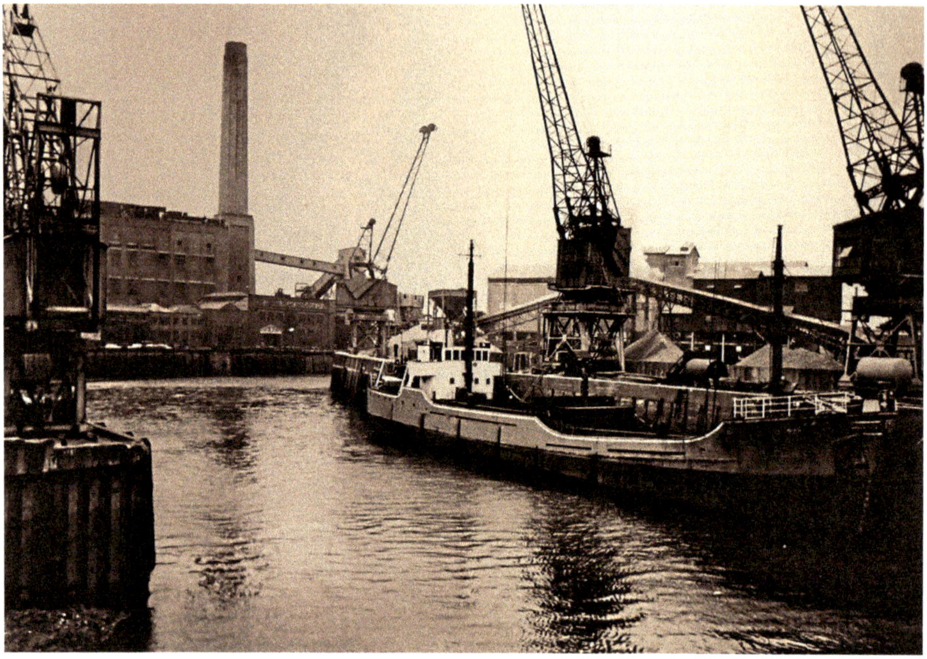

Deptford Creek

The River Ravensbourne is one of the few navigational creeks on the Thames. Coastal craft similar to the vessel tied up at Deptford Creek during the 1950s would sail up or down the river at high tide requiring the road bridge over the creek to open to allow passage through. Industries on the river included a tide mill, shipbuilder's, breweries, gas works, chemical works, candle factory, soap factory and power station. All have now gone as the land each side of the Creek is under redevelopment.

Inset: Plaque on the side of Deptford Creek Bridge control tower.

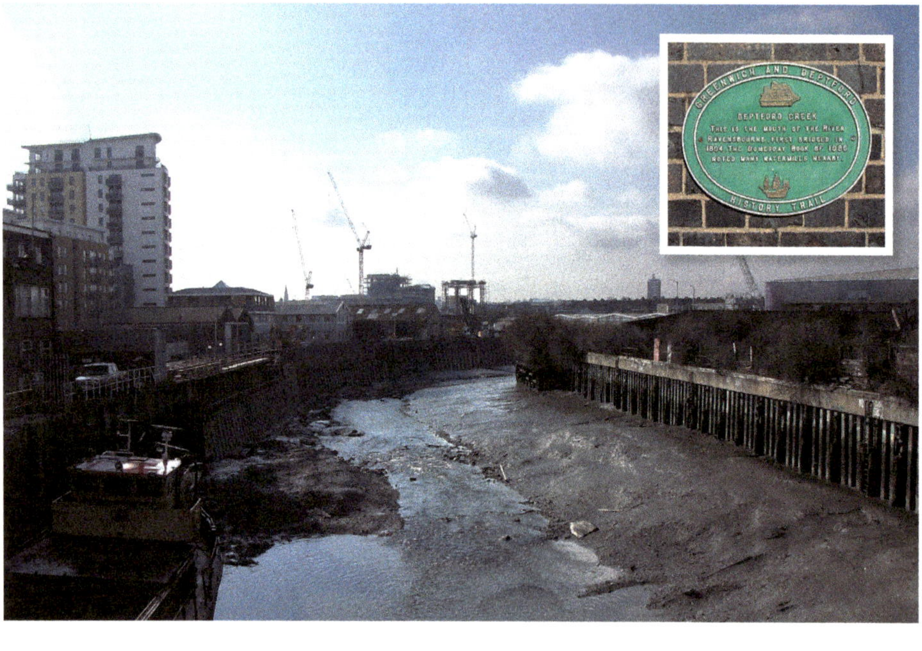

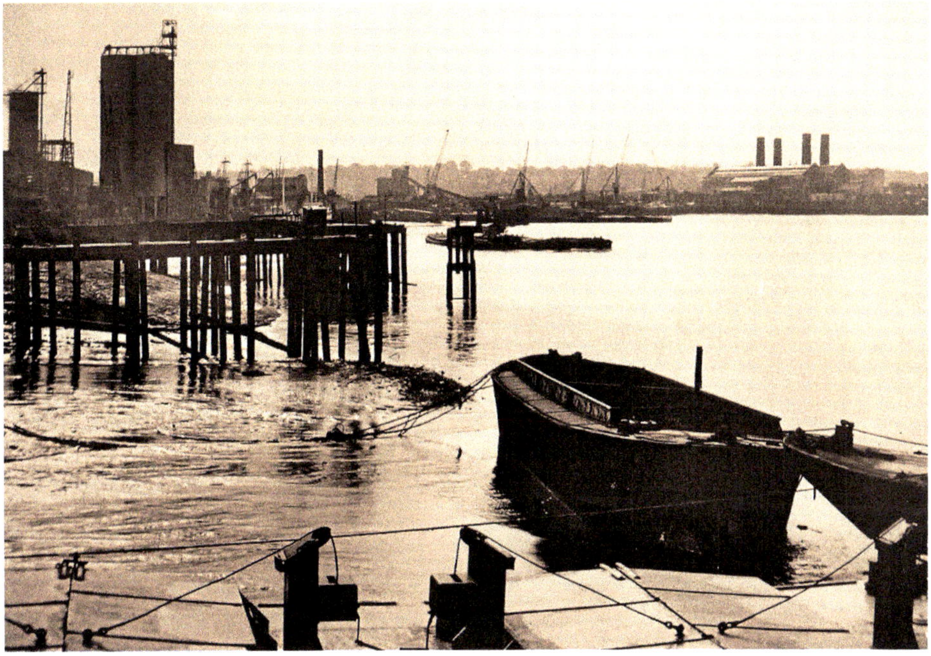

Blackwall Reach – River Thames

The decline of the industries on the south bank of the Thames from Blackwall Reach to Greenwich Reach can be seen when comparing a photograph taken during the mid 1900s the latest taken in 2010. The cranes of the riverside wharfs have been replaced by cranes moving building aggregates. Greenwich Power Station is still prominent in the far distance, but the river is empty of barges and shipping. The developments along this part of the riverfront will include housing, business parks, hotels and leisure facilities.

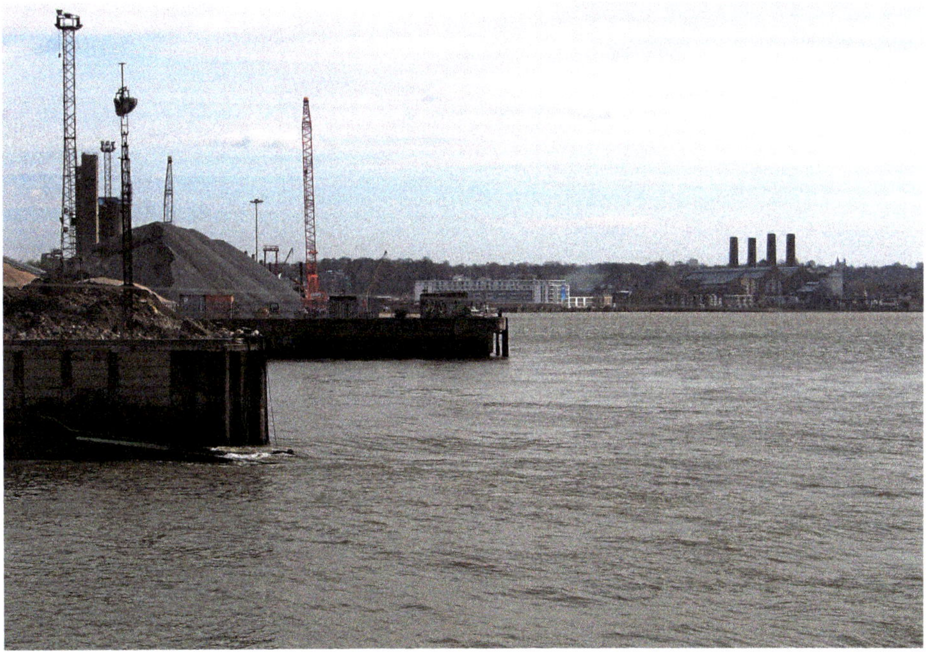

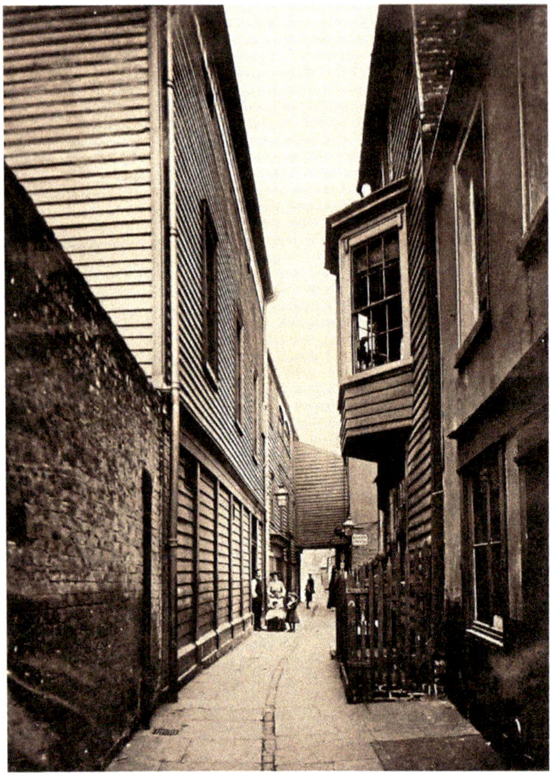

Crane Street – Highbridge Wharf

These historic weather-boarded riverside buildings of the late 1800s were situated each side of Crane Street which leads towards Highbridge Wharf. The street name has associations with a crane which stood on the site in 1730 used for unloading ships at the wharf. These historic riverside buildings were demolished and replaced by bland brick-built commercial workshops, most of which have recently been replaced by modern apartments and flats.

Insert: An inscription on the stones at the foot of a series of steps leading down to the river at Highbridge Wharf welcomes strangers arriving by boat.

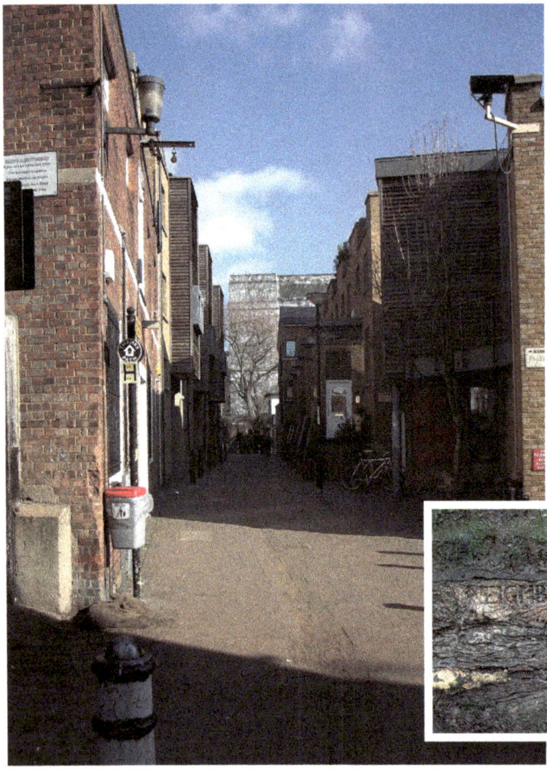

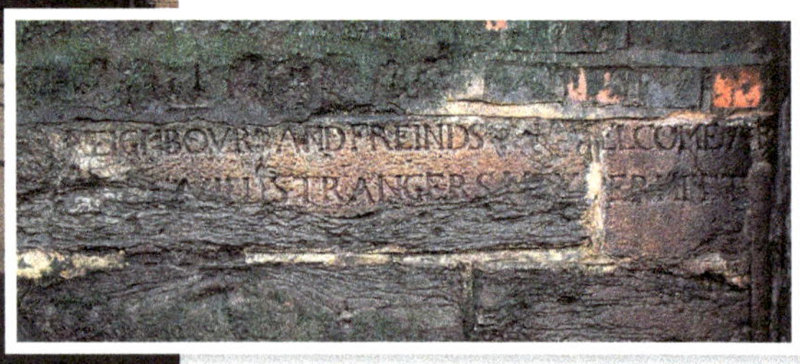

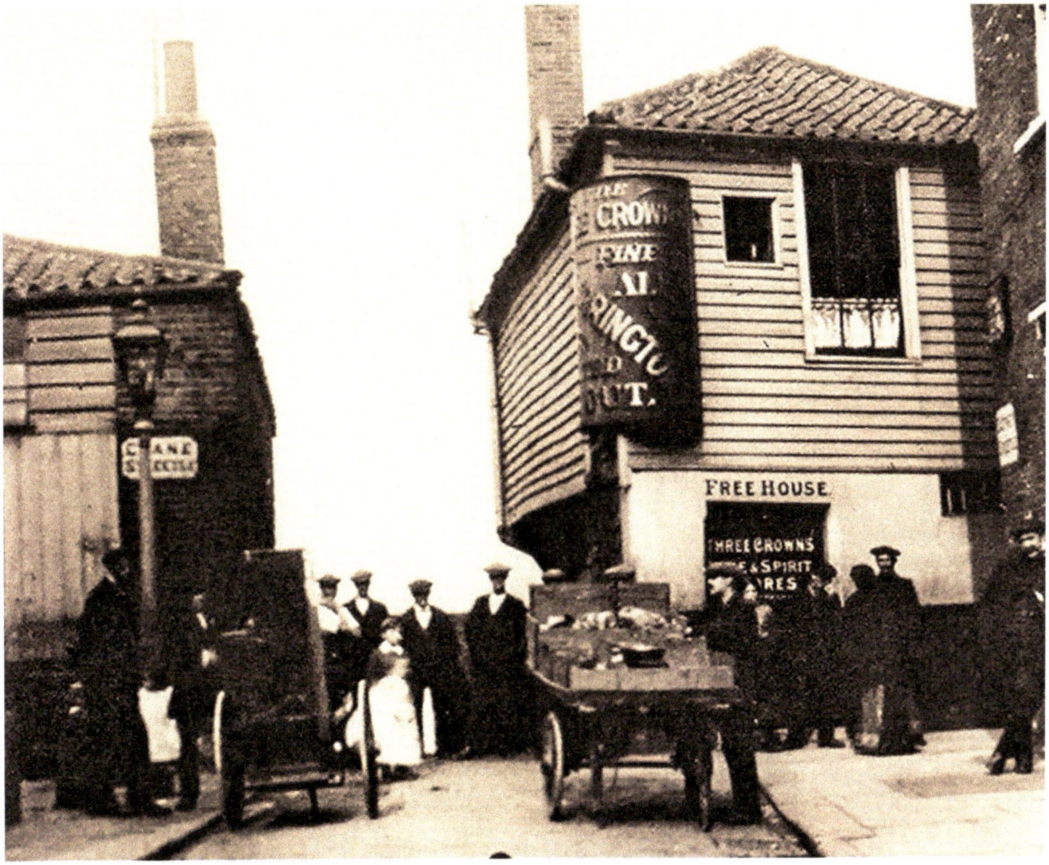

The Three Crowns – East Street

Street traders are selling their wares outside the inn during the early 1930s, the group of men behind the traders are standing in front of a heavy pair of wooden gates which lead down towards the Thames. The Three Crowns was demolished along with many other unique properties along this stretch of the riverfront. Some of these buildings were torn down after being damaged in the blitz, many others for redevelopment. The riverside gates are still in place and are open for access to the river for rowing club crews taking their boats down to the Thames. When we were children my friends and I would climb over the old river gates to go beach combing, where we would find Victorian clay pipes, bottles, bones and on vary rare occasions old coins.

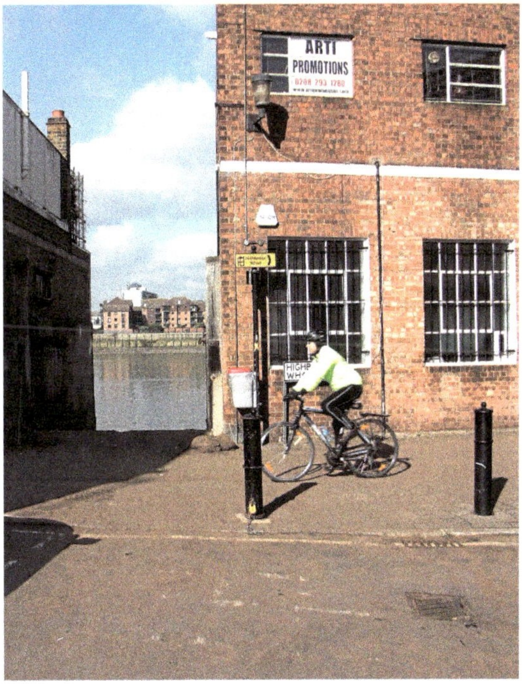

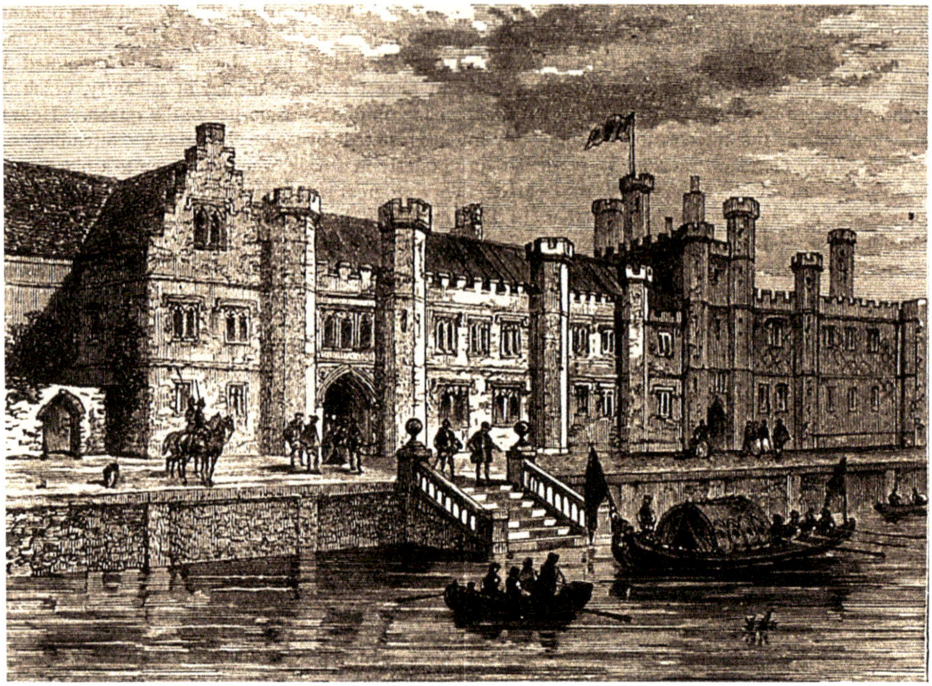

Greenwich Palace – Old Royal Naval College

The Palace at Greenwich was acquired by King Henry VII in 1487. Henry VIII was born at the palace where the king resided during a long period of his reign. The palace fell into disrepair and was demolished under the instruction of Charles II to make way for a new palace. Although never completed when William and Mary came to the throne the site was given over for the construction of a hospital for retired and injured seamen. During excavations at the site in the early 1970s the foundations of the Tudor Palace were discovered towards the east wing of the college adjacent to the Trafalgar Tavern.

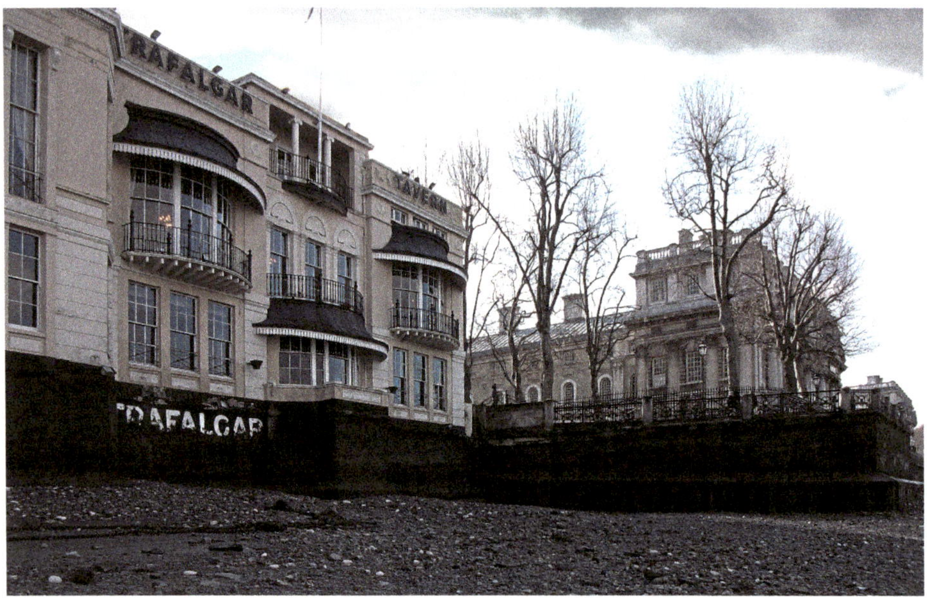

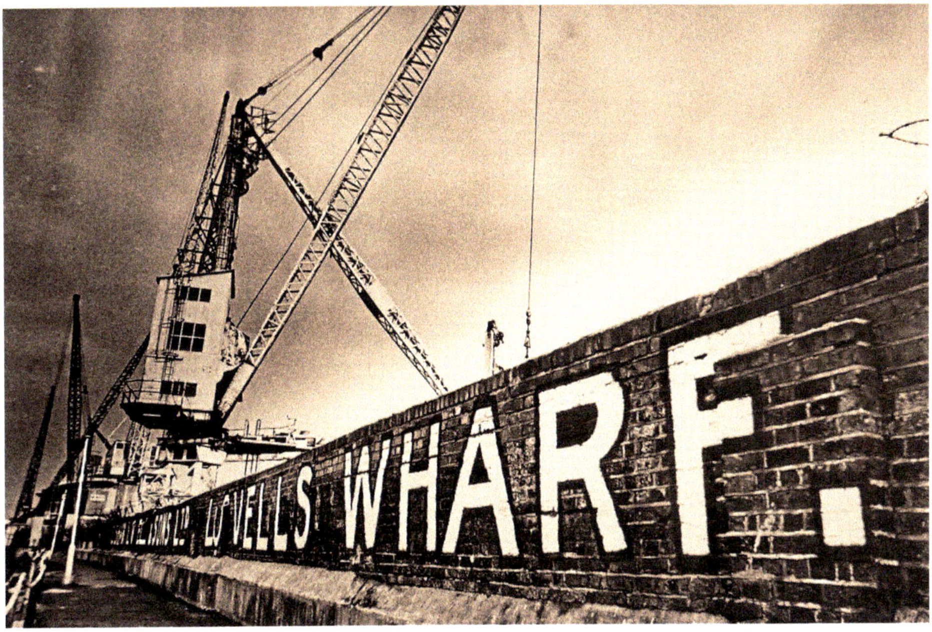

Lovell's Wharf

Lovell's Wharf, originally Greenwich Wharf, had been built to deal in coal until Shaw Lovell & Co took over the lease in the 1920s to handle shipments of non-ferrous metals. The two large cranes at the wharf, Scotch Derricks, were of historical and industrial interest but were removed along with the iconic brick wall after Lovell's moved out in the late 1980s. While the site was in the process of being redeveloped for housing archeologists discovered the remains of a twelfth-century tidal mill preserved in peat deposits when carrying out excavations at the wharf.

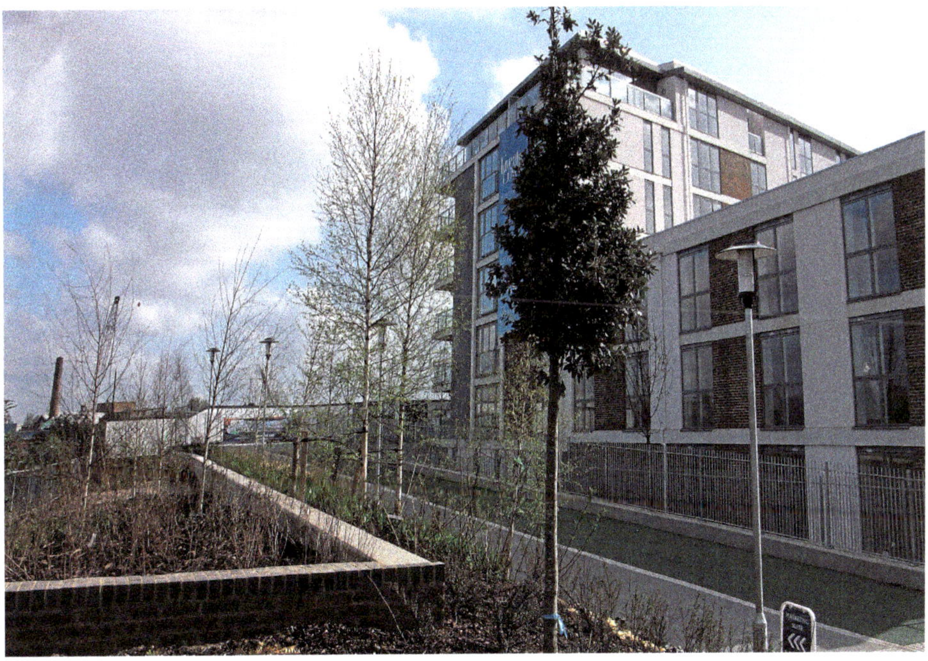

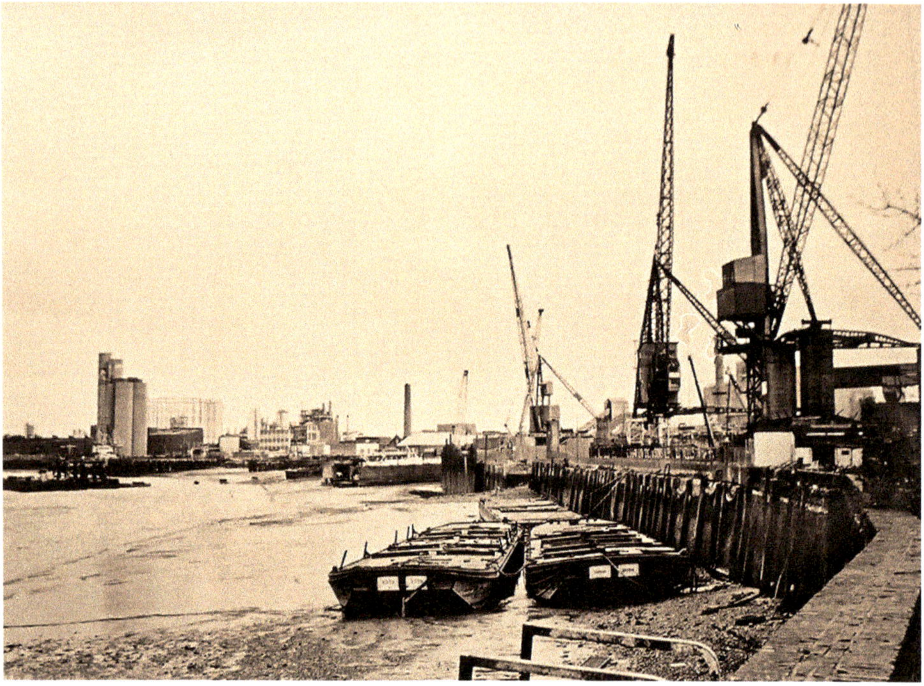

Morden Wharf – Greenwich Marsh

Morden College owned most of the land on the marsh. The charity was founded by Sir John Morden in 1695 to aid merchants who had lost their estates through accidents at sea. The charity's income came through trading and the buying and leasing of land. Morden Wharf, towards the centre of the picture, was named after the landowners by Charles Holcombe who had become a wealthy industrialist through business activities on the marsh. The Greenwich Dome, now the O_2 Arena, was built to the north of the lands owned by Morden College.

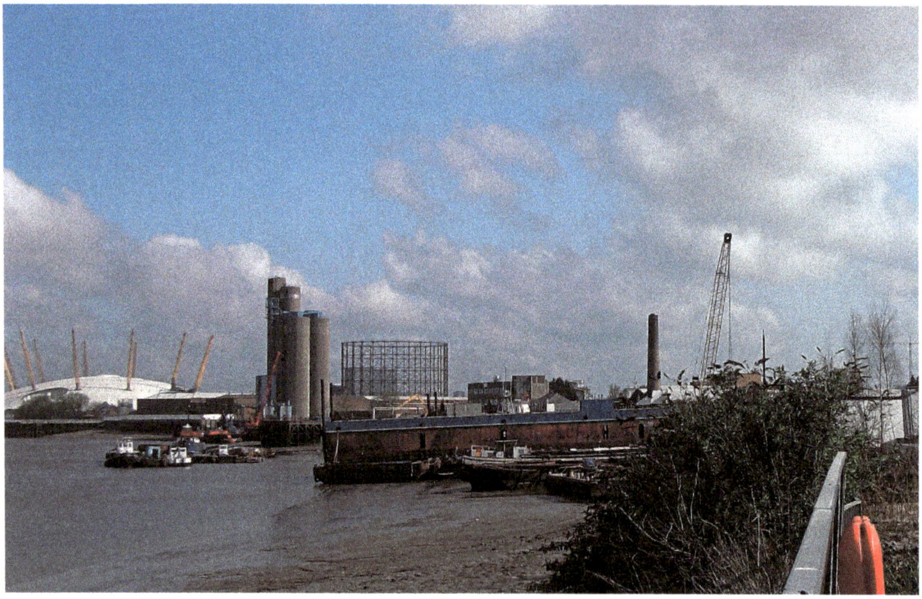

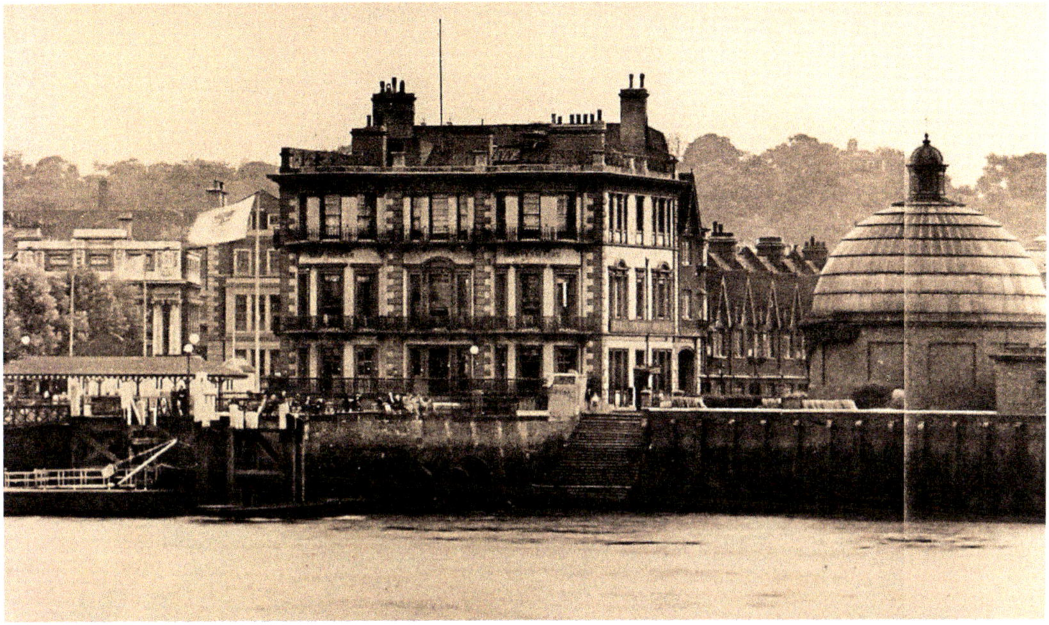

Greenwich Garden Stairs

A flight of steps leading down from the front of the Ship Tavern were used to access a passenger ferry running across the river from Greenwich to the Isle of Dogs. These ferries had been in operation since the early 1300s but eventually closed after the Greenwich foot tunnel opened in 1902. The foot tunnel entrances were housed under glass-domed buildings and the Greenwich entrance was to the right of the Ship Tavern. The tunnel is still used and the only ferries running from near Garden Stairs today are the tourist boats and river buses travelling up and down river from Greenwich Pier.

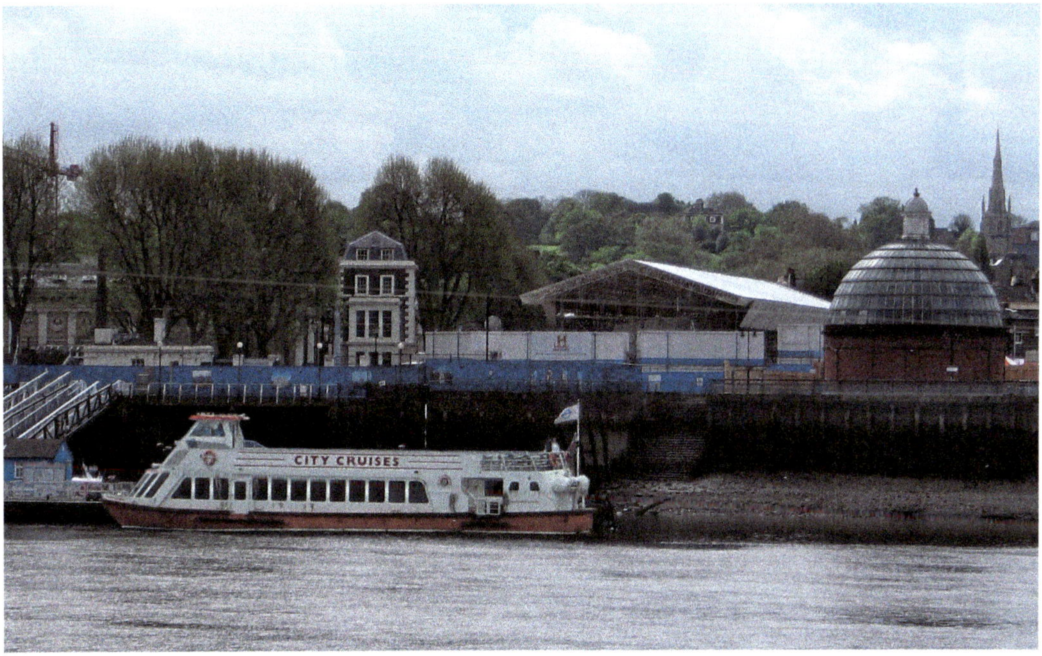

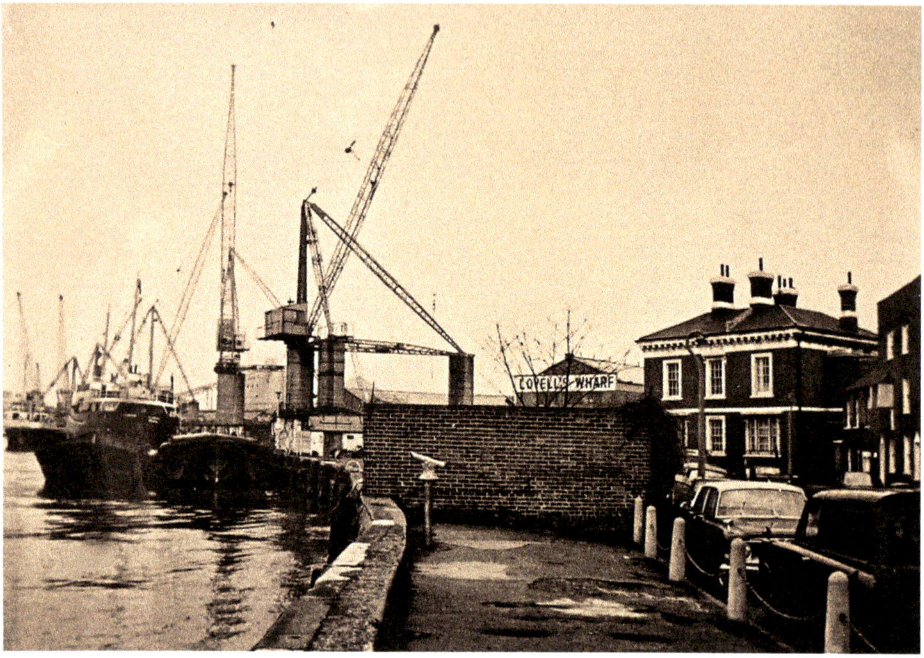

Ballast Quay – Union Wharf

Ships had been taking on ballast at the quay since the seventeenth century. After off-loading their cargo the vessel would need to load ballast for the return voyage. The quay was opposite the Union Tavern, now the Cutty Sark Tavern, used by merchant seamen, lightermen and watermen working on the Thames. With cargo vessels no longer needing to take on ballast at the quay, today's visitors are local residents and tourists taking on a few drinks while relaxing on the old quay overlooking the Thames.

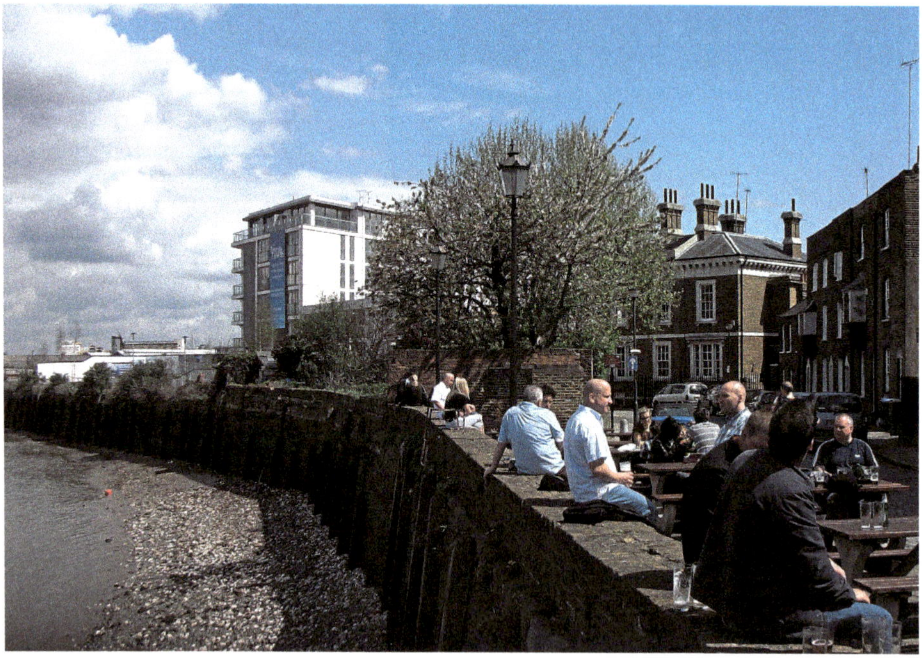

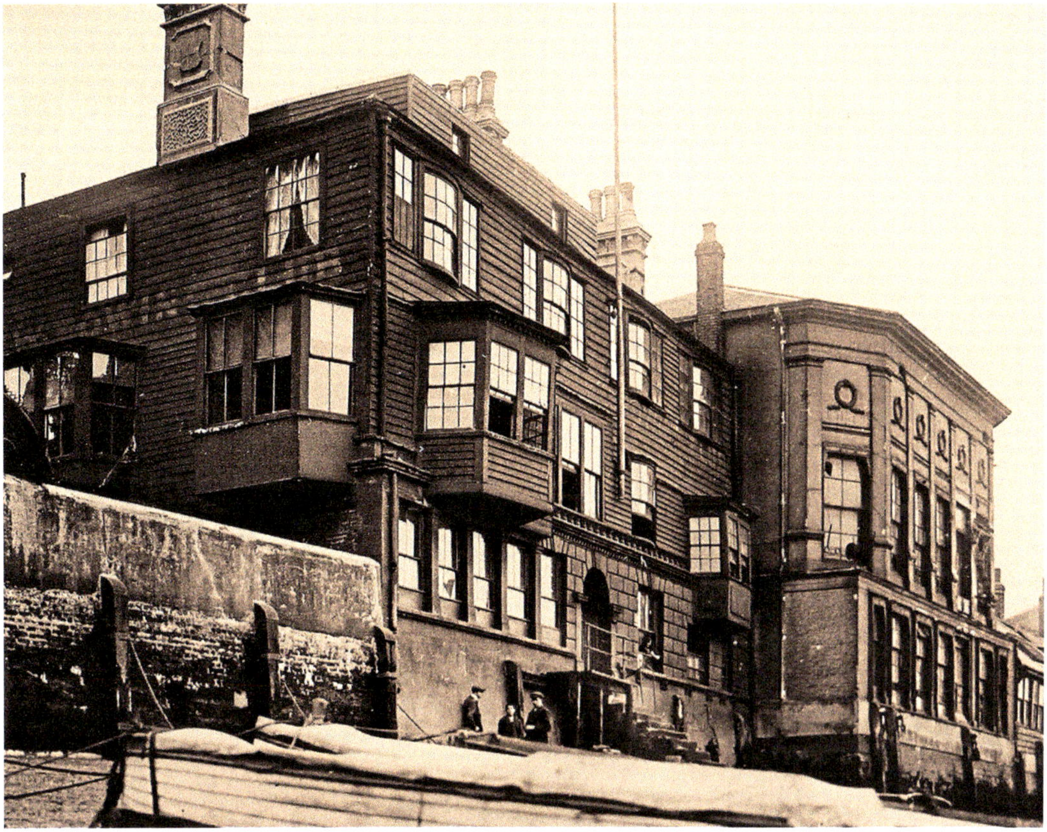

Crown & Sceptre – Highbridge Wharf

The weather-boarded public house was the headquarters of Curlew Rowing Club, the oldest rowing club on the tideway. In 1787 the rowing club, known then as Curley, took part in the first ever regatta on the Thames off Greenwich. When the Crown & Sceptre was demolished in 1934 the club rented out part of the Trafalgar Tavern. Riverfront workshops built on the site have been replaced by modern flats and apartments.

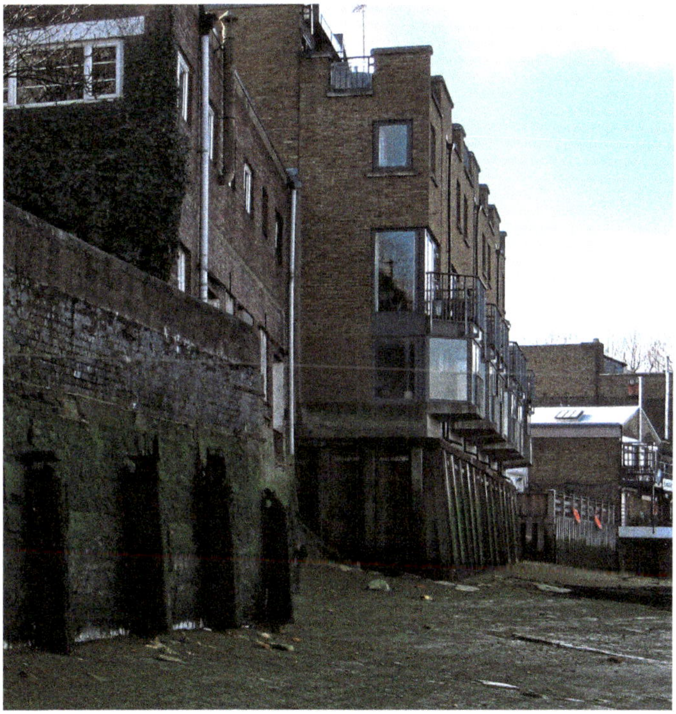

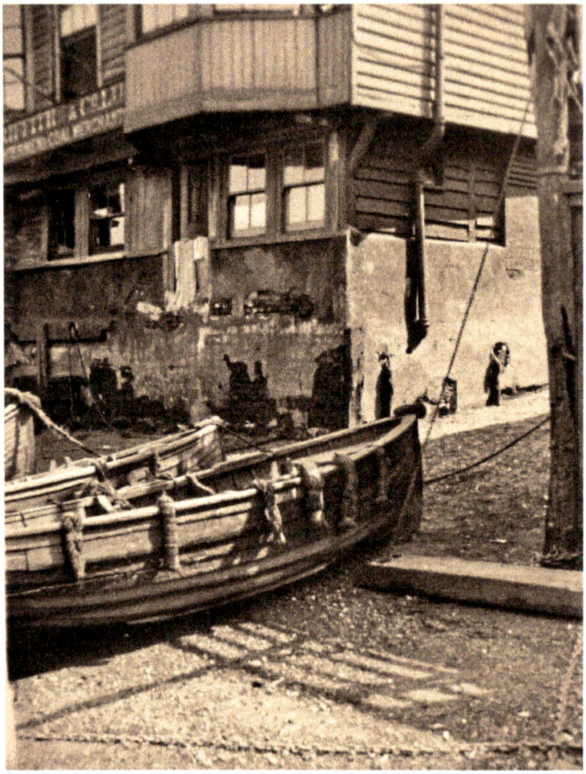

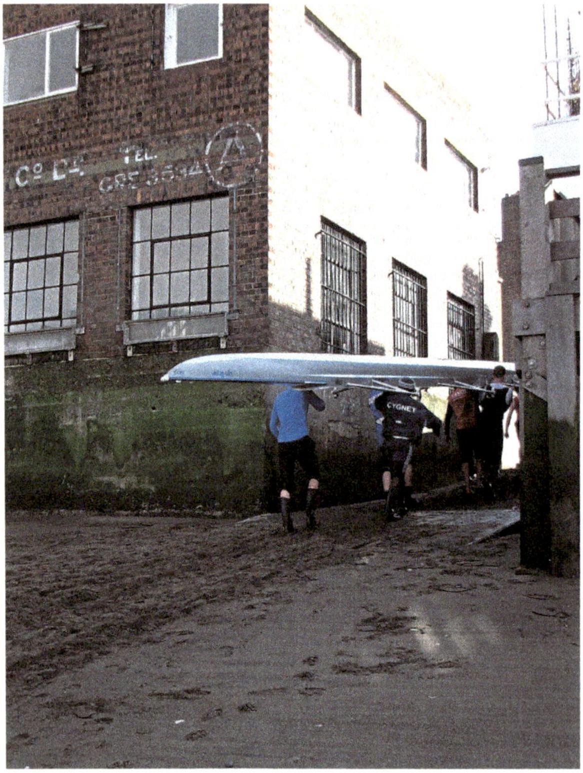

Work Boats and Rowing Boats – East Lane

A narrow slipway running from East Lane past the Three Crowns public house down to the Thames has been used as an access to the river for over two hundred years. Working rowboats and sailboats are tied up at this old slipway which has been used by crews from the nearby Curlew Rowing Club since the early 1800s. Most of the original riverfront buildings have now gone although Greenwich rowing crews still use the slipway to take their boats to and from the Thames.

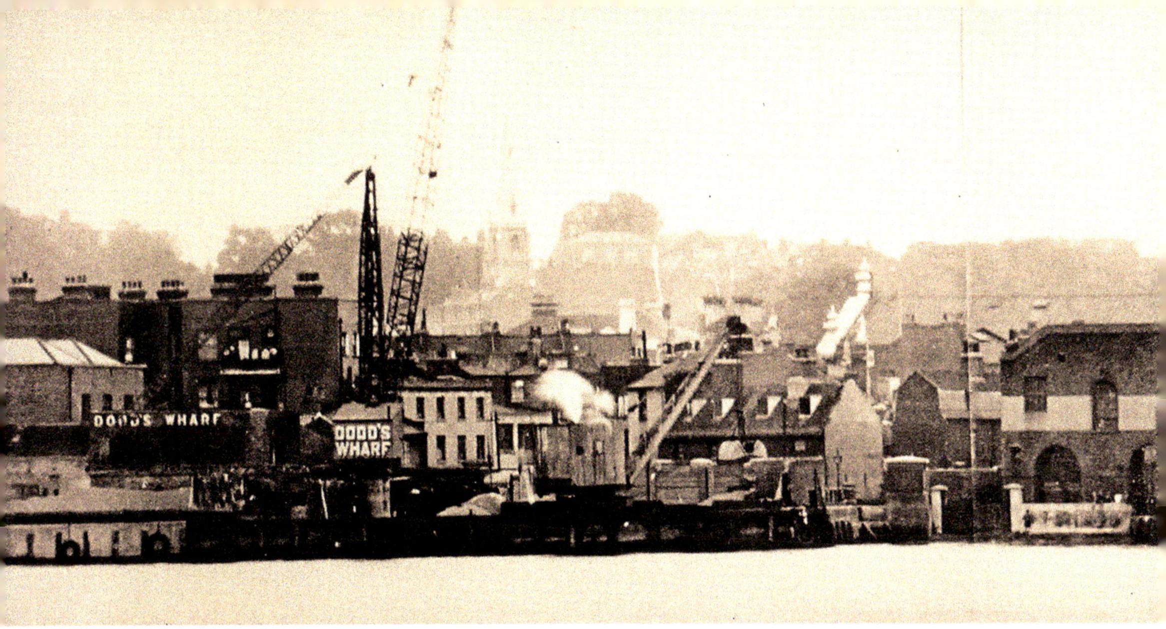

Dodds Wharf – Billingsgate Dock

During the early 1900s Dodds Wharf was built at the site of Billingsgate Dock. The dock had long associations with a fishing boat fleet which had sailed out of Greenwich into the north seas since Tudor times. After the fishing fleets had left, the dock was occupied by marine engineers, boiler makers, a ballast contractor, barge builders and boat repair yards. A council housing estate replaced the old wharfs, workshops and yards damaged during the blitz. The whole length of the riverfront towards Deptford Creek is now undergoing regeneration and redevelopment.

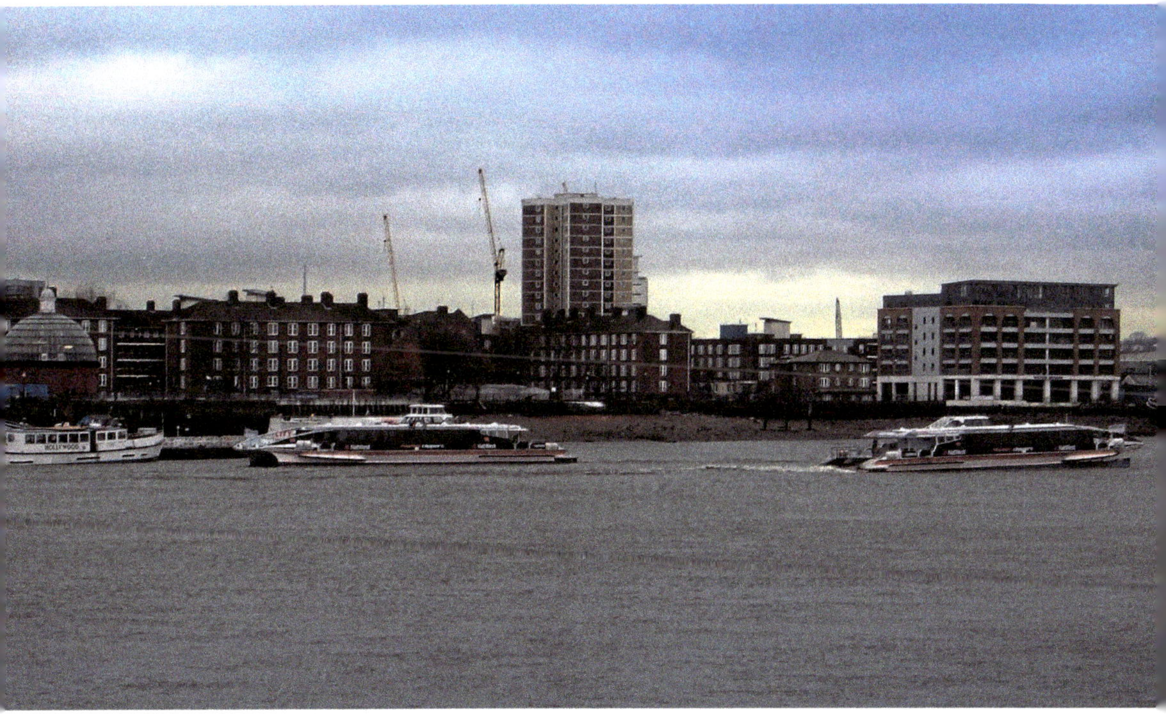

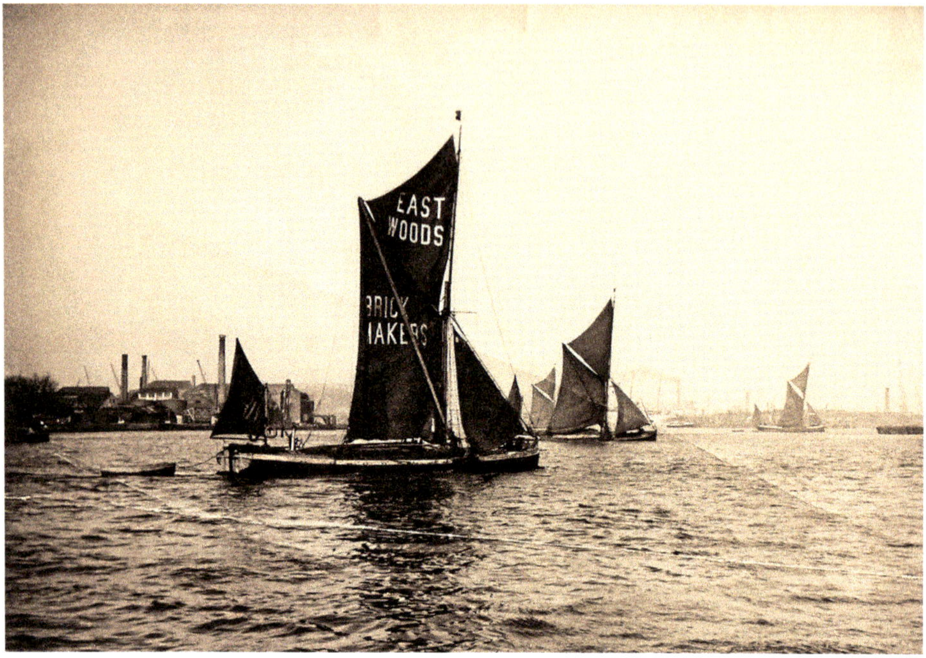

Thames Sailing Barge – Greenwich Reach

Many Thames sailing barges working on the Thames during the nineteenth century were built in yards at Greenwich. Constructed of wood and then later steel, their flat-bottomed design meant they were able to sail in the shallow waters of river estuaries and narrow creeks to load and unload their cargo. The days of sailing vessels working on the Thames came to an end during the mid 1900s which resulted in the demise of the local boat building industry. A few of the old working boats can still be found along the riverfront on display as a reminder of Greenwich's boat building heritage.

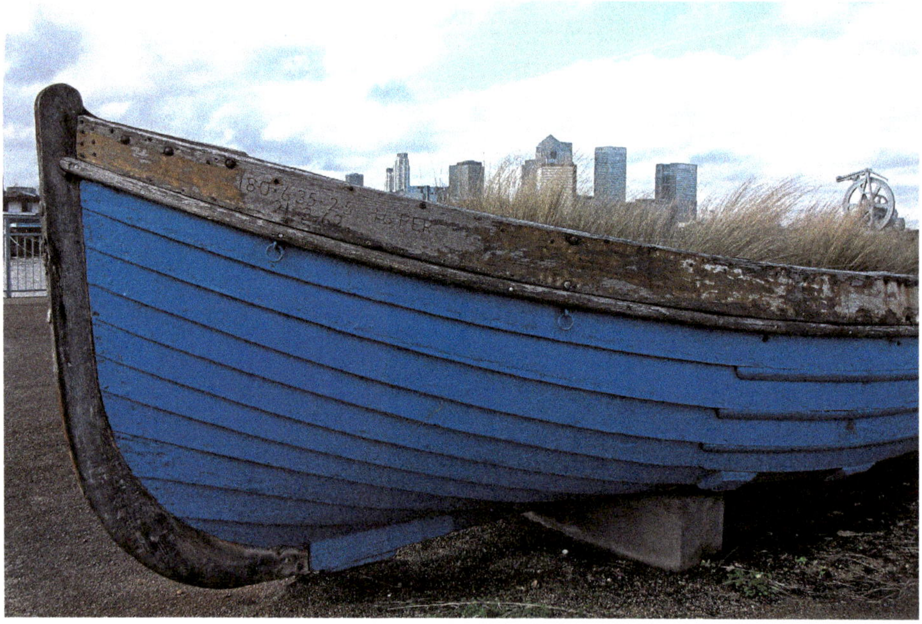

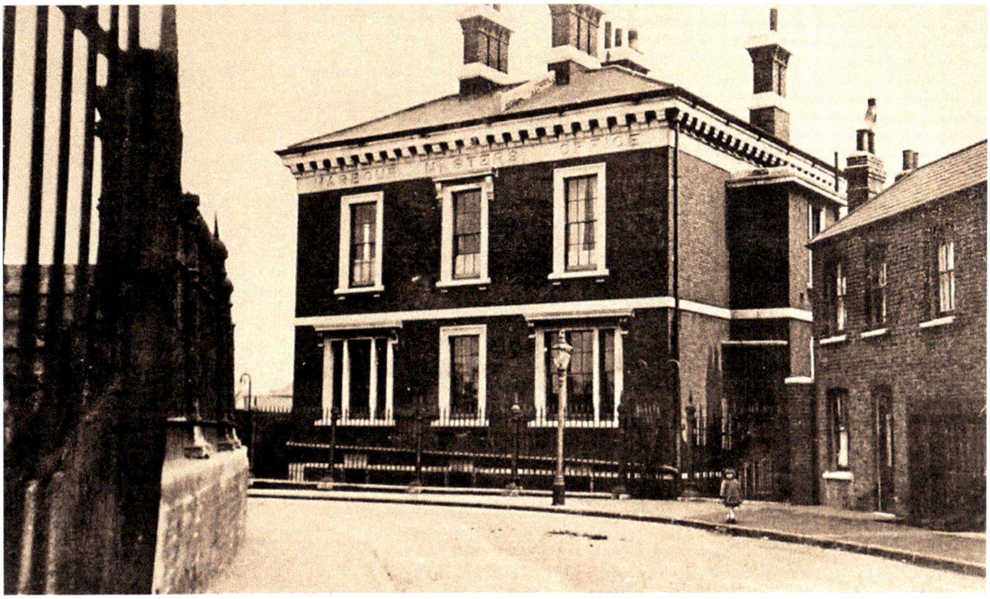

Harbour Master's Office – Port of London Wharf

The early Victorian listed building is another reminder of the days when the shipping industry at Greenwich was an important part of the town's heritage. Built in 1855 by local architect George Smith the building replaced an earlier Harbour Master's Office located near the Yacht Tavern. The office controlled the movement of all colliers on the Thames. The colliers brought in coal from the north east of the country to power the heavy industries along the river. The office closed in 1890 and the building is now a private residence.

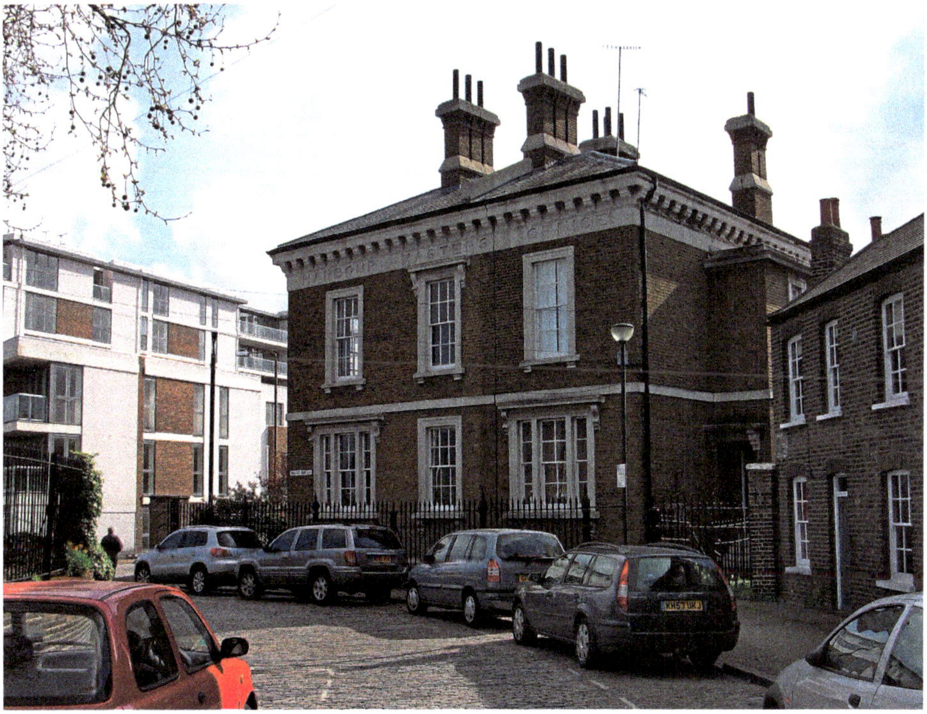

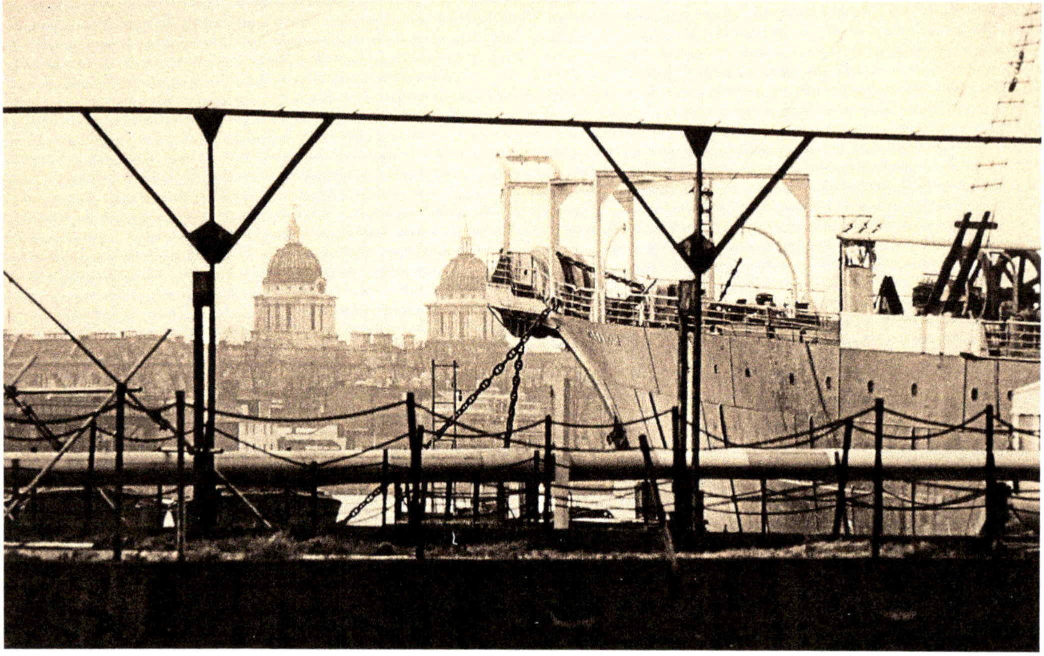

John W. Mackay – Enderby Wharf

The bow of the *John W. Mackay* can be seen to the right of the picture when the cable-laying ship was moored at Enderby Wharf in 1984. Commissioned in 1922 the ship had been laying and maintaining submarine cables for more than fifty years. The ship's cable-laying days were now over after the manufacture of submarine cable on the site came to an end in 1975. There were plans to turn this historic vessel into a museum but she was scrapped in yards at Sunderland. Remnants of the cable laying industry can still be seen on the wharf opposite the riverside path.

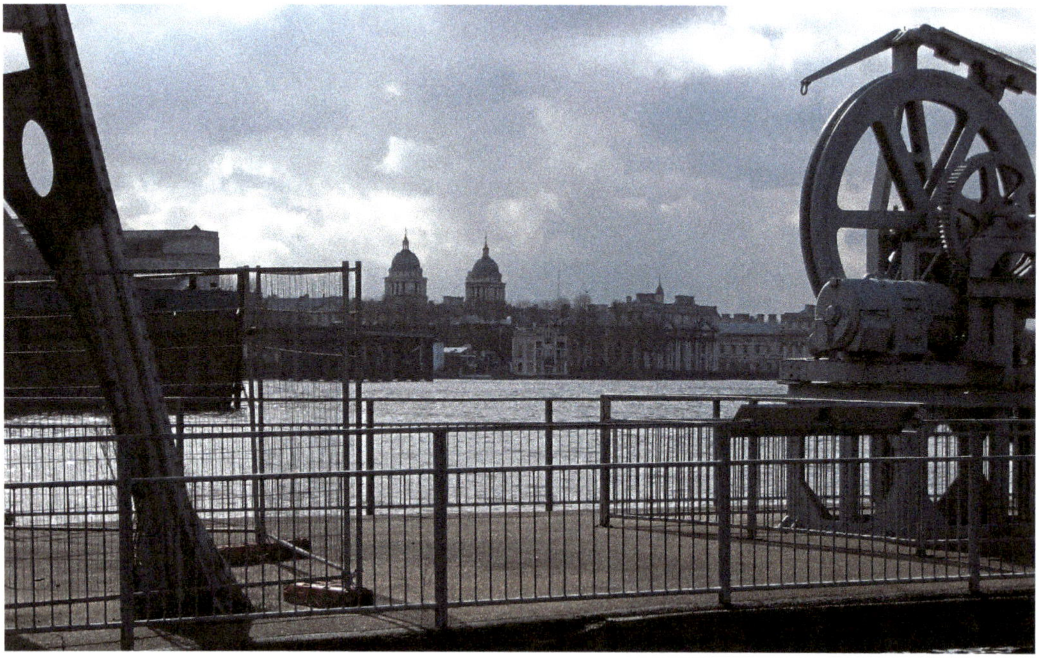

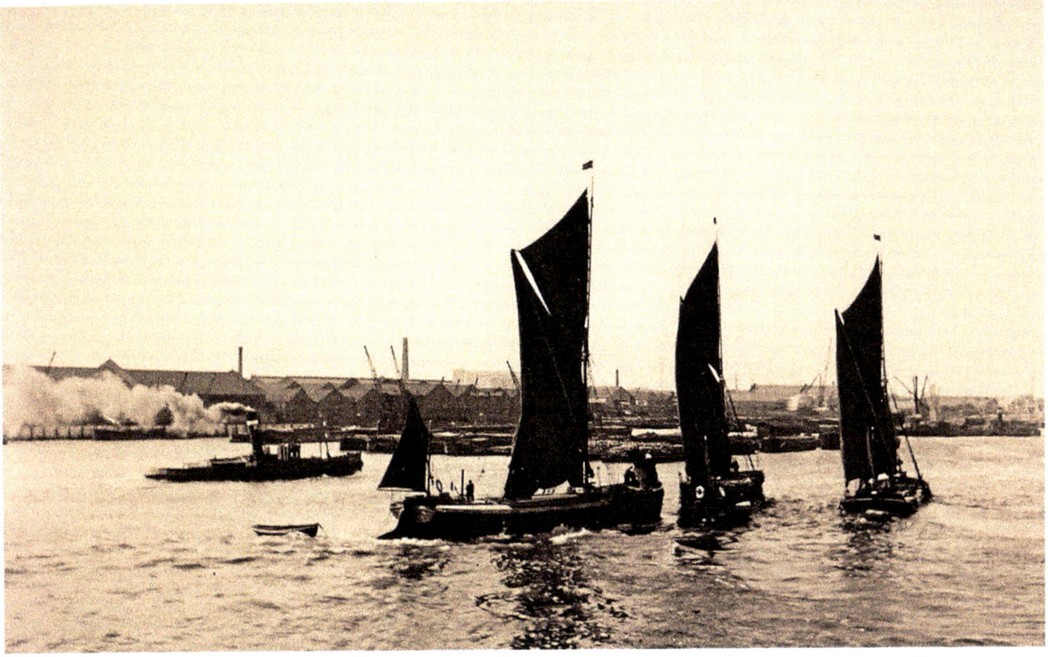

River Craft – Blackwall Reach

Thames sailing barges make their way down river during the 1950s towards Blackwall Point. The tug and container barges in the background would eventually make these historic working sail boats redundant. These river craft had relied upon trade created by the industries along the Thames but over recent years, as new regeneration projects replace the riverfront industries, there has been dramatic decline in all types of working river craft on the Thames. One working vessel which can still be found off Blackwall Reach is the 600-ton dredger *Arco Trent* turned into a static and permanent sculpture by Richard Wilson, titled Slice of Reality.

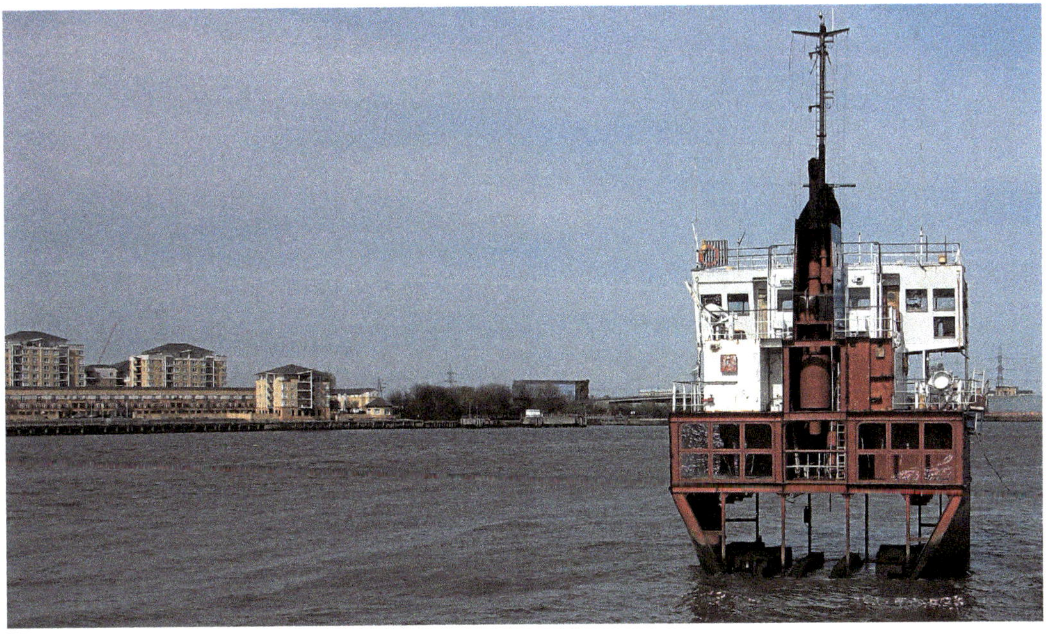

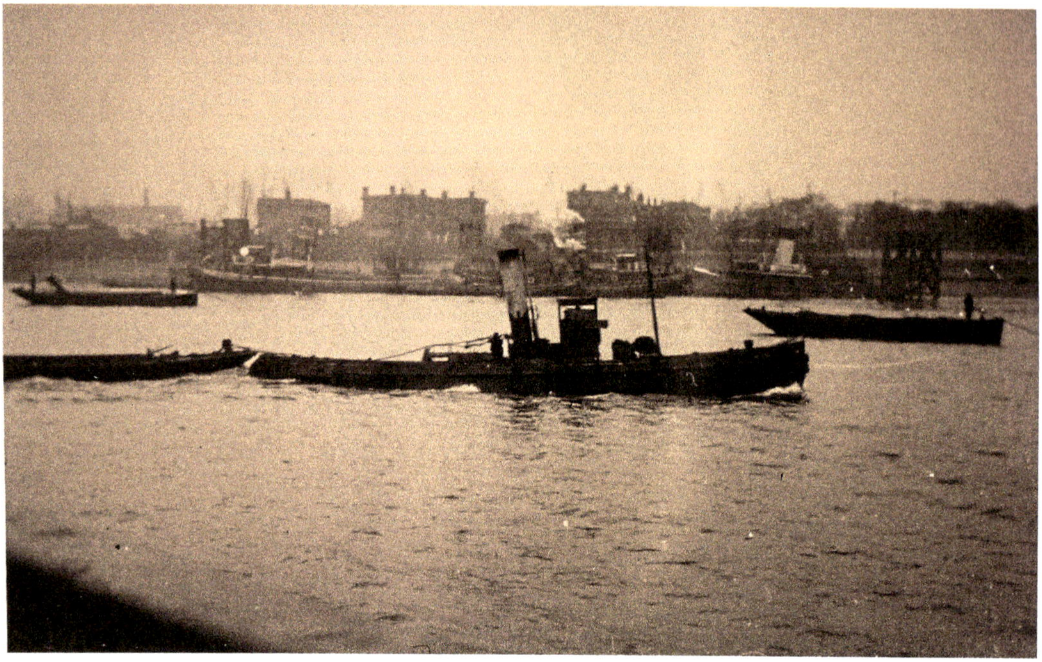

Steam Power *v.* Man Power – Greenwich Reach

A tug moves container barges across Greenwich Reach during 1934 as Thames lightermen manoeuvre their laden barges using just oars. The lightermen were extremely skillful in moving their loaded barges on the Thames from wharf to wharf and ship to shore using the flow of the river and a pair of 20ft oars. Although this technique is no longer used to move barges about the river, crews still practice these skills when navigating 30-ton barges along a seven mile stretch of the Thames from Greenwich to Westminster in an annual Barge Driving Match for Thames Watermen and Lightermen.

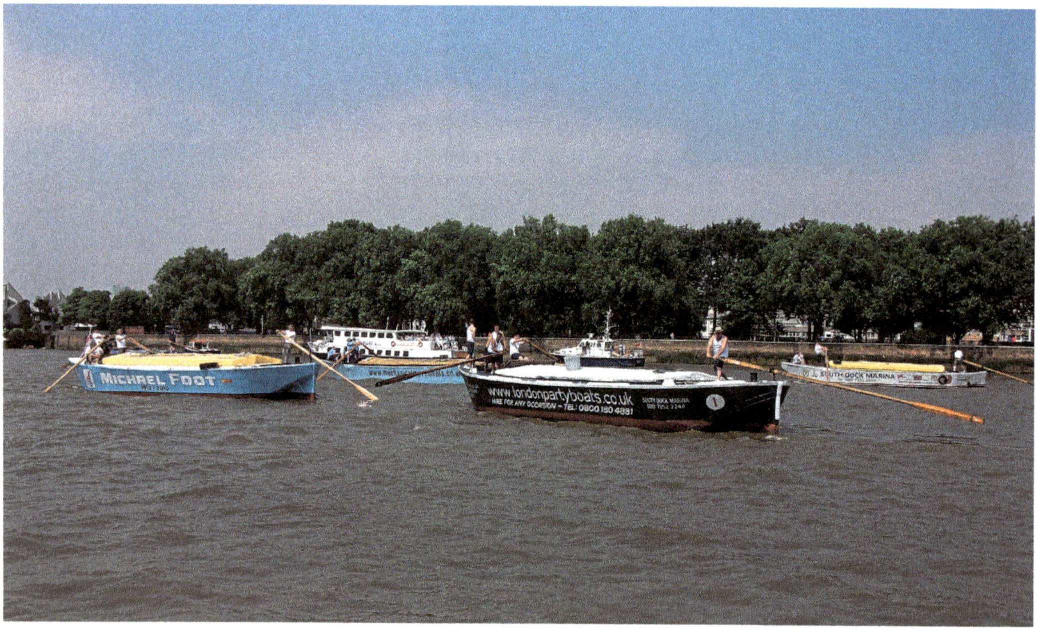

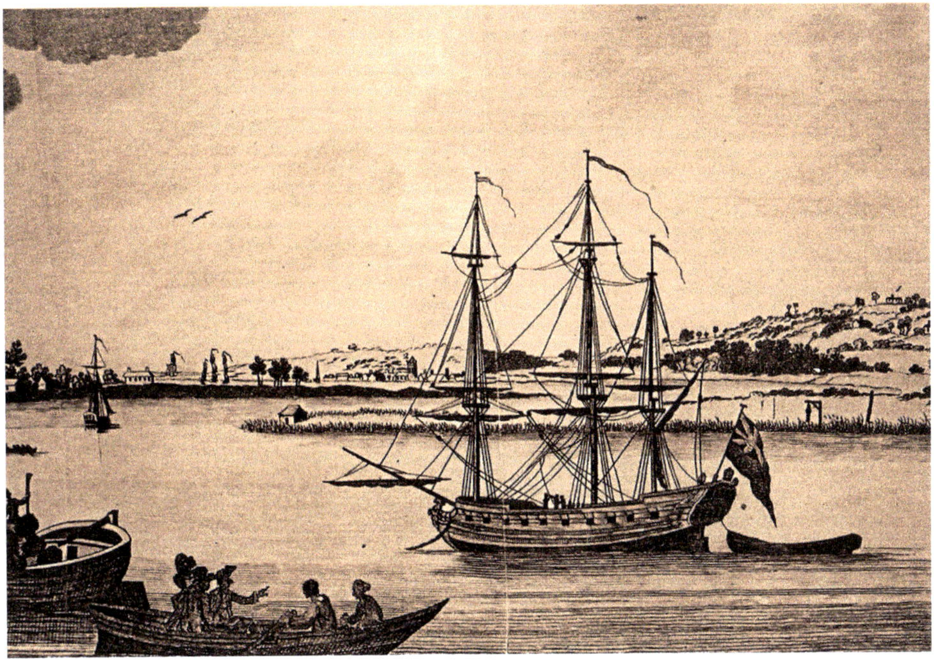

Blackwall Point – Greenwich Marsh

An eighteenth-century East Indiaman moored off Blackwall Point in 1782 opposite the gibbet on Greenwich Marsh where pirates' corpses were hung in chains. The last criminal hung on the gibbet was reported to have been in 1834. The marsh was drained for cattle grazing during the late seventeenth century and throughout the eighteenth and nineteenth centuries became heavily industrialised. By the end of the twentieth century the whole area began a program of regeneration. As those old industries close down new modern building developments similar to those across river at Canary Wharf will replace them.

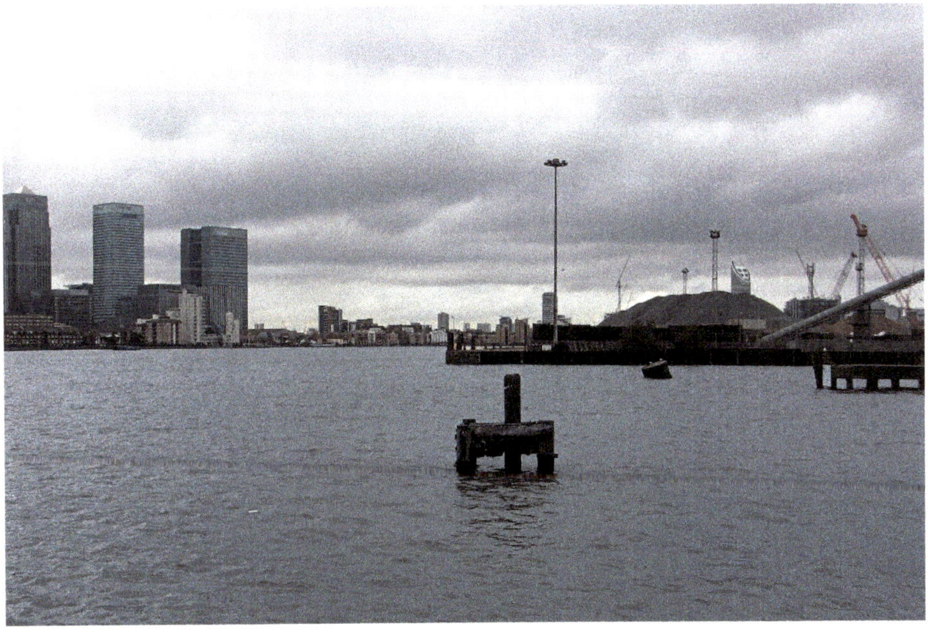

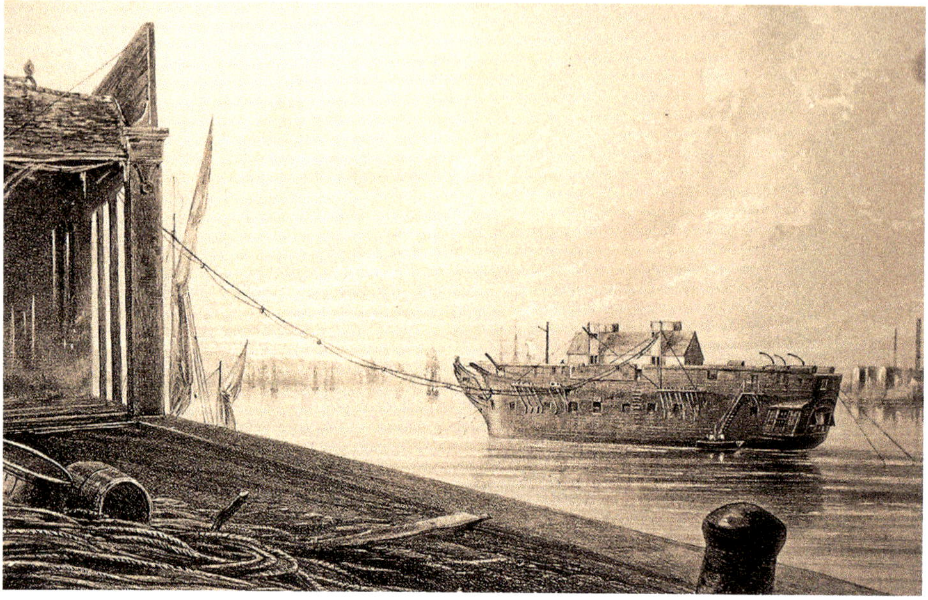

Man of War – Enderby Wharf

The *Amethyst* is loading telegraph cable while laying off shore at Enderby Wharf in 1865. The site had been acquired by the Enderby family for the production of ships rope and canvas. Next to the wharf are Enderby's ferry steps where ferrymen rowed crews to and from the cable ships. In the picture a small ferry boat can be seen arriving at the landing stage of the old hulk. Sculptor Richard Lawrence was commissioned to carve a new set of ferry steps depicting the industrial heritage of Greenwich Marsh and the Enderby site. An announcement was made in June 2010 that plans were being made to transform the site into a new cruise liner terminal.

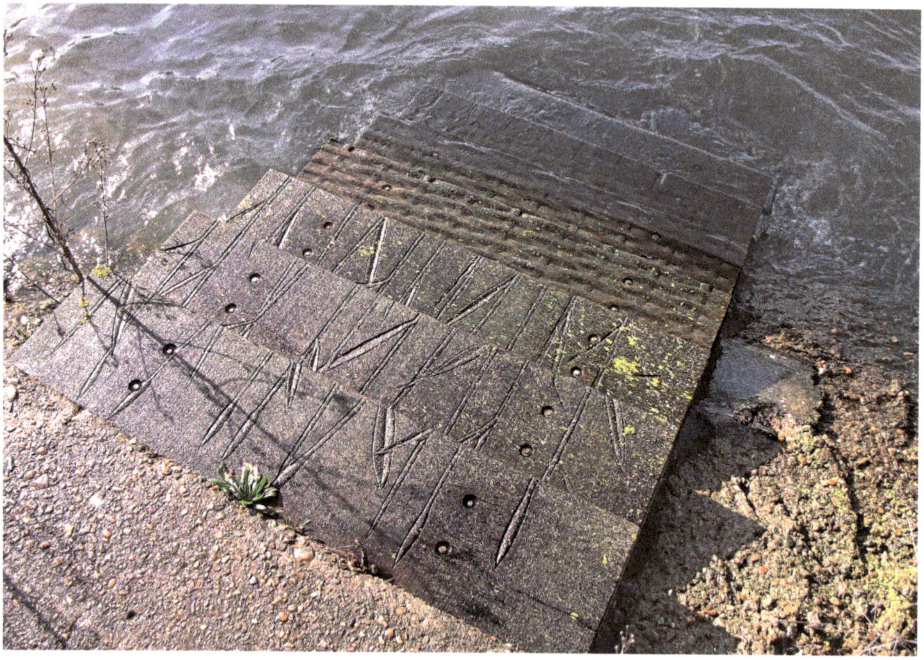

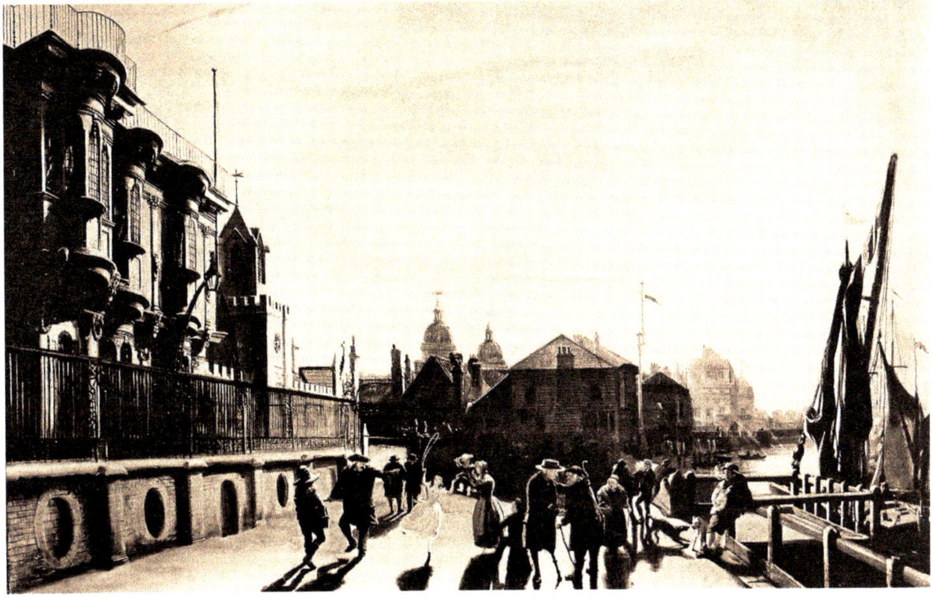

Crowley House – Anchor Iron Wharf

In 1647 London merchant Sir Andrew Cogan began building a property on land east of Greenwich Palace, which was completed after the Civil War by Parliamentarian Gregory Clement. The property was purchased by Newcastle ironfounder Sir Ambrose Crowley in 1704 who made his fortune producing anchors for the navy and shackles and chains for the slave trade. Crowley House was demolished in 1854 and Greenwich Power Station was built on the site. A three-dimensional story on the power station boundary wall, created by Amanda Hinge, tells of a boy's adventure by the river which takes me back to childhood memories of my own adventures by the Thames. The walkway running adjacent to this wall is crossed at the point where the story begins by the Greenwich Meridian Line, bringing together both western and eastern hemispheres, making Greenwich the centre of the world.

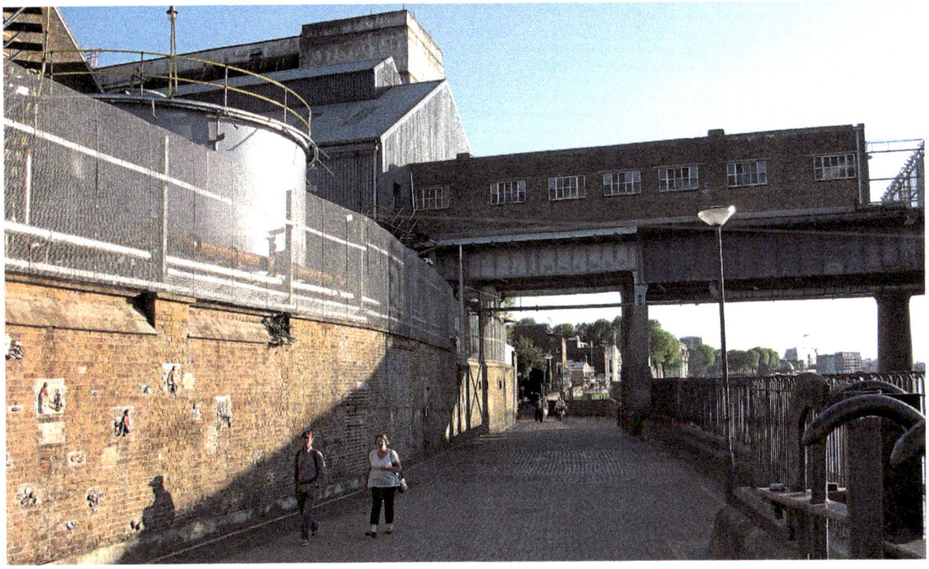

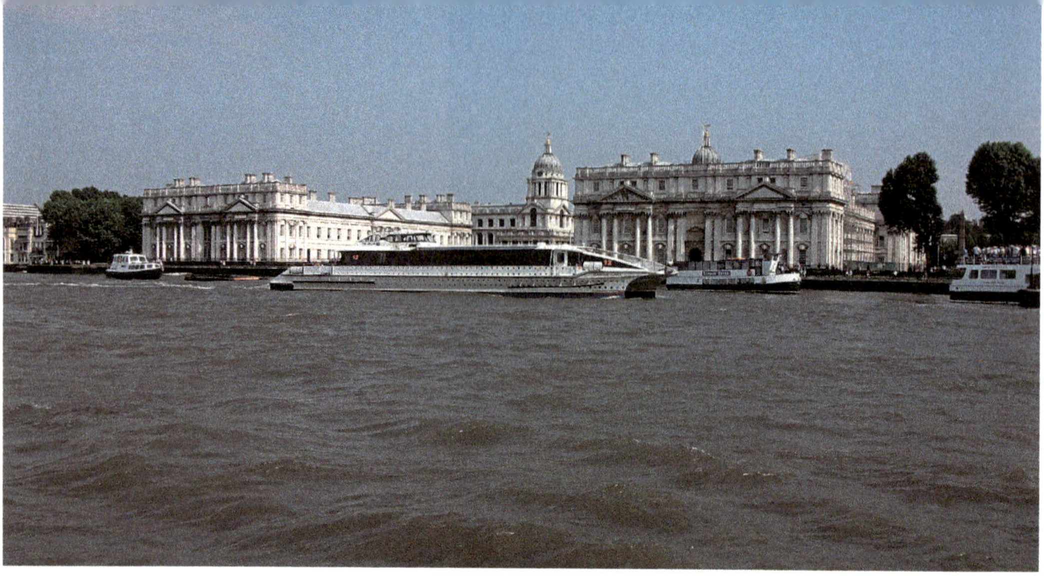

Old Royal Naval College – Greenwich
The maritime heritage of Greenwich has not only shaped the history of our nation; it has also shaped the history of the world. Greenwich is a Royal Borough and World Heritage Site.

Acknowledgements

This book is dedicated to Alex, Toby and Elizabeth.
The images of the past can have reflections on your future.

I should like to thank all those who have contributed to *Royal Greenwich Through Time* either by supplying images or memories which I have been able to use within the pages of this publication. Many of the period photographs have come from my own collection which I have gathered together over many years obtained from family members and friends, local history libraries, postcard fairs and antiquarian shops. The recent images were taken during my return trips to Greenwich over the previous year. I should also like to thank all those who have provided specific historical information or have given permission to use their images within the publication. If for any reason I have not accredited any images to people or organisations as necessary, or failed to trace any copyright holders, then I should like to apologise for any oversight.

I should also like to express my thanks to the following list of organisations and people without whose help I would not have been able to produce this publication:- The Local History Library at the Greenwich Heritage Centre, The Greenwich Industrial Heritage Society, the National Maritime Museum, The Cutty Sark Trust, 2nd Long Stratton Brownies Norfolk, Greenwich Foundation for the Old Naval College, Ray Gallagher, Andrew Lovibond, Jeff Rosenmeier Lovibonds Brewery Ltd, Bob Headley, Geoff and Barbara Billingsley and all of my family and friends.